Verill Ansel Swain
From Cleveland to Morrilton, Arkansas

By Marcia Swain Crossman   2024
Daughter of Ansel and Elizabeth Swain

Verill Ansel Swain
from
Cleveland to Morrilton, Arkansas

Research and writing by Marcia Swain Crossman, 2024
Daughter of Ansel & Elizabeth Swain

Ingram Spark Press
2024

ISBN 979-8-9885900-9-5

Table Of Contents

Appendices

Preface

It has given me great pleasure to research the life of my father, Verill Ansel Swain, and my mother, Elizabeth Ruth Hamlet.

Each bit of information I discovered along the way became a treasure of my heart. I hope all who read this book will keep safe their copies and pass them along to your descendants.

I want to thank my sister, Sherry Swain Borck for her contributions and help in proofreading.

I want to thank my spouse, Robert Owen Crossman for his constant encouragement, contributions and compiling together all the parts of the book for printing. Sincerely,

Marcia Gail Swain Crossman, 2024

mcrossman@conwaycorp.net

8 Sternwheel Dr. • Conway, Arkansas 72034

Ansel
and
The Early Years

"It began in Cleveland, Arkansas"

Section One

Ansel and The Early Years
"It began in Cleveland, Arkansas" Section One

Sherman Norton Swain and Stella Thomas Trimble

On the beautiful spring day of May 6, 1917, a young couple stand side by side to be married. Sherman Norton Swain was 23 years old; Stella Thomas Trimble was a mere 21. They were "of age." Was their family with them? Did they go to alone the courthouse to stand before a Justice of the Peace? Like most young couples they were serious about what life would become when they married.

Sam was not a rich boy. He was from the small community of Cleveland in Conway County, Arkansas. Young Sam had been taken away from public education due to the untimely death (suicide) of his father.

At age 15 years, he worked with his mother to care for the remaining children in the household. About the only thing he knew was farming. Was this how young Sam would support his future bride?

Stella, at 21 years old, was raised just one county away from Sam in Scotland, in Van Buren County, Arkansas. She was born just days after her father's untimely death. The family endured considerable hardships as their mother sought to raise them.

These two would become parents of two daughters and three sons. One son, Verill Ansel Swain, is who this book is about.

Sherman "Sam" Norton Swain 1894-1957
Stella Thomas Trimble 1896-1993

MARRIAGE LICENSE,

STATE OF ARKANSAS.

COUNTY OF CONWAY

To any Person authorized by Law to Solemnize Marriage
GREETING:

You are Hereby Commanded to solemnize the Rite and publish the Bans of Matrimony between Mr. *Sherman N Swain* of *Cleveland* in the County of *Conway* and State of *Arkansas* aged *Twenty Two* (22) years and Miss *Stella Trimble* of *Cleveland* in the County of *Conway* and State of *Arkansas* aged *Twenty* (20) years, according to law and do you officially sign and return this License to the parties herein named.

Witness my hand and Official Seal this *30th* day of *April 1917*

J. L. Williams County Clerk

D. C.

CERTIFICATE OF MARRIAGE

State of Arkansas.
COUNTY OF *Van Buren* I *J. G. Leavell* do hereby Certify that on the *6* day of *May 1917* I did duly and according to law as commanded in the foregoing License, solemnize the Rite and publish the Bans of Matrimony between the parties herein named.

Witness my hand this *7* day of *May 1917*

My Credentials are recorded in the Recorder's Office *Van Buren* Co. Ark, Book ____ Page ____

J. G. Leavell J.P.

Note-This License, with the Certificate duly executed and officially signed, must be returned to the office whence it is issued, within Sixty days from date of the License, under penalty of forfeiture of the License.

Marriage License of Stella Trimble and Sam Swain, April 30, 1917; married on May 6, 1917

CERTIFICATE OF RECORD.

STATE OF ARKANSAS,
County of CONWAY. I, J. L. WILLIAMS.

Clerk of the County Court of said County, certify that the above license for and Certificate of the Marriage of Mr. *Sherman N Swain* and *Miss Stella Trimble* was filed in my office on the 16 day of *May* *1917*, and the same is duly recorded on page *483* of Book "*U*" of Marriage Records.

WITNESS my hand and the seal of said Court this 16 day of *May* *1917*

J L Williams
Clerk.

By D.C.

Marriage Certification of Stella Trimble and Sam Swain, 1917
Back page of License

Stella Thomas Trimble Swain's Family

Source: Ancestry.com • Marcia Swain Crossman's Family Tree, 2024

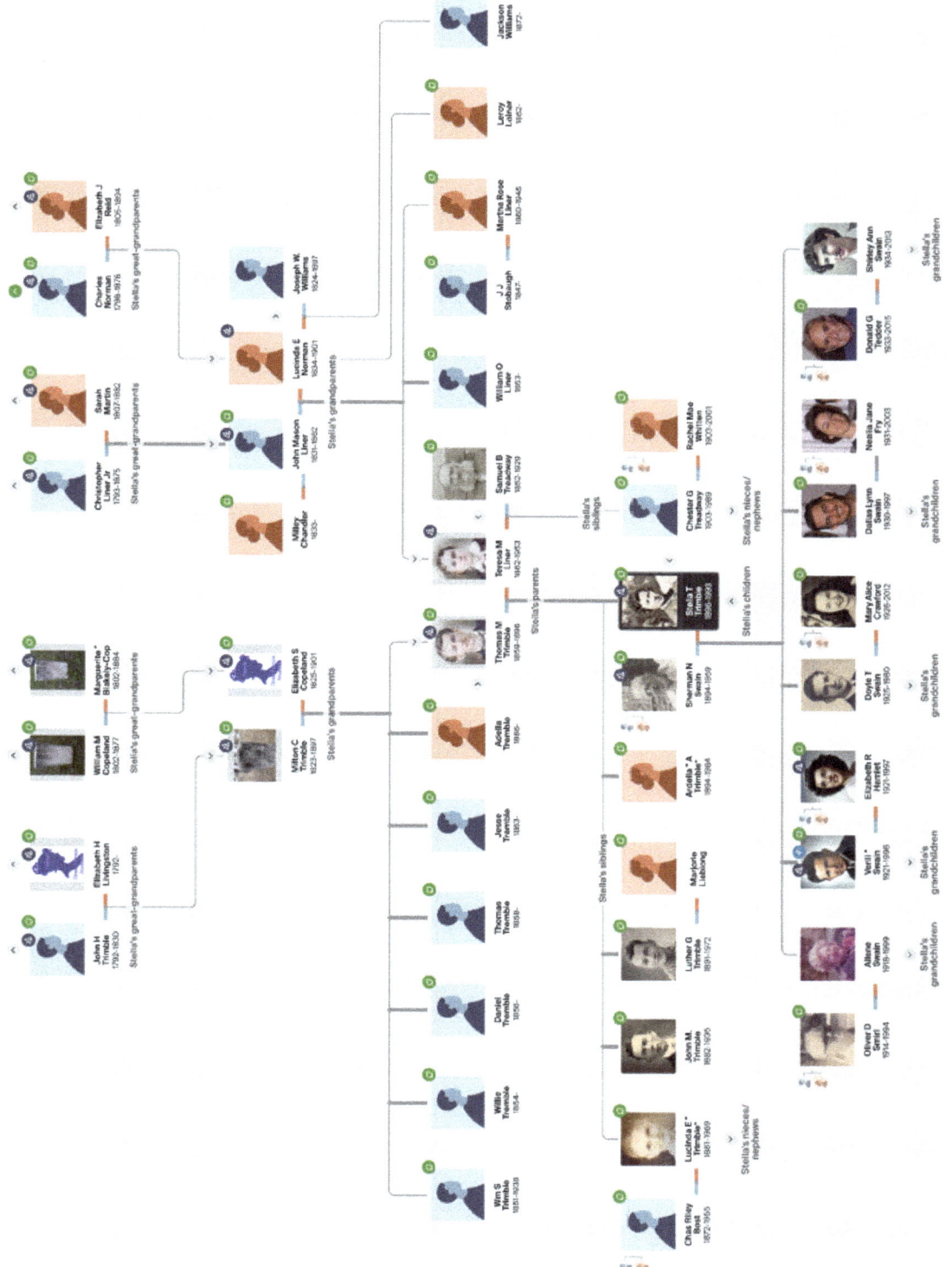

Sherman Norton Swain's Family

Source: Ancestry.com • Marcia Swain Crossman's Family Tree, 2024

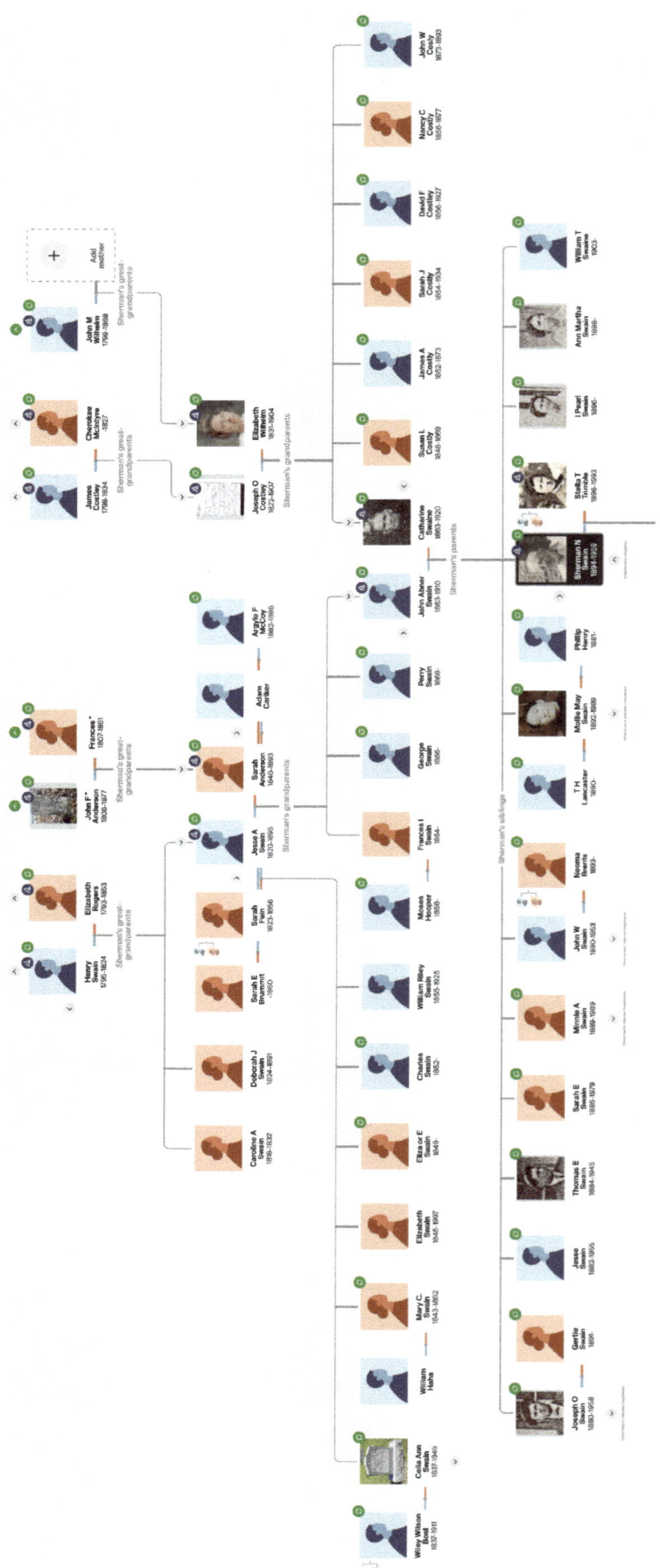

Verill Ansel Swain was the second child born to Stella and Sam Swain, April 13, 1921 in Cleveland, Arkansas

Stella
b. December 30, 1896.
m. May 6, 1917
Her age at marriage: 21

Stella birthed five children (most born in the spring). A typical birthing schedule for women in those days was two years between babies. Stella's time between birthing her children was unusual.

Her Children were:
Eunice Allene
b. April 22, 1918
Stella's age 22

Verill Ansel
b. April 13, 1921
Stella's age 25

Doyle Theron
b. March 24, 1924
Stella's age 28

Dallas Lynn
b. October 15, 1930
Stella's age 34

Shirley Ann
b. April 10, 1934
Stella's age 38

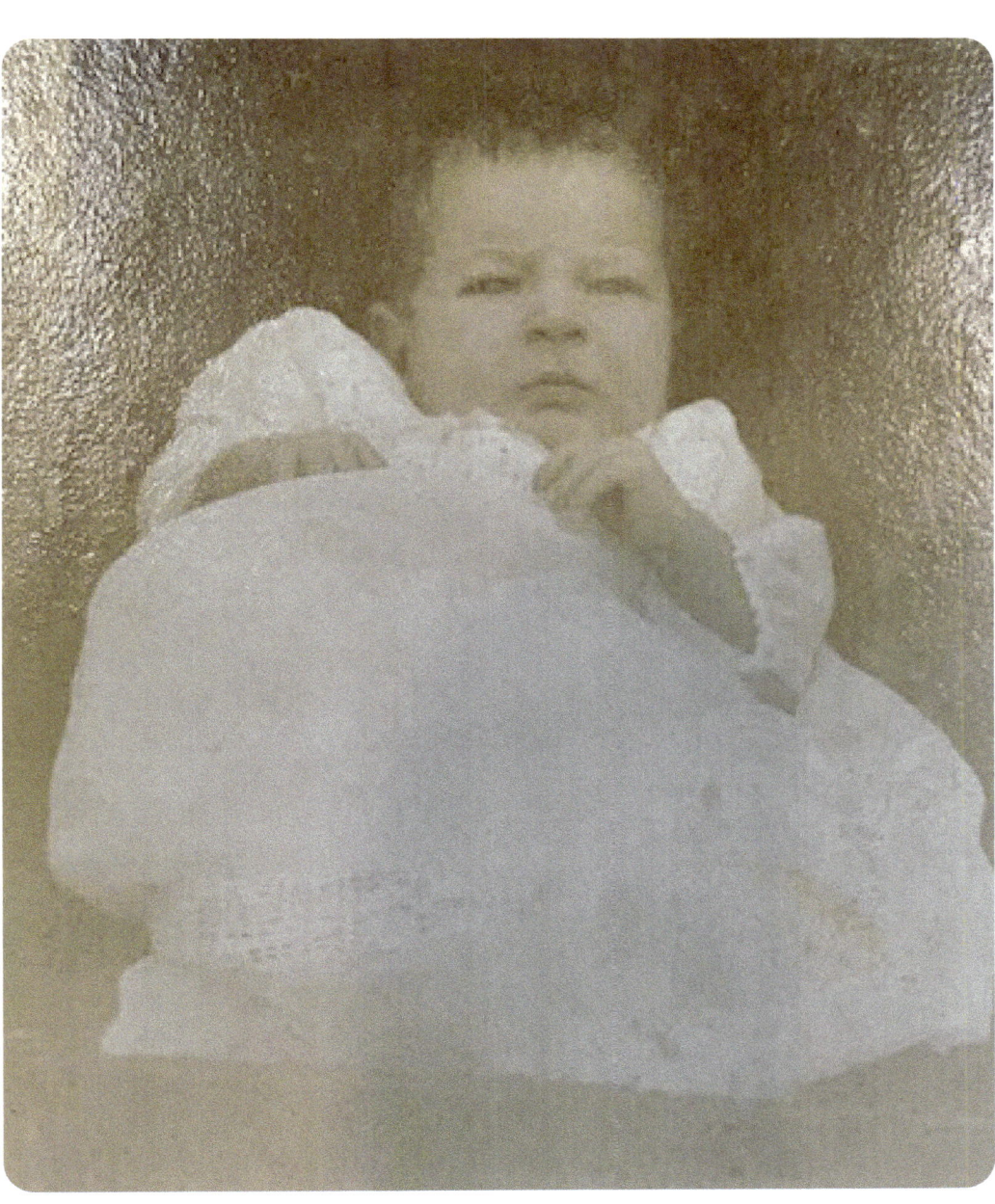

Verill Ansel Swain as a tiny baby in 1921.

When **Verill Ansel** called "Ansel" was a tiny baby, the family sent off for postcards with his baby picture. It was traditional in those days, to take pictures and send to friends and family when a person was sick and thought death was eminent. Postcards were a way to announce what was happening. Fortunately Ansel pulled out of what was ailing him and went on with the business of growing up.

Verill Ansel Swain's Ancestors

Source: Ancestry.com • Marcia Swain Crossman's Family Tree, 2024

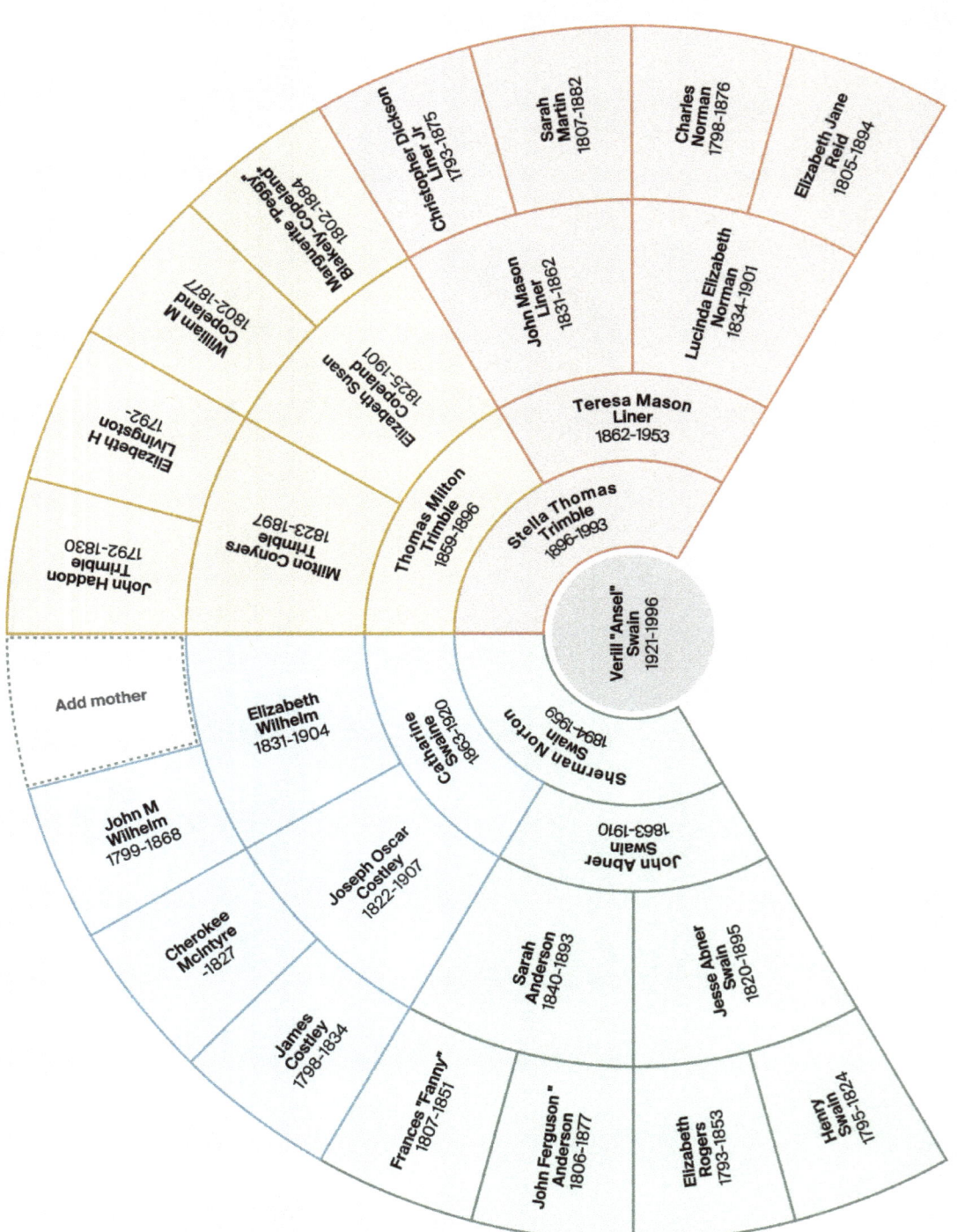

Ansel
"2nd child"
on left

Doyle
"3rd child"
in the
middle

Allene
"1st child"
on the
right

about
1925.

Baseball, with the other kids, was Ansel's favorite past time.

Ansel soon learned life was not all fun and games.

Children picking cotton, Library of Congress .gov

In order to financially assist the family, Ansel, as a boy, picked cotton in the heat of the Arkansas summers. A full bag of raw cotton was worth a nickle or so.

Ansel also did jobs around the store and home to help his parents. He moved and loaded animal feed, filled gas into cars, cleaned the house and out buildings, stocked shelves, retrieved the mail from the train and what ever was needed.

Ansel was back row on far right.

Ansel spent his childhood years attending school at Cleveland and Wonderview, Ark.

CLEVELAND SCHOOL 1934 — from left, top row, Lorain Knighten, Reba Brents, L. Reed, Versey Duncan, Geraldine Rhodes, Maxine Wells, Pauline Shumake, Harold Copland, Custer Poteet, Grady Swain, Harold Hatcher, Gerald Brents, Ira Brents, Harold Bowen, Edward Hatcher, Alma McCoy and Ancel Swain; second row, Huffman, Lois Wells, Mary E. Roberson, Captola Ring, Charline Brents, Christine Brents, Jewel Wells, Marvine Treadwell, unknown, unknown, Hazel Brents, Geraldine Phillips, Lill Halbrook, Loyd Brents and Jerry Roberson; bottom row, G. A. Walls, Leo Huffman, Cecil Reed, Stanley McCoy, Leo Wells, Hershall Wells, Tommy Wells, Lynn Brents, Ralph Ring and John Brock, Jr.

In a "Remember When" article, from the local newspaper out of Morrilton, Arkansas:
"S.N. Swain's Store in Blackwell some 30 years ago."

In the early years of Ansel's life his father, **Sam**, had been a farmer. In **1928** when Ansel was seven, his father, Sam, opened his first store in Cleveland, Arkansas. It was a small general merchandise store. This general merchandise store, during the late 1920's, took a considerable share of the trade in the area. It sold groceries, livestock feed, canned goods, and the basic necessities. **The Swains** lived in the area for some time. They were among the leading citizens. He was a member of the **Wonderview School Board** and served as president.

Unlike modern day Cleveland, the late 1920's Cleveland had good business in the community. There was a doctor, a cotton gin, gas stations and other small town entities. Many people moved there to make a home for their families.

Later, in **1935**, the family moved to the **Welborn Township**. This was essentially Morrilton, in Conway County, Arkansas. plus the surrounding areas which contained the community of Blackwell. *(US Census)* The above photo is **Swain's Store** in Blackwell, *Welborn Township*, Conway, County. Not exactly the same, but it gives us an idea of what the Cleveland store looked like. Sam is standing in the middle. Sam was very often involved in leading singing at community churches.

While **Sam** was at the store or away, **Stella** reared the children, raised gardens and small animals for food, dried and preserved fruit, completely remade old clothes for her children to wear. She often assisted other mothers by making clothing for their children. Older daughter, **Allene** assisted in home chores.

Sam Swain and Stella Trimble's Family Tree

Source: Ancestry.com • Marcia Swain Crossman's Family Tree, 2024

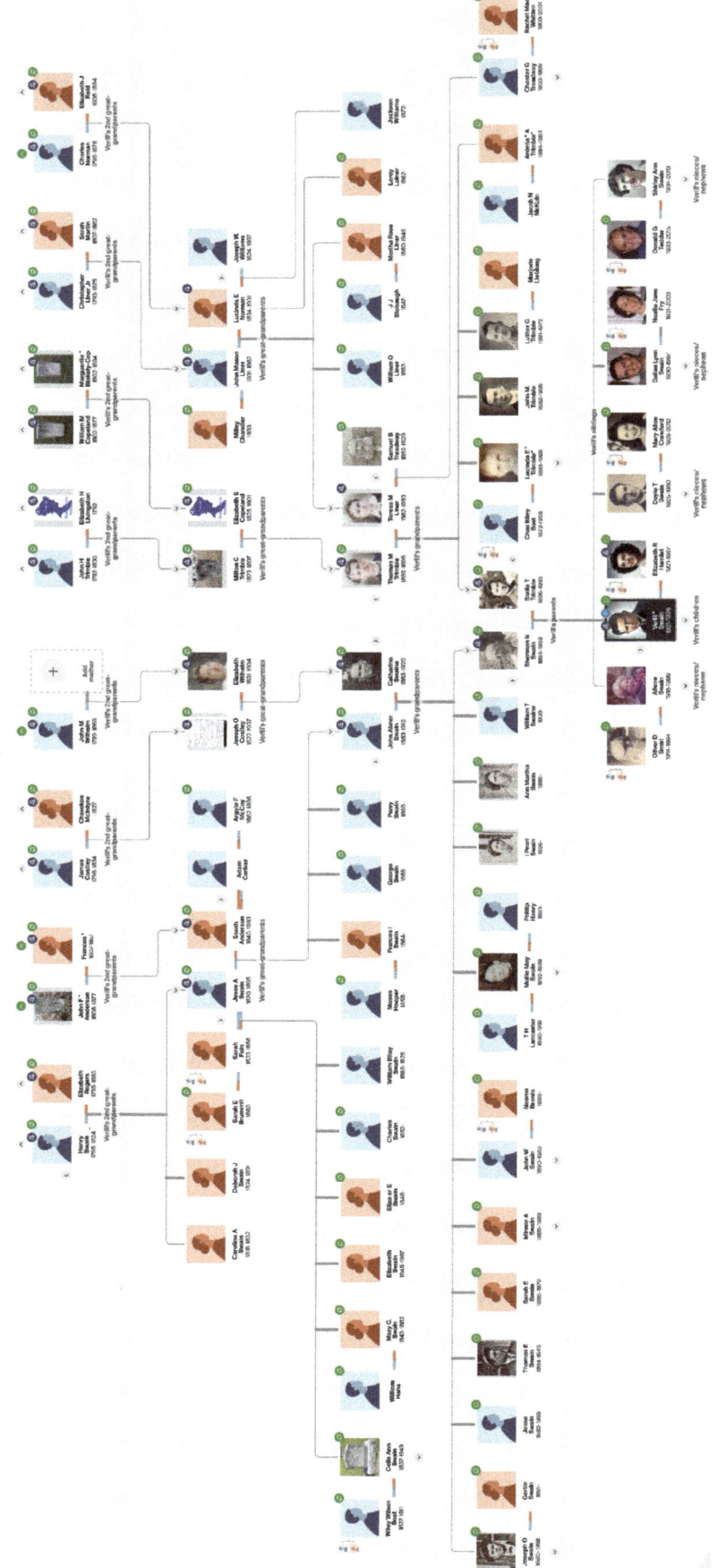

Memories of Ansel Swain's Family

Photo to Left:
Shirley (daughter) & her friend,

*Stella & Sam Swain,
location possibly Blackwell*

Family Photo Below:
*Ansel, Doyle & Dallas Swain,
(sons),*

*Sam Swain holding Joe Smirl &
Stella Swain (parents),*

*Allene Swain Smirl, & Shirley
Swain, (daughters)
Around 1940, during WWII*

Memories of Ansel Swain's Family

Left:
Allene, Stella, Shirley and Doyle Swain children of Sam and Stella Swain. Around 1942.

Right:
Stella Thomas Trimble Swain, Around 1960

Bottom Left:
Stella Swain's mother, Teresa Liner Trimble Treadaway, Stella, Allene standing & Shirley, daughters. Around 1941. **What beautiful hats!**

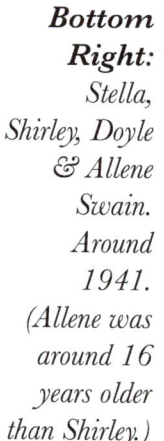

Bottom Right:
Stella, Shirley, Doyle & Allene Swain. Around 1941. (Allene was around 16 years older than Shirley.)

Memories of Ansel Swain's Family

Right: Sam-Swain with grand-daughters *Olivia Smirl, Sherry & Marcia Swain. Around 1955.*

Sherman Norton "Sam" Swain Sergeant, First Class, WWI, 1917-1919 Served in France in a medical base hospital company. His induction papers described him being tall, medium build, with light brown hair & blue eyes.

Note: John Abner Swain was father of Sam Swain.

Below: Sherman Swain in his last years.

Left to Right: Children of John Abner & Catherine Costley Swain: Pearle, Joe, Bill, Tom, Sam, & Annie with spouse Elbert Lentz

Memories of Ansel Swain's Family

"Rookies at Camp Pike: Myers, Harmbek, Swain & Harman, WWI. Around 1915"

"Camp Dix NJ: These soldiers were on a hike and found picknickers.
Swain with an "x", WWI. Around 1915"

Memories of Ansel Swain's Family

*Swain Family
Gathering
Left to Right
from first row up:
About 1957*

*John, Sam,
Marcia, Elizabeth,
Bill Swain,
Shirey (Swain) &
Don, Alan Teddar,
Sherry, Stella Swain,
Oliver & Allene
(Swain) Smirl,
Dallas Swain,
Joe & Olivia Smirl,
Mary & Doyle Swain*

*Swain Family
Gathering
Left to Right About
About 1953*

*Sam, Nealia Jane,
Doyle, Dallas
holding Bill Swain,
Stella holding
John Swain,
Joe Smirl, Marcia in
high chair, Ansel Swain,
Mary Swain, Oliver,
Allene & Olivia Smirl*

Memories of Ansel Swain's Family

Family Gathering:

Top Row: Oliver Smirl holding Sherry Swain; Sam Swain holding Tim Swain; Shirley (Swain) Teddar holding Alan Teddar.

Front Row: Marcia Swain, Olivia Smirl, Bill Swain, and John Swain. about 1954.

Location unsure, notice the tall ceilings.

Family Gathering:

Sam, Stella, Ansel, & Elizabeth (Hamlet) Swain,

Mary (Cranford) Swain (married to Doyle Swain),

Allene (Swain) Smirl (married to Oliver Smirl),

Shirley Swain (eventually married Donald Eugene Teddar),

The children are probably Olivia & Joe Smirl, children of Allene.

Location may be Ansel & Elizabeth's home in Morrilton on Church Street when first married in 1950.

Descendants of Sam and Stella Swain, Part One

Source: Ancestry.com • Marcia Swain Crossman's Family Tree, 2024

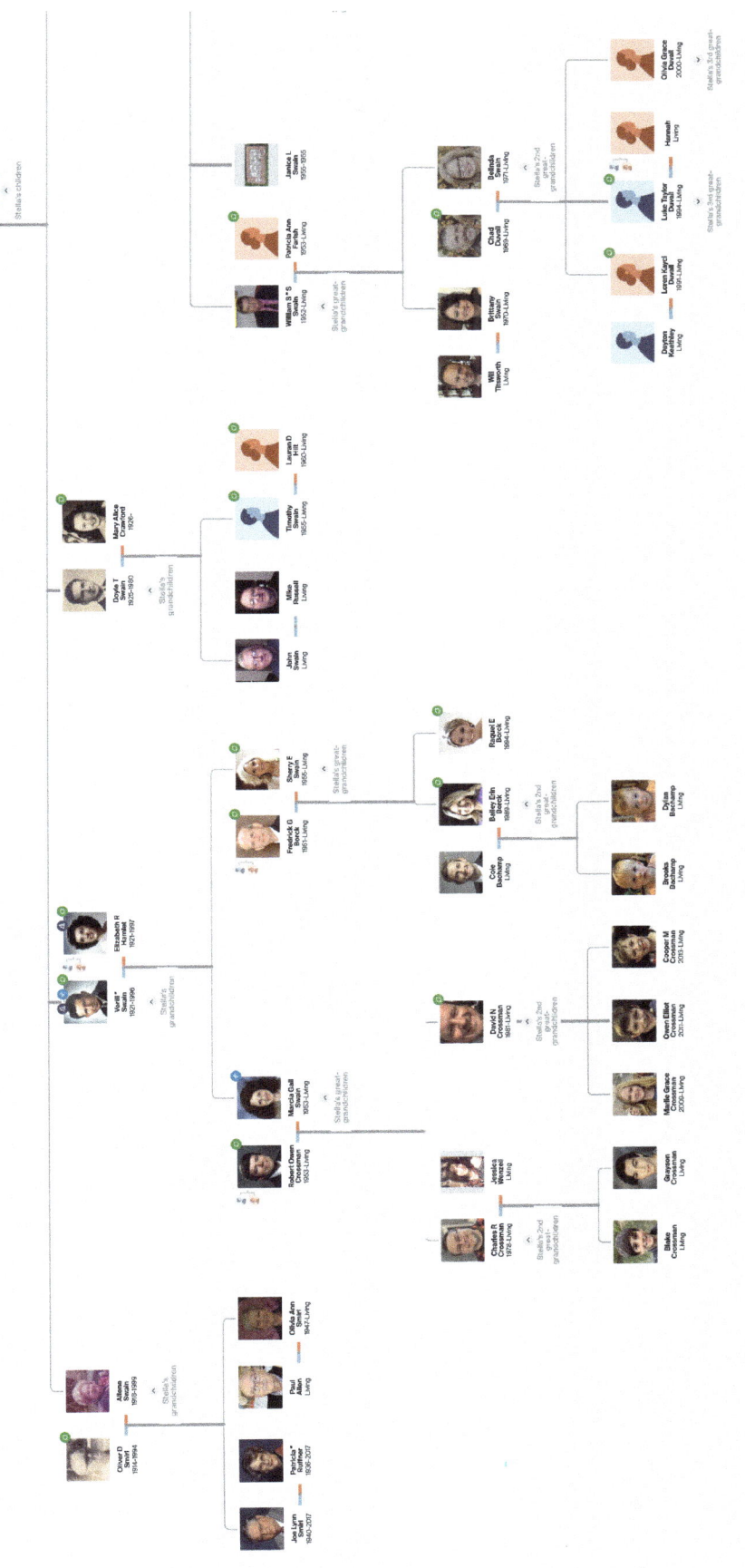

Descendants of Sam and Stella Swain, Part Two

Source: Ancestry.com • Marcia Swain Crossman's Family Tree, 2024

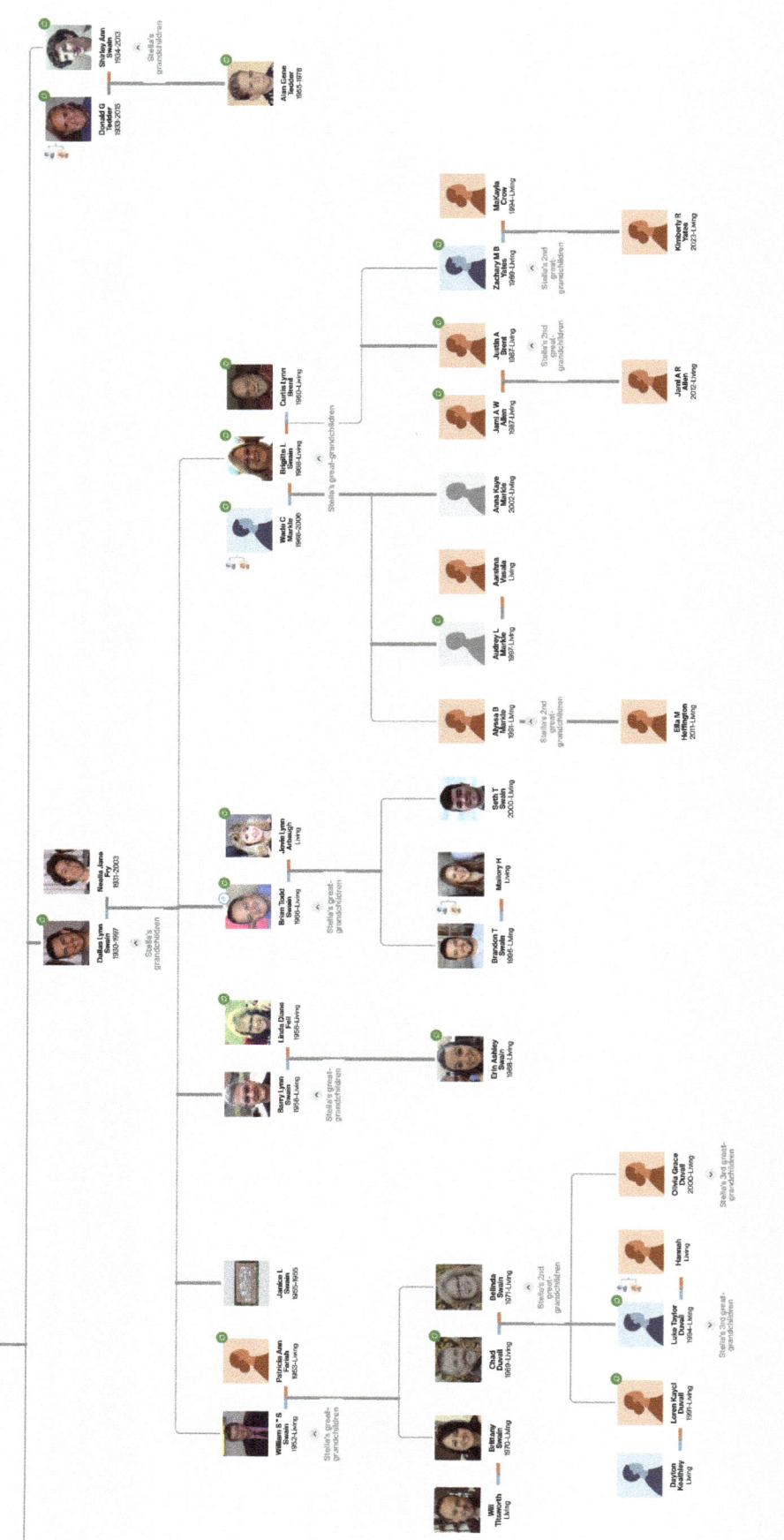

In Memory of Sam Swain and Stella Trimble

Sam Swain is buried at the Old Liberty Cemetery.

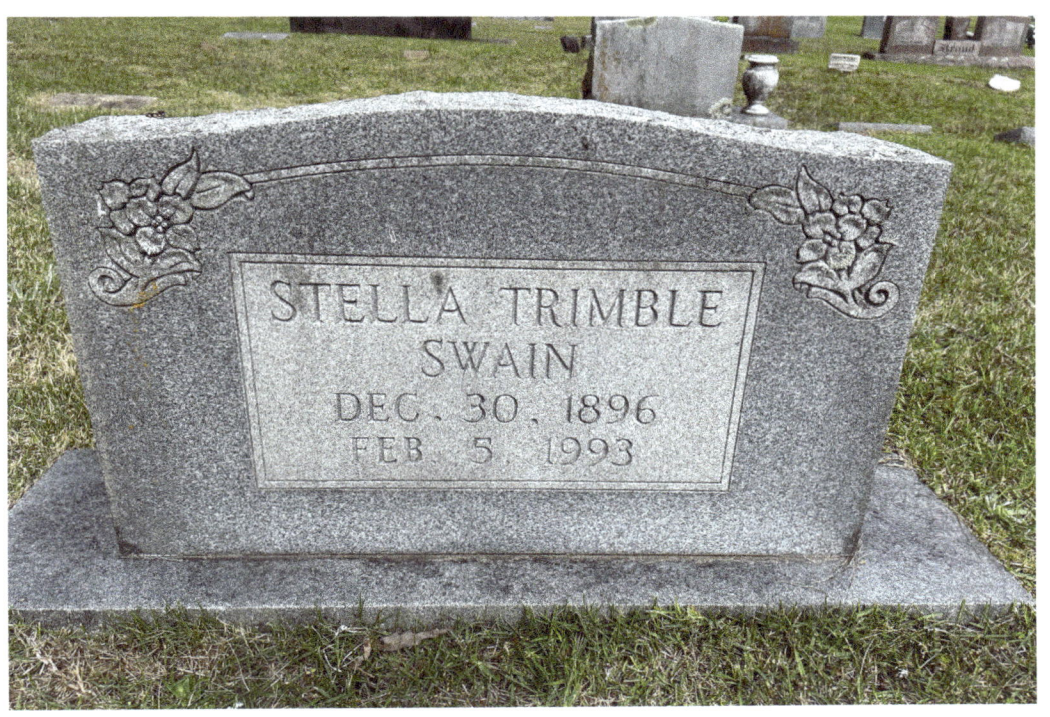

Stella Swain is buried at the Pleasant Grove Cemetery.

Obituary
Sherman
Norton Swain

Retired postmaster, born October 18, 1894, merchant of Blackwell died at age 64 in his home. He was a native of Cleveland, a veteran of WWI, a Mason and member of the Church of Christ where he lived for 21 years. He was married to Stella Trimble of Scotland. The burial was at the Old Liberty Cemetery near Scotland.

Obituary
Stella Thomas
Trimble Swain

Formerly of Blackwell, Stella Swain passed away at the age of 96. The widow of Sam Swain, she was born Dec. 30, 1896 in Scotland. She was a daughter of Thomas Trimble and Teresa Liner Trimble. She was a member of the New Liberty Church of Christ near Cleveland. She had five children, ten great grandchildren and one great great grandchild. Funeral services were at the Harris Funeral Home in Morrilon by Robert O. Crossman, (spouse of grandchild Marcia). Burial was at the Pleasant Grove Cemetery a few miles from Scotland where her husband was buried.

Ansel

and

The Civilian Conservation Corps

"The Great Depression"

Section Two

Ansel Enters The Civilian Conservation Corps
"The Great Depression" Section Two

"Amid the depression years of the 1930s, **"Ansel"** *(as he was called all his life)* **Swain** left Morrilton High School, after his 11th grade, to financially assist his family and entered the **Civilian Conservation Corps**. Ansel, at only sixteen, was accepted into the CCC's. Swain spent over two years in regular CCC service.

A Photo of Ansel in his teen years...

*I propose to create the **Civilian Conservation Corps** to be used in complex work, not interfering with abnormal employment, and confining itself to forestry, the prevention of soil erosion, flood control and similar projects.*

*I call your attention to the fact that this type of work is of **definite, practical value**, not only through the prevention of great present financial loss, but also as a **means of creating future national wealth**.*

PRESIDENT FRANKLIN D. ROOSEVELT

Going out to job sites...

What was the CCC's all about?

The great depression was raging. People were out of work. Families were hungry; children were not healthy. Crops were not growing.

The US Government under **President Franklin Roosevelt had an idea. We could call on young men ages 17-25 to fix this problem. Young men could be selected to live in tents and perform hard labor to help farmers control their soil and to build camps and parks all over the country.** *It would not be a pleasant thing. The government would send approximately $25 each month directly to the families of these boys.*

In turn, the **young men would be provided housing in tents, food, clothing and tools.** *Each boy had a tent with other youth, ate meals of plain and simple foods in groups, enough to sustain their needs and* **were given several pieces of clothes, enough to wash and keep clean. It was cold and it was hot.** *There was no air conditioning and no hot water.* **Labor lasted nine to ten hours a day, and even six days a week.** *There was work with* **pic axes, shovels and hoes, nothing fancy.** *But the boys labored on. They* **helped farmers gain control of their land,** *especially in Kansas which was the center of the dust bowl. Their work can still be seen in rock walls and state parks that we enjoy today. The work was hard and long, but most boys did it to help their families.* **They had no cars, snacks, recreation, or girls to keep their minds occupied. At night they slept well due to exhaustion. The morning would come. Most boys stayed at least two years.**

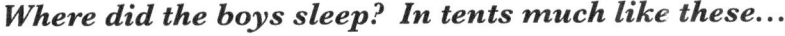

Where did the boys sleep? In tents much like these...

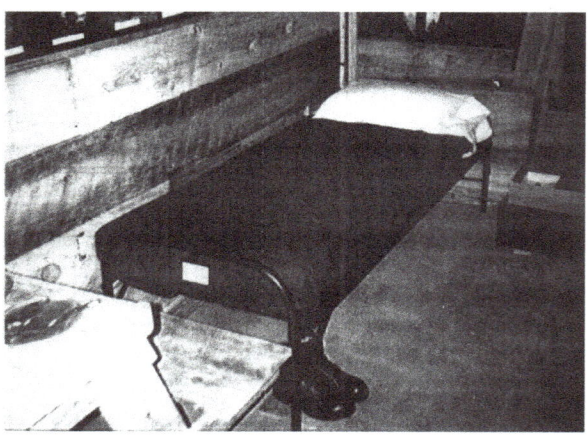

Boys slept on cots in tents.

After a year in the CCC's, Ansel was promoted to **hospital attendant**, Ansel, at one time, **sewed up the head of a young man who had received a blow from a pic axe into his head.**

When Ansel was around 18 years old, he was transferred to the Conservation Corps Base **Headquarters in the Medical Department** in Jacksonville, Ark. where he was employed as **Chief Clerk.**

While in Jacksonville, Ansel was able to **finish his high school education** in night school receiving his diploma.

If you were a teen back in those days, would you join the CCC's to help your family?

Ansel Swain's Trunk from the CCC's.

When our parents, **Ansel and Elizabeth Swain passed away,** *my sister, Sherry and I shared all their* **worldly possessions.** *Our parents wrote a letter to us before they died. When the time came, they wanted us to share their things in the most equal way.* **"Share and share alike,"** *they wrote us. We did this in the most amicable way. I ended up hauling an old wooden trunk home from this trade. I have always been attracted to the trunk. I felt the need to protect it and will never sell it or give it away.*

The trunk had our father's name on it. "V. A. Swain" was hand painted on the top in beautiful gold calligraphy. *The trunk is approximately 30" x 30" x 24" and made with brown stained wood. It is a basic box with metal hinges and latch for a lock on the outside. It is not a beautiful box but it was* **functional.** *This mysterious trunk was placed in the attic of my house for around 18 years. It was stored in other garages for seven years.*

I had no idea where it came from until my research into the CCC's. There, I found that the **young men were given these trunks to keep their belongings in.** *Footlockers were used by the CCC workers to hold their personal possessions. The trunks were then used to take their belongings with them when honorably discharged from the Corps.*

Trunks were built by the young men serving in the camps. The CCC camp was a temporary community structured to have barracks (initially Army tents) for 50 enrollees each, officer/technical staff quarters, medical dispensary, mess hall, recreation hall, educational building, lavatory and showers, technical/administrative offices, tool room/blacksmith shop and motor pool garages. Along with these places of work was a place to build these trunks.

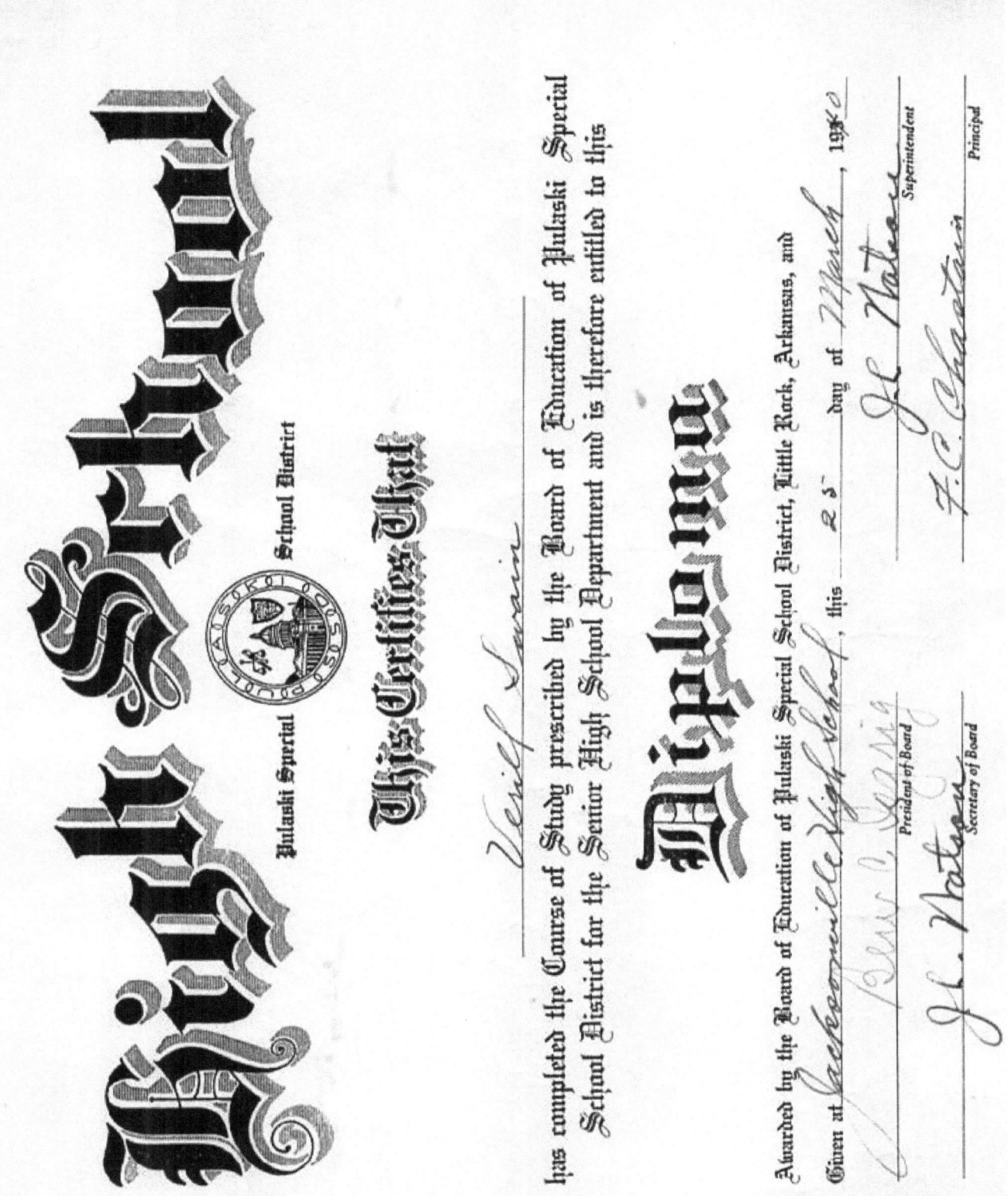

Ansel earned his high school diploma in night school in the CCC's

Graduating from Jacksonville High School while in the CCC's, Ansel became **assistant to the camp physician**. On his **19th** birthday, in 1940, he was appointed **Civilian Clerk** in the War Department in Little Rock. He was later given the job of **Chief Clerk** in the District Physician's office where he stayed until enlistment in the Seabees. He was called in November. Following a school for Yeomen and Storekeeper, Swain was transferred and trained for service in the **64th U.S. Naval Battalion**.

Verill Ansel Swain was around 21 years old
when he left the Civilian Conservation Corps.

Would you like to know more about the Civilian Conservation Corps?

Wikipedia has excellent information along with the Butler Central for Arkansas Research. arkansas-ccc.com/ccc/camps-in-arkansas This is information compiled from these sources.

The CCC's was started in early 1932 to use young men from the lists of the unemployed to improve existing reforestation areas. It was a voluntary government work relief program that ran from 1933 to 1942 in the United States for unemployed, unmarried men ages 18–25 and expanded to ages 17–28. Upon conception of the New Deal Program by Franklin D. Roosevelt, the CCC provided a sense of immediate relief to the citizens of the state of Arkansas and other states.

It promised to provide 250,000 young men with meals, housing, work wear, and medical care for working in the national forests and other government properties. Sources written at the time claimed an individual's enrollment in the CCC led to improved physical condition, heightened morale, and increased employability. The temporary tent camps had developed to include wooden barracks. An education program had been established, emphasizing job training and literacy.

The typical CCC enrollee was a US citizen, unmarried, unemployed male, 18–25 years of age. Normally his family was sent directly $25 (about equivalent to $570 in 2022). The worker/ dependent was provided housing, food, clothing, and medical care. Each enrollee volunteered. Upon passing a physical exam and/or a period of conditioning, was required to serve a minimum six-month period, with the option to serve as many as four periods, or up to two years, if employment outside the Corps was not possible. Enrollees worked 40 hours per week over five days, sometimes including Saturdays if poor weather dictated.

Nationwide approximately 55% of enrollees were from rural communities, a majority of which were non-farm and 45% came from urban areas. Level of education for the enrollee averaged 3% illiterate, 38% had less than

eight years of school, 48% did not complete high school and 11% were high school graduates. At the time of entry, 70% of enrollees were malnourished and poorly clothed. Few had work experience beyond occasional odd jobs.

An implicit goal of the CCC was to restore morale in an era of 25% unemployment for all men and higher rates for poorly educated teenagers. Through a regime of heavy manual labor, civic and political education, and an all-male living and working environment, the CCC tried to build "better men" who would be economically independent and self-reliant. In the U.S., the largest

Shovels and pic axes, not power tools . . .

enrollment nationwide, at any one, time was 300,000.

Through the course of its nine years, three million young men took part in the CCC's, which provided them with shelter, clothing, and food, together with a wage of $20-$30, equivalent to $678 in today's dollars value. ($25 per month had to be sent home to their families). The CCC was designed to supply jobs for young white men and to relieve families who had difficulty finding jobs during the Great Depression in the United States. The CCC provided a sense of immediate relief to the citizens of the state of Arkansas.

The CCC disbanded one year earlier than planned, as the 77th United States Congress ceased funding it.

Operations were formally concluded at the end of the federal fiscal year on June 30, 1942. The end of the CCC program and closing of the camps involved arrangements to leave the incomplete work projects in

the best possible state, the separation of about 1,800 appointed employees, the transfer of CCC property to the War and Navy Departments and other agencies. Some former CCC sites in good condition were reactivated from 1941 to 1947 as Civilian Public Service camps where conscientious objectors performed "work of national importance" as an alternative to military service. Approximately 47 young men died while in this line of duty.

General Douglas MacArthur was placed in charge of the program, but said that the number of army officers and soldiers assigned to the camps was affecting the readiness of the regular army. However, the army also found numerous benefits in the program. When the draft began in 1940, the policy was to make CCC alumni corporals and sergeants. The CCC also provided command experience to Organized Reserve Corps officers. Through the CCC, the regular army could assess the leadership performance of both regular and reserve officers. The CCC provided lessons which the army used in developing its wartime mobilization plans for training camps.

Because of the power of conservative "Solid South," white Democrats in Congress, insisted on racial segregation. Most New Deal programs were racially segregated. Blacks and whites

rarely worked alongside each other. At this time, all the states disenfranchised most blacks. Because of discrimination by white officials at the local and state levels, blacks in the South did not receive as many benefits as whites from New Deal programs. In the first few weeks of operation, CCC camps in the North were integrated. By July 1935, however, all camps in the United States were segregated. Enrollment peaked at the end of 1935, when there were 500,000 men in 2,600 camps in operation in all states. All received equal pay and housing. Black leaders lobbied to secure leadership roles. Adult white men held the major leadership roles in all the camps. Director Fechner refused to appoint black adults to any supervisory positions except that of education director in the all-black camps.

In 1933, veterans from World War I were qualified These men received additional pay ranging from $36 to $45 per month depending on their rating. They could be any age, physical condition and married or single as long as they were in need of work. Veterans in Arkansas were generally assigned to four camps. Enrollees were eligible for positions to help with camp administration: senior leader, mess steward, storekeeper and two cooks; assistant leader, company clerk, assistant educational advisor and three second cooks.

Hard labor was typical in the camps.

```
                HEADQUARTERS SEVENTH CORPS AREA
                Office of the Corps Area Commander


                                              Omaha, Nebraska
                                              June 8, 1942


    Name: _____ Verill A. Swain _____

    Employed in: Medical Section, Hq. Arkansas District CCC,
                 Little Rock, Arkansas.

    Position: ____ Junior Clerk _____

    Service: ____ CAF _____ Grade: ___ 2 __

    Roll:   Civilian Conservation Corps


            Your efficiency rating for the period ending March 31, 1942,

    is ____1_____ ___Excellent_____.
       numerical rating   adjective rating


            Final approval of this rating has been given by the Efficiency
    Rating Committee.


                                              John A. Shaw
                                              JOHN A. SHAW
                                              Colonel, Infantry
                                              Acting Assistant Adjutant General
```

Adjective Rating	Numerical Rating
Excellent	1
Very Good	2 or 3
Good	4, 5 or 6
Fair	7 or 8
Unsatisfactory	9

JUN 15 1942
C.C.C., ARK
SURG. DIST. ARK.

Efficiency Rating June 8, 1942 for Ansel Swain.
Ansel rated a 2 for very good as a junior clerk.

Arkansas CCC companies were allowed to remain in the largely rural state since there were so many forest and recreation projects underway.

The greatest legacy left in Arkansas by the CCC was their work in the development of state parks.

The CCC build infrastructure at **Petit Jean State Park**,

The CCC also built infrastructure at state parks that included **Mount Nebo, Crowley's Ridge, Devil's Den, Lake Catherine, and Buffalo River State Park**, which is now part of the Buffalo National River and known as Buffalo Point.

Grandfather Sherman Norton Swain *participated in a CCC camp as a WWI veteran. He was later honorably discharged. This was before the family moved to Blackwell, Ark. Sam and Stella Swain had four children by that time. Veterans were given leadership roles in the camps earning around $50 a month to be sent back home to their families.*

Ansel and The US Navy

64th Seabees Navy Battalion

"World War II"

Section Three

Ansel and The US Navy
64th Seabees Navy Battalion

"World War II" Section Three

Verill Ansel Swain was called to the US Armed Forces.

"Men born on or after Feb. 17, 1897 and on or before Dec. 31, 1921 must register for the draft."

Ansel was born on April 13, 1921.

Verill Ansel Swain - From Cleveland to Morrilton, Arkansas

Registration Card for US Armed Forces

Ansel is third from the left.

— 41 —

Report for Induction

ORDER TO REPORT FOR INDUCTION

JUL 10 '42
(Date of mailing)

OARD A
COUNTY
. ARKANSAS
(OCAL BOARD)

...e United States,

To .... Verill .... A .... Swain
(First name)   (Middle name)   (Last name)

Order No. 10497

GREETING:

Having submitted yourself to a Local Board composed of your neighbors for the purpose of deter-
...ning your availability for training and service in the armed forces of the United States, you are hereby

...l that you have now been selected for training and service in the .... Army
(Army, Navy, Marine Corps)

...will, therefore, report to the Local Board named above at .... 723 Boyle Bldg
(Place of reporting)

...00 A. m., on the .... 20 .... day of July .... , 1942
(Hour of reporting)

This Local Board will furnish transportation to an induction station of the service for which you have been selected.
You will there be examined and if accepted for training and service, you will then be inducted into the stated branch of the
service.

Persons reporting to the induction station in some instances may be rejected for physical or other reasons. It is well
...eep this in mind in arranging your affairs, to prevent any undue hardship if you are rejected at the induction station.
...u are employed, you should advise your employer of this notice and of the possibility that you may not be accepted at
...duction station. Your employer can then be prepared to replace you if you are accepted, or to continue your
...ent if you are rejected.

...u are not accepted, you will be furnished transportation to the place where you were living when ordered to report
...tion by this Local Board.

...ful failure to report promptly to this Local Board at the hour and on the day named in this notice is a violation of
...ctive Training and Service Act of 1940 and subjects the violator to fine and imprisonment. Bring with you sufficient
...for 3 days.

...ou must keep this form and bring it with you when you report to the Local Board.

If you are so far removed from your own Local Board that reporting in compliance with this Order will be a serious
...ship and you desire to report to a Local Board in the area of which you are now located, go immediately to that Local
...rd and make written request for transfer of your delivery for induction, taking this Order with you.

D. S. S. Form 150
(Revised 6/2/41)

16—18271

...of Local Board.

Clerk

V. Ansel Swain registered to serve in the US Armed Forces. He then received orders:
- Report for Induction July 20, 1942 -

Having submitted yourself to a Local Board composed of your neighbors for the purpose of determining your availability for training and service in the Armed Forces, (Army, Navy, Marine Corps), you will therefore, report to the Local Board named above at 723 Boyle Building in Little Rock, Arkansas, on the 20th day of July 1942. The Board will furnish transportation to induction station where you will be examined. If accepted you will be inducted to your branch of the Army. Failure to report to the Local Board is a violation of the Service act of 1940 and will lead to fine and imprisonment.

*V. Ansel Swain
reported
to the
US Armed Services
for induction
on
July 20, 1942*

*Notice of
Classification
from the
Local Board in
Little Rock, AR
had come on
July 1, 1942.
Ansel
was to be
1-A.*

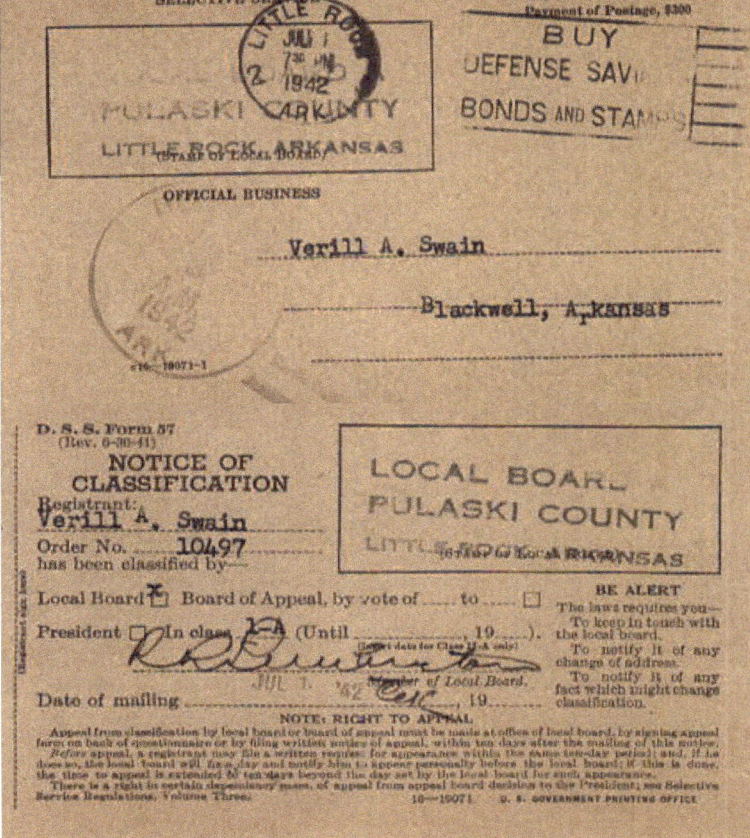

What did Ansel Swain tell his family about the US Navy?
What was 1942-1945 like in his life?

The only thing our dad told us about the Navy was how he got home, sitting on the top of a Navy carrier ship.

Ansel never spoke of the Navy during family time. There was never a mention around the dinner table or conversations with old Navy buddies. Our family never discussed what our dad did in the Navy. Ansel never told us his story of the 64th Naval Battalion.

Back then, we though we knew what the US Navy was all about. My sister and I had seen enough **Saturday movies** to think the Navy men floated the oceans drinking coffee in the canteen and playing cards in the bunks.

Possibly we had seen enough **John Wayne** *movies to envision the sailors, with their white hats, floating onto the shores of Hawaii, sitting on top of big guns and bombing the Japanese.* Did our father do that in the Navy?

Ansel's Navy photos always revealed a smile on his face. He wasn't unhappy there. Even though he was drafted, I believe he wanted to go. His father had served in WWI. His brothers, Doyle and Dallas went in the Navy. Many Americans went to war for freedom, some because they were forced to. But our dad had good American values and one was to keep our country safe.

For Ansel, it was about people back home. He wanted to get married, have a family, be part of a community and go to church. Life with others was important. He wanted a good job and to be in service back home.

Where did I learn what our father did in the Navy Seabees?

When we packed our parents home to sell we found a very old **box of books** that belonged to our father. The small collection was composed of books from the Civilian Conservation Corps, the Navy Seabees, yearbooks and books on the history and mechanism for producing corduroy. There was also a ragged old scrapbook, tied up to keep loose pages inside. *This **library in a box** traveled from their basement, to my attic and later to our garage.*

In 2023, I dug into the traveling library and found a book that explained much to me about our dad. **"The History of the 64th Naval Construction Battalion, 1942-1945."** Looking much like a high school year book, it contains what the **Seabees** did during in the Navy. It is a lasting tribute of the experience of the 64th Battalion. *It is a lasting memory of the life of Ansel Swain.*

"The Uniform Years" in the 64th Battalion history, tells about what these soldiers did in the Navy. **Most recruits arrived at induction by train after many hours of riding across the country.** We don't know where Ansel traveled from. He had lived and worked in Little Rock after the CCC's. Maybe he traveled from Little Rock. There were train stations around his parent's home in Blackwell. Where ever the recruits came from, all tracks led to **Little Creek, Virginia**, the place where there was boot camp.

Men arrived in Virginia in crowded trains. They were marched from the train to **Camp Bradford**, Virginia. Orders were given to cut hair and line up for clothing. **Mercurochrome**, *which has now been proved to be a poison*, names were written across the men's chests. Recruits were cautioned to purchase life insurance. $10,000 was recommended. Your own clothes could be shipped back home for 82 cents. Photos were made for ID cards. Chow...Drill... Demonstrations were given for poison gas masks, hand grenades, and how to use bayonets. At the end of boot camp was liberty.

Last, in the history book is a list of all the the men in the 64th and their home addresses.

Verill Ansel's home was listed simply as "Blackwell, Arkansas."

We owe a great deal of thanks for those who wrote and compiled the "History of the 64th Naval Construction Battalion, 1942-1945." Those who contributed their time and talents to the assembling of this were: Owen L. Shanreau, Leonard E. Gyllenhaal, John Howard Riley, Louis S. Casalini, James L. Dale, Robert H. Halff, Leonard Garner, Howard F. Moore, Melvin H. Pope, James R. Holland, Thomas M. Ansbro, B. G. Ryals, William P. Walker and the Naval Pictorial Publishers.

Next stop was Williamsburg, Virginia for Basic Training.

The big day, January 8, 1942, arrived. The recruits were moved to Williamsburg, Virginia. Basic training had begun.

There was **technical** training, heavy equipment operation, chemical **warfare** operations, hikes, drills, crawling through barbed wire, over walls, abandoning ship drills, crawling through pipes and other unpleasantnesses. Shots...March... Hike...

Basic training was finally over in two months. The sailors were given leave, but were quickly called back.

Friends in the Seabees, maybe from back home...

Argentia, Newfoundland - the Land of Snow and Winter

On March 24, 1943, the 64th Battalion was shipped out to **Newfoundland**. On their way they encountered a **Code Red** in the Atlantic. Life jackets were worn. A German submarine had just sunk a ship nearby. Finally there was an "all clear."

The Battalion arrived on March 27th at Argentia, Newfoundland to **ten** feet of snow. Strict discipline was applied as cargo was unloaded. The men went in pairs to keep from getting lost in the drift and snow.

The schedule included marching, drills, and hikes in the rain and snow. The 64th built roads, walks, and railroad tracks. Gasoline refueling piers, additional barracks, mess halls, and storage buildings were built to hold ammunition. Their tasks were unending.

All went well until one night when bombs began to fall. Flames and fires on planes began to soar. Finally the air raid came to an end.

Were Ansel's teeth chattering from the cold?

These Seabees look cold!

Travel in pairs! Get the winter gear! In Newfoundland, they built a ship house, industrial shop, docks and a wharf. They built roads, barracks, and a train depot station. Airway and roads were extended. The Seabees worked night and day to support the US Armed forces.

Ansel is front row on the right.

The 64th was finally leaving the land of snow and ice.

Where would the 64th be sent next?

Liberty! A 25 day leave in Providence, RI was well earned.

Then, there would be a long train ride across the country from the east coast to the west coast of the US. The next stop was the islands of the Pacific Ocean.

Ansel on the beach

Ansel standing on the right above

Pearl Harbor, Hawaii

This time the 64th would be **shoving off again** into the Pacific. On October 25, 1944 the Sea-bees boarded Army water transport boats. Their destination was **Pearl Harbor, Hawaii**. There was five days on board with *no lights above or below the decks while they traveled.*

One of their duties was to build barracks for the Lady Marines. There were other Seabees Units around that assisted in this. Most of the Seabees would remember the **liberties**. There was enter-tainment abound in Hawaii, anything a person desired. **Recreation at camp** included programs back at the base. Then followed shots and training on jungle diseases. Even though the men enjoyed the beautiful island of Hawaii and all it offered, there was still more training and building to be done in **Samar, Philippines**.

Ansel in the center above

Ansel on the left

On the way to the Philippines the 64th would be stopping over in **Tokyo, Japan and other islands**.

Much care was taken as pockets of Japanese were still left in the islands.

Ansel, on the left, with a buddy

Tubabao Island, Philippians

On April 28, 1945, the 64th arrived in **Tubabao Island in the Philippines**.

Their biggest mission lay ahead-to finish building an entire US Naval Receiving Station which had been begun by the 54th Naval Construction Battalion. It would mean that every man would have to work as long and hard as humanly possible. With work, there was **rain, malaria and heat** to deal with. This went on for four months of backbreaking labor. There were six areas dupli-cated for accommodating 1,500 men each, in total for supporting 9,000 service men.

Completely Created an Island

The 64th also built quarters for the officers, mess halls, laundries, sick bay and chapel. Added to this was a **movie theater, handball and basketball** courts, game rooms and a wonderful **baseball** field. Rocks were blasted from the island and concrete was made. Roads and waterfronts were made.

Ansel was right side, middle.

Ansel driving truck.

*With friends,
Ansel is in the middle.*

A close up....

***Ansel
and
Navy
friends***

*The men
built two
training
ships,* the
Invasion
and the
Libertar-
ian.

***Ansel is
3rd from
the right.***

64th Navy Battalion Baseball Team. This was Ansel's favorite activities in the Philippians.

Ansel is shown on row one, second from right.

On Their Way Home...

One night while the men were watching a real movie, news came through. ***The Japanese made a peace offering***. There were days of anticipation for more news. Hirohito would now take his military orders from the Allied Supreme Command.

Time passed. Around **400 of the 950 in the 64th** had gained points in a release system, the old 64th, so faithful to their service, was on their way to release.

Though the 64th had seen no active engagements, they **helped make victory a reality**. The 64th Battalion, as a unit, would be no more. **It was time for each to make his way home to families, wives, and children.**

Each was grateful for helping to bring victory and peace to the world once more.

350 Seabees units were formed during the Second World War.

It was said of the Seabees: They were soldiers in sailors uniform, with marine training, doing civilian work at WPA wages.

The USS Antaeus was the ship that transported the 64th Battalion.

The original name of this ship, between 1932 and 1941, was the Saint John. It was owned as a shipping and commercial passenger boat. The ship was acquired by the US Navy on April 24, 1941.

This ship was commissioned as the **USS Antaeus and carried the 64th Battalion.** The Antaeus served in the Pacific. She was given two battle stars for her role in World War II service. After the war, the Antaeus was recommissioned on April 29, 1946 to become a Navy rescue or hospital ship at the Brooklyn Navy Yard. She was decommissioned in 1946.

Placed in Permanent Reserve on September 28, 1948, the Antaeus was ultimately advertised for sale on September 12, 1958. Bids opened on September 12, 1958. The following day, the vessel was sold as scrap to a steel production plant in Washington.

Verill A. Swain
age 23
of
Blackwell, Ark.
was
honored
in
CAN DO
a publication
of the
Navy
Seabees

This photo
appeared in the
newspaper
article
on the
next page.

Naval Publication Honors Verill A. Swain of Blackwell

In North Atlantic

Naval Publication Honors Verill A. Swain Of Blackwell.

CAN DO, official publication of the 64th Naval Construction Battalion, Fleet Post Office, New York, N. Y. in the issue of December 17 carried on the front page a picture of Verill A. Swain, SK2c, son of Mr. and Mrs. Sam Swain of Blackwell, one of the circulation managers of the publication, with this story:

"Verill A. Swain, SK2c, who so pleasantly handles his job in the Disbursing Office, is a typical American youth whose normal progress in life has been interrupted by war.

"Growing up in the little town of Cleveland, Arkansas where his father was in the general mercantile business, Swain had a normal small town boyhood. After school hours, he helped his father around the store and whenever possible gathered the neighborhood boys on a corner lot for a loud voice game of scrub baseball. He loved the game and played it well enough to make the American Legion team which placed second in the state race in 1936.

"Graduated from High School in 1938, he went to work on the CCC soil conservation program as a laborer. After six months he became assistant to the camp physician and a year later, on his nineteenth birthday, he was appointed Civilian Clerk in the War Department District Headquarters at Little Rock, where he worked for the next twelve months. Verill was then given the job as Chief Clerk in the District Physician's Office at Little Rock where he stayed until enlisting in the Seabees in July, 1942.

"He was called in November and went through 'boot' at Allen and Bradford with the 47th as a SK3c. Following a course in the school for Yeomen and Storekeepers, Swain was transferred to the 64th, and you are all familiar with what the 64th has done and seen.

"Neither married nor contemplating marriage, he plans after the war is over to go into the automobile supply business in central Arkansas with his younger brother, Doyle, who is now a HA1c at the Great Lakes Naval Training Station. With his pleasant smile and willingness to work CAN DO predicts a successful future for the now nebulous Swain Brothers' firm. If you need a spark plug in Arkansas after the war look them up. With the plug you'll get a lot of reminicing about the 64th, but that won't cost any extra."

"Storekeeper Swain 23, of Blackwell, Arkansas is with the North Atlantic Fleet. **CAN DO**, official publication of the 64th Naval Construction Battalion. Fleet Post Office, New York, N.Y. carried on its front page a picture of Verill A. Swain SK2c, son of Mr. and Mrs. Sam Swain of Blackwell, Ark., one of the circulation managers of the publication with this story:

Verill A. Swain, who so pleasantly handles his job in the Disbursing Office, is a typical American youth whose normal progress in life has been interrupted by war.

Growing up in the little town of Cleveland, Arkansas where his father was in the general merchandise business, Swain had a normal small town boyhood. After school hours, he helped his father around the store. Whenever possible he gathered the neighborhood boys on a corner lot for a loud voice game of scrub baseball.

He loved the game and made the American Legion team which placed 2nd in State in 1936 when Ansel was 15 years old.

Graduating from high school in 1938, he went to work on the CCC soil conservation program as a laborer. After six months, he became **Assistant** to the camp physician. On his 19th birthday he was appointed **Civilian Clerk** in the War Department in Little Rock where he worked for the next 12 months. Verill was later given the job of **Chief Clerk** in the District Physician's office where he stayed until enlistment in the Seabees in July 1942.

He was called in November and went through boot at Allen and Bradford with the 47th as a SK3c. Following a course in the school for Yeomen and Storekeeper, Swain was transferred into the 64th. And, you are all familiar with what the 64th has done and seen.

Neither married, nor contemplating marriage, Verill plans after the war to go into the automotive business in Central Arkansas with his younger brother, Doyle Swain, who is currently in Naval training at Great Lakes Naval Training Station.

With his **pleasant smile** and **willingness to work**, CAN DO predicts a successful future for the nebulous Swain Brothers firm."

"If you need a spark plug in Arkansas after the war look up the Swain Brothers.

With the plug, you'll get a lot of reminiscing about the 64th, but that won't cost you any extra."

HEADQUARTERS

ARKANSAS MILITARY DISTRICT

OFFICE OF THE EXECUTIVE

PORBECK BUILDING, 515 EAST SECOND STREET

LITTLE ROCK, ARKANSAS

MEB/mm

28 July 1953

AKMAR 201-SWAIN, Verill A. (Enl)
ER 18 334 568

SUBJECT: Discharge by reason of Expiration Term of Service

TO: SFC Verill A. Swain
        507 E. Church
        Morrilton, Arkansas

        Inclosed herewith is your Honorable Discharge which evidences your separation from the Enlisted Reserve Corps per expiration term of service.

        BY ORDER OF COLONEL MCCONE:

Even though Ansel came home from the Navy in 1945, he was not officially discharged from the reserves until 1953.

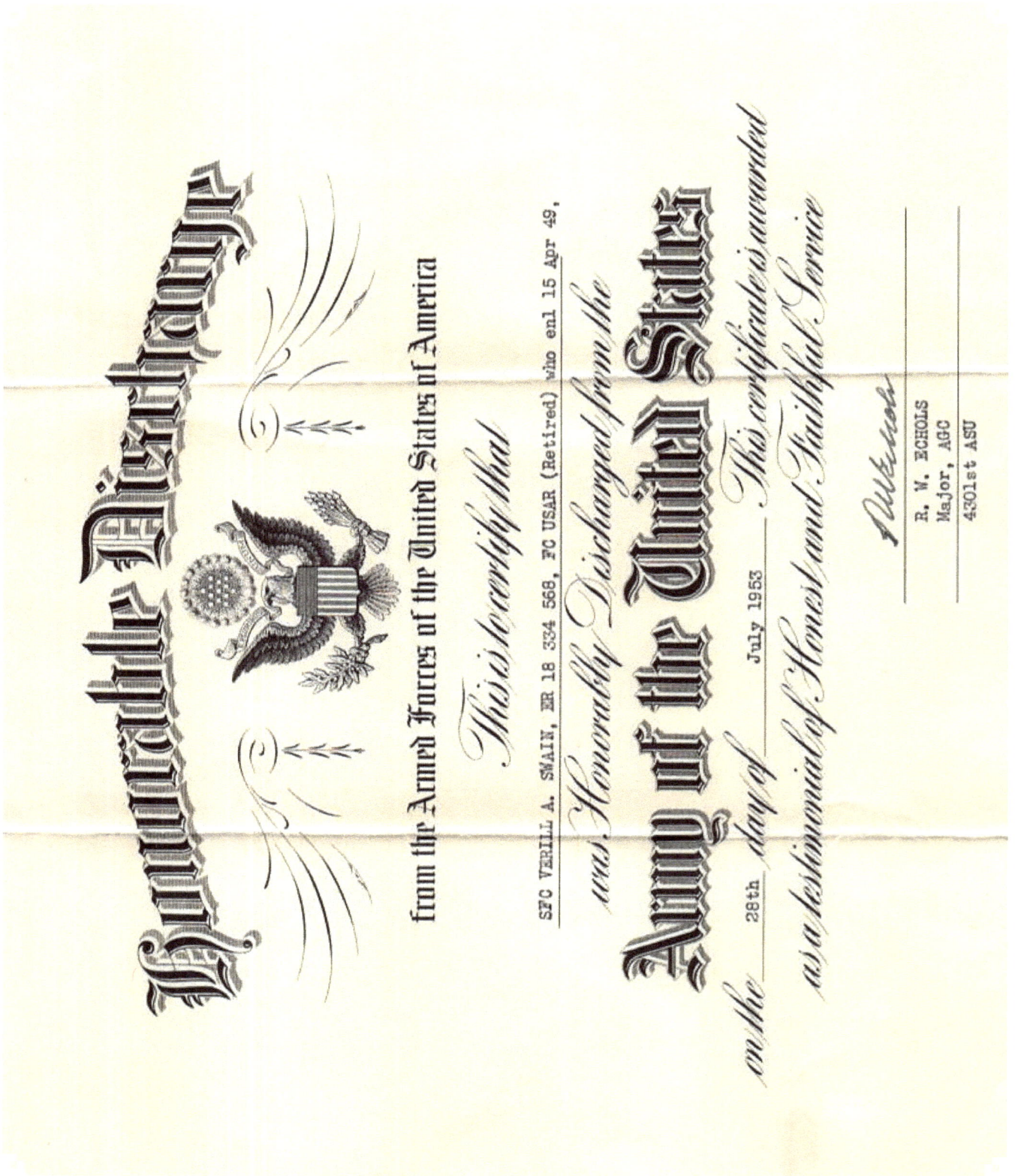

Honorable Army Discharge

from the Armed Forces of the United States of America

This is to certify that

SFC VERILL A. SWAIN, ER 18 334 568, FC USAR (Retired) who enl 15 Apr 49,

was Honorably Discharged from the

Army of the United States

on the _____ 28th _____ day of _____ July 1953 _____   *This certificate is awarded*

as a testimonial of Honest and Faithful Service

R. W. ECHOLS
Major, AGC
4301st ASU

Honorable Navy Discharge paper for Ansel Swain.

VERILL A. SWAIN

To you who answered the call of your country and served in its Armed Forces to bring about the total defeat of the enemy, I extend the heartfelt thanks of a grateful Nation. As one of the Nation's finest, you undertook the most severe task one can be called upon to perform. Because you demonstrated the fortitude, resourcefulness and calm judgment necessary to carry out that task, we now look to you for leadership and example in further exalting our country in peace.

Harry Truman

THE WHITE HOUSE

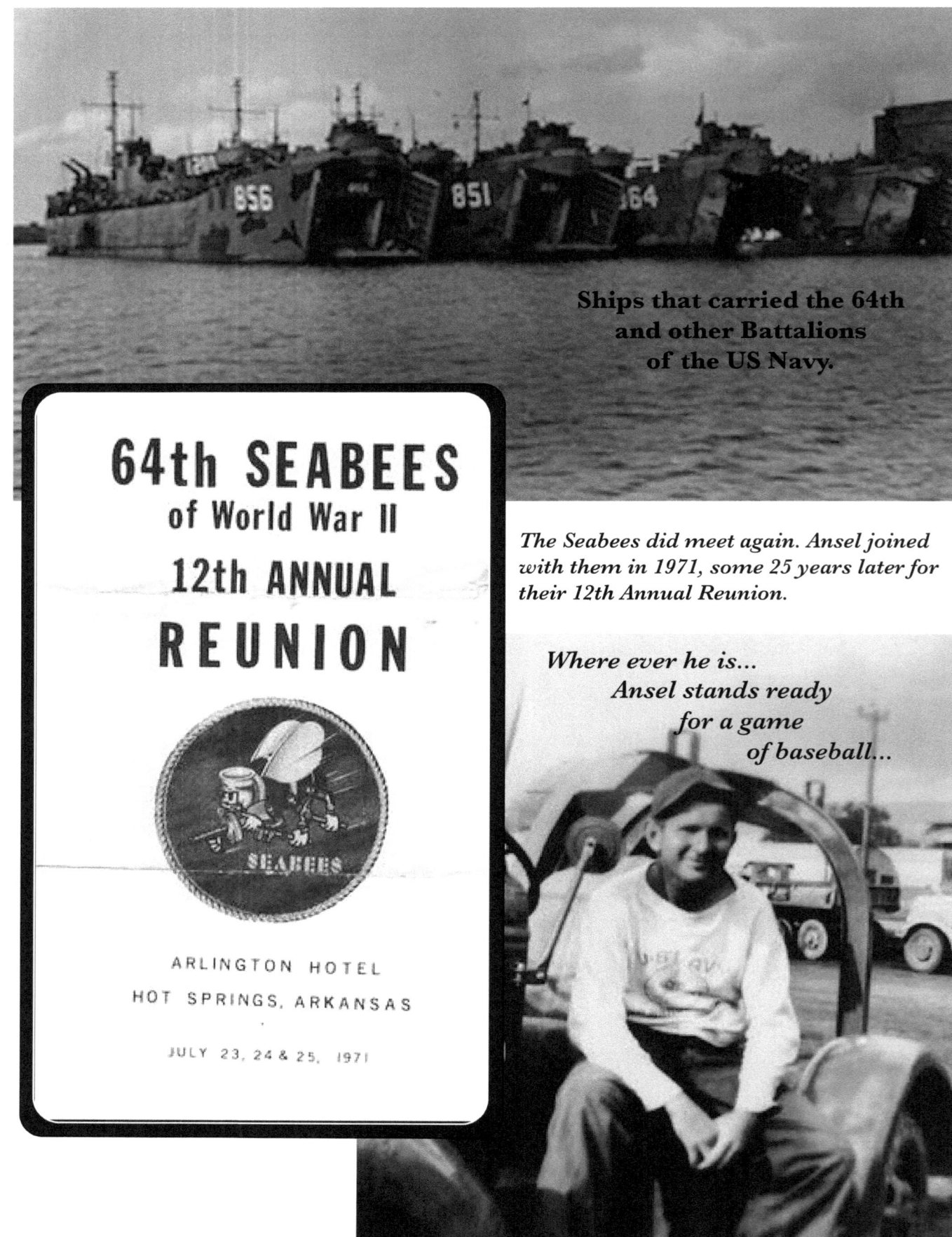

Ships that carried the 64th
and other Battalions
of the US Navy.

64th SEABEES
of World War II
12th ANNUAL
REUNION

SEABEES

ARLINGTON HOTEL
HOT SPRINGS, ARKANSAS

JULY 23, 24 & 25, 1971

*The Seabees did meet again. Ansel joined
with them in 1971, some 25 years later for
their 12th Annual Reunion.*

*Where ever he is...
Ansel stands ready
for a game
of baseball...*

An additional interesting photo...

ITALY OUT OF THE WAR

Ansel

and

Swain's Roller Rink

"Ansel Comes Home From The War"

Section Four

Ansel and Swain's Roller Rink

"Ansel Comes Home From the War" Section Four

Ansel met his bride to be at his favorite place ...

Elizabeth Hamlet Kimberlin and Ansel dance the nights away ...

"With the return to civilian life in 1946, Ansel attended **Arkansas Polytechnic College in Russellville, Arkansas** and the **Arkansas State Teachers College in Conway, Arkansas**. The schools are now known as Arkansas Tech University and the University of Central Arkansas.

Between the years 1947 and 1957, Ansel bought land in Blackwell, Arkansas, near his parent's home, built and operated **Swain Roller Rink**. It was a modern roller rink for skaters and parties from all over the county and beyond.

Ansel's father, **Sherman Norton Swain**, and his brother, **John Wesley "Wes" Swain**, assisted Ansel in building the rink. After the rink was opened **Uncle Wes Swain** assisted in running and cleaning the rink.

In the 1950 US Census, it records this about John Wesley Swain: "John Wesley Swain's occupation was listed as Skating Rink Attendant, hours worked per week, 60." Wes Swain died in 1953 and is buried at Old Liberty near Scotland, Ark. near many other Swains.

Advertising and Operations at the Roller Rink

Grand Opening

You Are Cordially Invited To Attend

OPEN HOUSE

—at—

SWAIN'S

New and Ultra-Modern

ROLLER RINK

Blackwell, On Highway 64

Tuesday Night, September 23, 1947

FREE

Skating Sessions Held Hourly 7-8-9 p. m. in order to accommodate all guests.

Your presence is urgently needed in making this a successful occasion!

OPENING
*Y*ou are cordially invited to attend an

OPEN HOUSE at SWAIN'S ROLLER RINK.

New and Ultra Modern.

Located in Blackwell, on Highway 64,

Tuesday Night, September 23, 1947.

FREE Skating Sessions Held Hourly 7-8-9 p.m. in order to accommodate all guests.

Your presence is urgently needed in making this a successful occasion!

Morrilton Headlight

With a ticket, one could skate for one to two hours by themselves or with a group

Singles and Groups came from as far as Russellville and Little Rock

Rental of the rink's new slates were included in tickets. .

SWAIN'S ROLLER RINK

Let's Go Roller Skatin'!

Blackwell, Arkansas
April 20, 1949

President
Junior Class,
Danville High School,
Danville, Arkansas

Dear Sir:

Quite soon another school year will be at an end and along with it, the date for the annual class trip that you've long waited for. Probably already you have selected and made reservations at the city or site where you shall spend your class vacation.

If your plans include visiting in our particular vicinity, or if your itinerary shall require that you pass by our rink, may we suggest and invite you to include a roller skating session in your schedule.

Located on U. S. Highway No. 64, eight miles West of Morrilton, Arkansas, our rink is considered by skating authorities to be one of Arkansas' outstanding and rates among the highest from a standpoint of patronage and entertainment. The rink floor has recently been re-surfaced and our skates are kept in the very best possible condition.

We shall be able to accomodate your class during any of the week days, Monday through Saturday, 10:00 a.m. until 9:30 p.m., with the exclusion of Tuesday and Thursday nights. A reservation need not be made, however, to insure a guarantee of the rink for your class, we would appreciate your making such request by letter should you definitely conclude that you would like a skating party.

Your presentation and discussion of the above subject with your class will be greatly appreciated.

Very truly yours,

ANSEL SWAIN, Owner
Swain's Roller Rink
Blackwell, Arkansas

Ansel skating ...

Letters were sent to schools and organizations to come and book sessions.

After WWII and through the 1960's Everybody Loved to Skate

Dance Skating

Everyone Skating

Children Skating

In the Mid 1950's Ansel Sold his Roller Rink

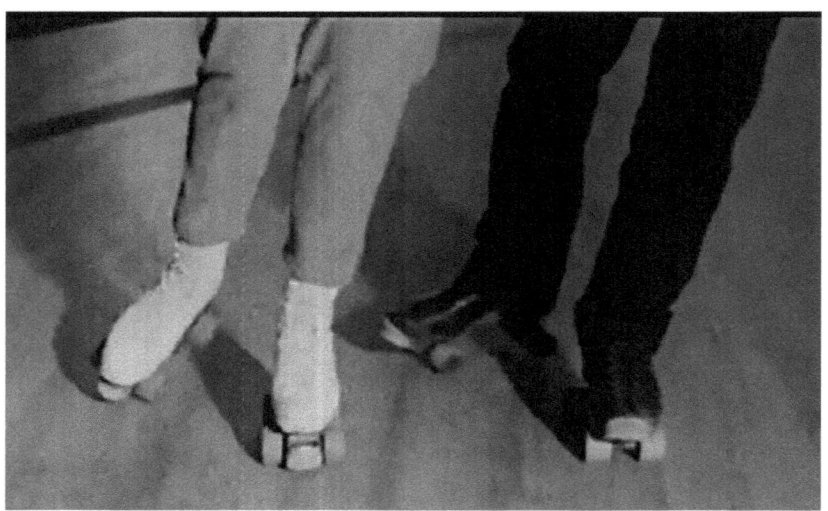

Skates, back in that day, were much like very tight boots. The boots of the skates came up from the toe and over your ankles or mid calves. Men wore black skates and women wore white. On the bottom of the boots were metal soles that attached two sets of rollers. **Roller skate wheels** were made of wood or hard rubber. Contact with the rink floor would quickly wear them out. **One of the expenses that Ansel had was keeping new wheels on the skates.**

Getting the skates on people's feet was a challenge. As one entered the rink, the "pay and rent skates" window was on the right. Here you would purchase your ticket for a two hour session. Then you would be asked, "What size shoe do you wear"? You would be loaned a set of skates that corresponded with your shoe size. Frequent skaters owned their own skates.

When Ansel owned the rink, he hired **teen boys to assist in getting skates on**. One might lace their own skates or ask an attendant to help.

In my adult years, at Crossman Printing in Conway, Ark., customers would come in with stories of **working for Ansel and lacing up skates**. Skates were laced up from the toe end up. Very long laces were criss-crossed on hooks over and over until the top of the skates were reached. The laces then went around the skate a few times and tied in a bow at the top front.

Then there were the skate keys. A skate key would allow an attendant to loosen the wheels for the skater to travel at the fastest speed possible. Only the bravest of skaters wanted this option. There were rubber stops on the skate toes to stop skating. Or, one could stop at the short wall in front of the stands where people were sitting.

Long after our father sold the rink, my sister, Sherry, and I learned to roller skate there. Even though we lived in Morrilton, Blackwell was just a short seven mile trip up Highway 64 west. It was one of the places to have a birthday, church, class or school party. Many people from all communities around Blackwell still reserved the rink for all occasions. Remembering back, many of the little girls who skated there had costumes. An outfit I wore as a child was a short dress made of red corduroy. Silver sequins formed swirl patterns to make it fancy. My mother had made it for me.

Looking back at the rink from my childhood, it seemed like a huge building. Actually it was not much larger than a big house and probably made of wood and concrete blocks. There were posts much like telephone poles, in the center of the building that held up the roof. People skated on a large wood floor. Large fans were placed to around the rink to keep skaters cool on warm days. Three sides of the rink were surrounded by a short wall that would stop the skaters from running into persons resting and sitting on benches behind it. Music played constantly over a speaker. What great memories of friends and parties we went to as children!

Driving through Blackwell Ark., **the old skating rink is just a memory**. In my younger days, one could recognize the "footprint" of the building where it stood. Now it is no longer there ... *just a memory of our dad and mom dance skating in their early days together.*

Ansel and Elizabeth

Courtship and Marriage

"Let's Get Together Tonight"

Section Five

Ansel and Elizabeth Courtship and Marriage

"Courtship and Marriage, 1949-1950" Section Five

Dearest Darling,

I know you are sick and tired of promises, of waiting and never seeming to get any closer to what we really want in life. I come to realize more and more just how much you mean to me. You've been understanding about the whole thing and you never complain about our situation. I appreciate that. A man hates to be in a position where he can't give the woman he loves most of the things she wants. It's painful to his ego - mine anyway. I'd like more than anything to move you into the finest hone in Morrilton - to be able to say to the outsiders, "Look, this is ours." The fact that I can't do something like that accounts for my being so slow in making a move of any sort. It's much nicer to back up words with security than to say, "Honey, marry me and some day I'll give you everything."

I love you, honey. Ansel
September 20, 1949

Letters from Ansel to Elizabeth

A small bundle of personal letters, from Ansel to Elizabeth, written between *January 3, 1949* and *June 14, 1950* still survives today. Those letters were in my possession for 24 years before I opened them. Perhaps I was waiting for courage to open those letters. I hoped, maybe, the letters might be full of sweet talk and swooning. There was some of that going on.

Much of a letter written on *October 25, 1949* has words that are of such a personal matter that I cannot include them. Only my sister and I will ever share the reading of these words.

Dearest Lib,

Having someone as beautiful as you are to love is really a wonderful possession. I will always be proud of you for your beauty, for the nice manner of the way you dress and the way you wear your clothes. It gives me pride just to have you with me because I like to show you off a whole lot more than any worldly possession that I've ever owned.

The most beautiful part of our existence together and the thing I am most sincerely proud of is the fact that you have given me your love and affection without reservation. That factor alone is as much proof of your love, more so, than all the acts of kindness that you could bestow upon me in a normal lifetime. I pledge myself to you and only you.

I love you, Ansel
October 25, 1949

We can only guess . . .

We can only guess how Ansel and Elizabeth met. Looking back, we have to say it was by chance from life's circumstances. They lived in a small geographical area. It was post WWII when young adults were rebuilding their lives after the war.

Before Elizabeth met Ansel, tragedy had struck her life. Elizabeth first married Donald Eugene Kimberlin, a lifelong beau and classmate from Atkins High School. Being the bride of a US Air Force training pilot held a bright future for the young couple.

The Kimberlins moved to California for Donald's Air Force pilot training. Tragedy struck when Donald and other young officers were killed in a crash in the mountains. Their bodies were located and returned home for burial six months after their deaths. Elizabeth moved back to Atkins to live with her parents. She relocated to Little Rock, where she held a position with the Veteran's Administration.

Elizabeth's Early History

The hometown of Elizabeth Ruth Hamlet was Atkins, Arkansas, just a few miles west of Blackwell, Arkansas where Ansel Swain had grown up. She was born in 1921, the same year that Ansel was born. Elizabeth was the only child of **John Turner Hamlet** and **Velma Kate Johnson**. She was raised in a middle class family. The family were very active members of the Methodist Episcopal Church, South. Her father and uncle, **Tom Hamlet** who lived with them, were small business and mercantile owners in the downtown of Atkins. Elizabeth's parents were very involved in community groups and post WWI American Legion activities. Her mother, Velma, was a homemaker. Velma served as president of the Arkansas Chapter of the women's division of the American Legion traveling by train to other states in her capacity as president, often taking Elizabeth with her. Elizabeth graduated from Atkins High School in 1939.

Wheels on the Road and Wheels on the Feet

As a war widow, Elizabeth had been approved to purchase her own car. Elizabeth commuted back and forth many times on Arkansas State Highway 64 between her job in Little Rock and her parent's home in Atkins, AR.

Elizabeth passed by, and surely would have stopped, at **Swain's Roller Rink** located in Blackwell, AR right beside the highway. As skating was a popular entertainment, Elizabeth and her friends from Atkins probably drove the short distance from Atkins to Blackwell on weekends.

This is likely where Ansel and Elizabeth came to know each other. The details of their meeting remains unknown.

Marriage and Finances

For the young couple, the desire to marry was met with the challenge of having the money to do so. Ansel's only means of income was the roller rink. Maintaining the roller rink meant expensive repairs to the building and equipment. Groups would make reservations and cancel at the last minute. Ansel was also a student at Arkansas State Teacher's College in Conway, AR the fall of 1950.

In the mean time, Elizabeth had transferred her employment position to the Russellville, AR Veterans Administration from which she had a small income. The couple wanted to move to Morrilton, buy a small house and make it their home. Yet this was not enough income. *Where would the money come from?*

The idea of a **career in county politics** would come forward. No doubt, Ansel had made many friends and supporters at the skating rink. His father, **Sam Swain**, a businessman, was involved in local politics. Being a young Navy veteran and a person quick to make friends with everyone he met, Ansel found himself running for **Conway County Clerk**.

Ansel would run and win the election for County Clerk enabling a greater financial security.

This four room frame house on Church Street in Morrilton was the first home of Elizabeth and Ansel.

Elizabeth and Ansel were married September 3, 1950.

Wedding Attendants included Raymond Johnson, uncle of Elizabeth,
Nealia Jane Fry Swain, sister in law of Ansel,
Doyle Theron Swain, brother of Ansel and an unidentified person.

A Reception was held at First Methodist Church in Atkins after the wedding.

It was a happy day for Elizabeth and Ansel Swain.
It was the beginning of 46 years of marriage.

Marriage License

STATE OF ARKANSAS

COUNTY OF CONWAY

TO ANY PERSON AUTHORIZED BY LAW TO SOLEMNIZE MARRIAGE, GREETING:

You are hereby commanded to solemnize the rite and publish the banns of Matrimony between Mr. *Verill Ansel Swain* of *Blackwell* in the County of *Conway* and State of *Arkansas* aged *29* years and Mrs *Elizabeth Ruth Kimberlin* of *Atkins* in the County of *Pope* and State of *Arkansas* aged *29* years according to law, and do you officially sign and return this License to the parties herein named.

Witness my hand and official seal this *2nd* day of *September 1950*

Jim H. Huitt
County Clerk.

Ansel Swain
D. C.

CERTIFICATE OF MARRIAGE

State of Arkansas,
County of *Pope* } I *H. C. Minnis* do hereby certify, that on the *3* day of *September 1950* I did, duly and according to law, as commanded in the foregoing License, solemnize the rite and publish the banns of Matrimony between the parties therein named.

Witness my hand, this *3* day of *September 1950*

My Credentials are recorded in Recorder's Office, *Fulton* County, Ark.

Book *1* Page *63*

H. C. Minnis
Minister Methodist Church

NOTE—This License with the Certificate duly executed and officially signed, must be returned to the office whence it is issued within sixty days from the date of License, under penalty of forfeiture of the bond.

BANARD ST LOUIS

FORM No. 3546

Certificate of Marriage for Elizabeth and Ansel

CERTIFICATE OF RECORD.

STATE OF ARKANSAS,

County of Conway   I,   JIM H. HUETT,

Clerk of the County Court of said County, certify that the above license for and Certificate of the Marriage of Mr. _Verill Ansel Swain_ and Mrs. _Elizabeth Ruth Kimberlin_ was filed in my office on the 11th day of _September_ 1950, and the same is duly recorded on page 145 of Book 37 of Marriage Records.

WITNESS my hand and the seal of said Court this 11th day of _September_ 1950

Jim H. Huett
            Clerk.

By _Verill Ansel Swain_ D.C.

Back of Certificate of Marriage for Elizabeth and Ansel

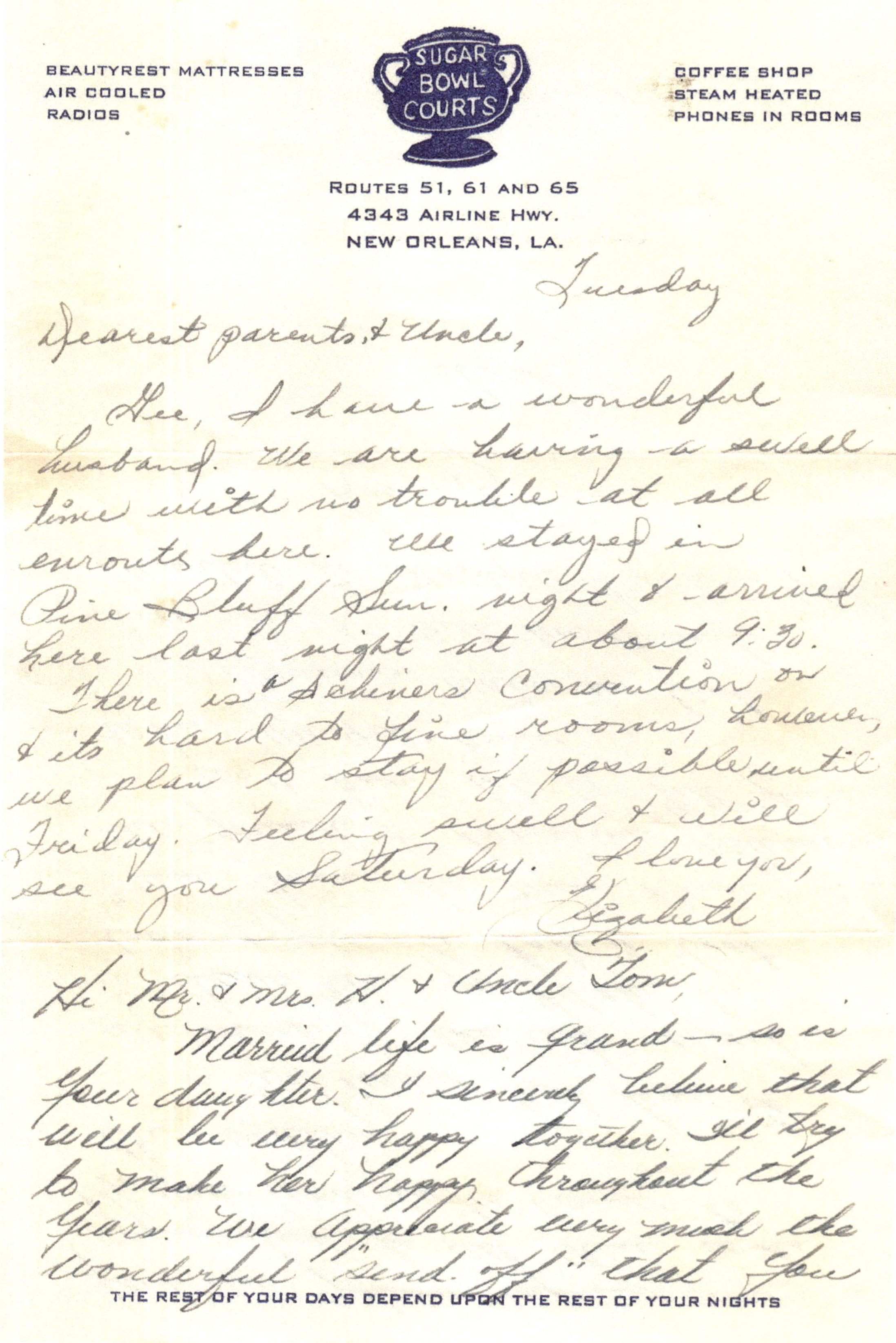

BEAUTYREST MATTRESSES
AIR COOLED
RADIOS

SUGAR BOWL COURTS

COFFEE SHOP
STEAM HEATED
PHONES IN ROOMS

ROUTES 51, 61 AND 65
4343 AIRLINE HWY.
NEW ORLEANS, LA.

Tuesday

Dearest parents & Uncle,

Gee, I have a wonderful husband. We are having a swell time with no trouble at all enroute here. We stayed in Pine Bluff Sun. night & arrived here last night at about 9:30.

There is a Shriners Convention on & its hard to find rooms, however, we plan to stay if possible until Friday. Feeling swell & will see you Saturday. I love you,

Elizabeth

Hi Mr. & Mrs. H. & Uncle Tom,

Married life is grand — so is your daughter. I sincerely believe that we will be very happy together. I'll try to make her happy throughout the years. We appreciate very much the wonderful "send off" that you

THE REST OF YOUR DAYS DEPEND UPON THE REST OF YOUR NIGHTS

Page 1 of honeymoon letter to the Elizabeth's parents and uncle from the Sugar Bowl Courts Motel in New Orleans.

gave us. Please express our appreciation to all those who helped and who came to the wedding.

We haven't had time to see much of the city - expect to drive seen part of the town today & plan to take a boat cruise down the Miss. River on the "President" tomorrow afternoon.

We'll have lots to tell you when we get home.

Louisiana water tastes like h_l, but we haven't resorted to stronger drink — yet.

Lovingly,

AWS

Page 2 of honeymoon letter to the Elizabeth's parents and uncle from the Sugar Bowl Courts Motel in New Orleans.

RECENT BRIDE

From one of the Morrilton Newspapers.

Mrs. Ansel Swain

Mrs. Swain was married Sunday, September 3, in the Atkins Methodist Church. The bride, the former Mrs. Elizabeth Hamlet Kimberlin, is the daughter of Mr. and Mrs. Turner Hamlet of Atkins. The bridegroom is the son of Mr. and Mrs. S. N. Swain who is county and probate clerk-elect.

Ansel Elected County Clerk

"Election to Conway County Office"

Section Six

Ansel Swain

Ansel Swain Announces for County and Probate Clerk

Announces For County Clerk

Ansel Swain

Ansel Swain of Blackwell, who formally announced as a candidate for County Clerk of Conway County last week. is seeking his political job. Mr. Swain is 28 years old and was born in Cleveland, Conway County. He served as finance clerk in the Navy during World War II and for the past year was clerk of the Conway County draft board.

What does a County Clerk Do?

The **County Clerk** serves as the official **Voter Registrar** of the county, and is responsible for issuing **Marriage Licenses** and **Doing Business Under Assumed Name** certificates, as well as recording **Minister's Credentials**, incorporation **documents issued by the Arkansas Secretary of State, and county court documents**.

As Arkansas grew, it established **laws and statutes** governing county governments. Many states decided that county clerks should be **county-wide elected officials**.

County Clerks are generally responsible for maintaining records of all governing body transactions including resolutions and ordinances. They are responsible for **keeping records of deeds and marriage licenses** and most **other public records**. They also issue permits for various parades and parties, as well as other licenses.

Every Clerk needs a Deputy ...

Elizabeth Swain, newly married to Ansel Swain, was employed as the **Deputy County Clerk**. She became pregnant in 1952 and often said, the large books were heavy and difficult to carry. She served with Ansel until he was employed by **Crompton Arkansas Mills**.

Your Support Is Sincerely Desired

ANSEL SWAIN
CANDIDATE FOR
CONWAY COUNTY CLERK
VETERAN WORLD WAR II
EXPERIENCED -- HONEST -- QUALIFIED

Subject to Democratic Primary August 8, 1950

Conway County Courthouse

Ansel Swain Elected as County and Probate Clerk

County Clerk

County Clerk Ansel Swain was born at Cleveland, the son of Mr. and Mrs. Sam Swain. The Swains moved to Blackwell in April, 1937, where young Swain made his home until last November when he and his wife moved to Morrilton.

He joined the CCC program in the late 30's and while in this work completed his high school education at the Jacksonville High School where he graduated in April, 1940. He then joined the state CCC headquarters office at Little Rock and during a portion of this time he attended night school at Draughon's Business College. He joined the United States Navy in July 1942 and was discharged with the rank of storekkeeper 1st class on March 6, 1946.

Mr. Swain attended Arkansas Tech in 1946-47, and was a student at Arkansas State Teachers College at Conway the fall semester in 1950.

He was nominated to the first term as county and probate clerk without opposition last August. He is a member of the Blackwell Baptist church, and F. & A. Masonic Lodge No. 172 of Atkins.

Mr. Swain married Mrs. Elizabeth Ruth Kimberlin, daughter of Mr. and Mrs. Turner Hamlet of Atkins, September 3, 1950. Mr. and Mrs. Swain moved to Morrilton in November.

Mr. Swain and his father, Sam Swain, built one of the most modern skating rinks in the Arkansas River Valley at Blackwell in the fall of 1947, which he operated until he became county clerk.

—0—

In the newspapers …

"Withdrawals and New Candidates Filing Create Surprises as Conway County Political Campaigns Shape Up"

"**County Clerk Ansel Swain** was born at **Cleveland**, the son of **Mr. and Mrs. Sam Swain**. The Swains moved to **Blackwell** in April **1937**, where young Swain made his home until last November when he and his wife, Elizabeth Swain, moved to **Morrilton**.

He joined the **CCC program in the late 30's** and while in this work completed his high school education at the Jacksonville High School where he graduated in April **1940**. He then joined the state CCC **headquarters office at Little Rock** and during a portion of this time he attended night school at **Draughon's Business College**. He joined the **United States Navy Seabees** in July **1942** and was discharged with the rank of **storekeeper 1st class** on March 6, **1946**.

Mr. Swain attended **Arkansas Tech**, Russelleville, in **1946-7** and was a student at **Arkansas State Teachers College** at Conway the fall semester in **1950**.

He was **nominated the first term as county and probate clerk without opposition last August**. He is a member of the Blackwell Baptist Church, and F. & A. Masonic Lodge No. 172 of Atkins.

Mr. Swain **married Mrs. Elizabeth Ruth Kimberlin**, daughter of Mr. and Mrs. Turner Hamlet of Atkins, September 3, 1950. Mr. and Mrs. Swain moved to Morrilton in November.

Mr. Swain and his father, Sam Swain, **built one of the most modern skating rinks in the Arkansas River Valley at Blackwell** in the fall of **1947**, which he operated until he became county clerk."

Ansel Swain officially became County and Probate Clerk on January 1, 1951

STATE OF ARKANSAS

To All to Whom These Presents Shall Come - Greeting:

Know Ye, That Whereas, It appears that

ANSEL SWAIN *was duly elected*

COUNTY CLERK

in and for the County of CONWAY

in the State of Arkansas, at an election held in said County on the seventh day of November 1950

Therefore I, Sid McMath, Governor of the State of Arkansas, in the name and by authority of the people of the State of Arkansas, vested in me by the Constitution and the laws of said State, do hereby Commission him

County Clerk

in and for the County aforesaid for and during the term prescribed by the laws of the State.

He is therefore, hereby authorized to do and perform all and singular the duties incumbent upon him as said

County Clerk

in and for the County aforesaid, according to law and the trust reposed in him.

In Testimony Whereof, I have hereunto set my hand and caused the Great Seal of the State of Arkansas to be affixed at Little Rock, this the first day of January, in the Year of Our Lord, One Thousand Nine Hundred and Fifty One

_____
GOVERNOR

_____
SECRETARY OF STATE.

BY _____
DEPUTY

The Certificate of County Clerk

... He is therefore hereby authorized to do and perform all and singular the duties incumbent upon him as said in and for the County, according to law and the trust reposed in him.

I, _Ansel Swain_

do solemnly swear (or affirm) that I will support

the Constitution of the United States and the

Constitution of the State of Arkansas, and that I

will faithfully discharge the duties of the office of

County & Probate Clerk

in and for the _County of Conway_

on which I am about to enter.

Ansel Swain

Sworn and subscribed to before me _1st_

Audrey Stout Circuit Judge in and for

the County of _Conway_

this, the _1st_ day of _Jan._

One Thousand Nine Hundred and _51_

Audrey Stout

DOUGCRAT P. & L. CO., LITTLE ROCK

On The Back of Certificate

... Ansel Swain solemnly swore to **support the Constitution of the United States,**

and the **Constitution of the State of Arkansas,**

in and for the County of Conway

swearing before a Circuit Judge January 1, 1951.

... **All elected officials in every capacity in the United States of America** *swear to uphold he Constitution ...*

Withdrawal of Candidacy

In November of 1952, Ansel Swain withdrew his name for reelection. Ansel had accepted a new position with the Morrilton Cotton Mill as **Personnel Manager.**

The History of the Conway County Court House in Morrilton

From the Encyclopedia of Arkansas

Conway County Courthouse

Where did Ansel Swain work as the County and Probate Clerk?

The current court house was designed in **1929** by **Frank W. Gibb** in a fusion of Greek, Roman, and Italian Renaissance architectural styles, exhibiting the diminishing popularity of the Classical Revival style during the early twentieth century. **Before the Morrilton site was chosen for the county seat, court proceedings had been held in four previous locations**. In 1825, when Conway County was created, the town of **Cadron** was selected as the first established seat of county government. In **1829**, the county seat was moved from Cadron to **Harrisburg** *(then the house of Stephen Harris in Welborn Township)*. An election ordered by the Arkansas General Assembly in **1829** resulted in a new courthouse

and jail being built in Harrisburg. In **1831**, Dr. Nimrod Menifee donated land and erected a courthouse in the town of **Lewisburg** *(Conway County)*. The courthouse remained at Lewisburg until **1850**, when a new courthouse was constructed in the town of **Springfield** *(Conway County)*. Three courthouses were built in Springfield between **1858** and **1869**, with the original structure being destroyed by a tornado and the second building destroyed by a fire in **1864** during the Civil War. In June **1873**, the county seat was moved back to Lewisburg, with the town of Lewisburg promising to erect a courthouse of a similar high quality as the former one at Springfield. In **1883**, the county seat was taken from Lewisburg and moved to **Morrilton**.

The present-day **Conway County Courthouse** has been located at the corner of Moose and Church streets in Morrilton since the **first structure was built in 1883**. *The original courthouse in Morrilton consisted of a two-story brick structure with a hipped and decked roof.* On January 2, **1927**, the structure burned, and a replacement courthouse was built on the same site in **1929**.

Gibb was hired to design the new courthouse at Morrilton at an agreed amount of **$1,800**. **John P. Jones,** a Hot Springs *(Garland County)* contractor, submitted the winning bid for the construction of the **new building at a cost of $97,000**. **Sam Davies**, who played a key role in developing Petit Jean Mountain into Arkansas's first state park, was employed as the supervisor of construction, representing the county's interest in the project. *The courthouse was financed by taxes generated after an amendment was adopted to the state constitution in **1928** granting counties the freedom to vote on special taxes to build courthouses and jails.*

The two-story building's features include heavy, three-dimensional details and half-round Doric columns. The design is characteristic of Gibb's influence in architecture around Arkansas and the nation, particularly in the design of public buildings.

On November 13 **1989,** the **Conway County Courthouse** has received grants totaling **$528,092** from the **Arkansas Historic Preservation Program** for upkeep and maintenance.

Elizabeth Ruth Hamlet Swain

"Our Mother, Our Friend"

Section Seven

Elizabeth Ruth Hamlet Swain

"Our Mother, Our Friend" Section Seven

BIRTH
14 January 1921
Atkins, Pope Co., Arkansas

MARRIAGE TO ANSEL
3 September 1950 Atkins, Pope
Co., Arkansas

DEATH
4 JANUARY 1997 Conway,
Faulkner Co, Arkansas

When **Elizabeth Ruth Hamlet** was born January 14, 1921, in Atkins, Arkansas. Her father, **John Turner Hamlet**, was 33 years old, and her mother, **Velma Kate Johnson**, was 23 years old.

Years before Elizabeth's parents were married, her father, **Turner Hamlet**, and his older brother **Wm. Thomas Hamlet**, lived and worked for many years in Pope County, Arkansas. Along with the two of them, another brother, **Charles Hamlet**, owned a store near the Arkansas River where they traded in cotton, farm goods and household items. **Turner** and **Tom** lived together with their mother until she died. After Turner returned home from WWI, he and Tom moved their business, W.T. Hamlet & Company to downtown, Atkins.

Brothers Tom & Turner Hamlet

Elizabeth with mother, Velma Hamlet

Elizabeth's mother, **Velma Kate Johnson**, grew up on a farm outside Atkins, her family having deep roots in Pope County, Arkansas. **Velma** graduated from Atkins High School in 1919. She held an Arkansas State Teacher's License. Before her marriage to Turner, she was employed by the Atkins Public Schools. Turner and Velma met after he had returned home from WWI. The couple were ten years difference in age. When **Velma** married **Turner**, she also *"married"* his brother **Wm. Thomas Hamlet**. "Uncle Tom," remained unmarried and lived with his brother, Velma and Elizabeth for the remainder of his life. The family loved **"Uncle Tom"** and valued the love and support he brought to the family, especially to Elizabeth.

Velma, Elizabeth & Turner Hamlet

As an only child Elizabeth was overwhelmed with love and affection by her parents. **Velma Hamlet**, mother of Elizabeth, was a good role model for her daughter. She taught Elizabeth to be quite independent and always stand up for herself. **Velma** was a hard worker caring for the family of four.

In her spare time **Velma** was active in the **American Legion Auxiliary** and **Methodist Church** activities. The American Legion Auxiliary were supporters of WWI veterans. In her years as a member of the Auxiliary, Velma rose to the office of president of the Arkansas Chapter. She traveling to other states, supporting WWI veterans. Velma even traveled to New York City where she rode in a Veteran's Day parade on behalf of the American Legion Auxiliary of the State of Arkansas. Elizabeth had the opportunity to travel with her as she served as page to her mother.

Elizabeth was blessed by her mother's extended Johnson family. In 1921, when Elizabeth was born, her grandparents, **Flonnie Evans Johnson** and **Horace Lafayette Johnson**, in their older years, gave birth to a son. Their son was **Raymond Horace Johnson.** Elizabeth's uncle, Raymond, was more of a brother to her. The two were the same age and in the same high school class in Atkins.

Elizabeth also had the unbounding love and support of **Ruth Johnson** and her husband, **John Ernest Lemley**. Ruth was Velma's only sister. **Ruth** and **Johnny**, having no children of their own, gave time, love and affection to Elizabeth. They gave her gifts and often took her on trips with them.

Looking back on Elizabeth's childhood, it was the environment of post WWI. The country was coming out of a post economic depression era. From family stories, we recall the Hamlet brothers assisting many families in need.

Elizabeth Ruth Hamlet around age 17 in 1938.

Elizabeth did not grow up in a wealthy family. Her family lived in a small frame home near downtown, Atkins. Elizabeth's family was very middle class. Her education came from a small school where she enjoyed being on the school basketball team. Her parents made life choices for her, enrolling her in a typing class over popular school activities. The family dressed well and owned a nice car. Elizabeth was given everything she needed in terms of material possessions. More important, she was showered with love and affection from her extended family, cousins and friends. After high school, Elizabeth attended college for one semester down the road from Atkins at Arkansas Tech in Russellville.

Elizabeth left college to marry her Atkins high classmate and sweetheart, **Donald Eugene Kimberlin**. The young Kimberlin couple moved to California to allow Donald to serve in the US Air Force in pilot school. Elizabeth was active in various groups and served in the USO while Donald trained. In a tragic accident, Donald and several young men were killed when their plane went down in the mountains in California. Elizabeth moved back to Atkins after becoming a widow.

During the remainder of WWII, Elizabeth worked two years with the Office of Price Administration, and five years with the Veteran's Administration first in Little Rock then in Russellville, Arkansas.

It was during this time when Elizabeth met **Verill Ansel Swain**, a Navy Seabee who returned to Blackwell after his service in WWII. Between his continued education in college and owning a roller rink in Blackwell the two began courting and talking marriage. They married on Sept. 3, 1950 and spent the next 46 years, until their deaths, in Morrilton, Arkansas. *More of their story is in the previous section.* **Elizabeth** and **Ansel** became the parents of two daughters, **Marcia Gail Swain Crossman**, born April 26, 1953 and **Sherry Elizabeth Swain Borck**, born May 6, 1955.

The Swains were an active family in **Morrilton First United Methodist Church**. Elizabeth was a member of the choir for many years. She was also a member and two year president of the Women's Society of Christian Service later named **United Methodist Women**. When she received her Life Membership Award, the announcement read,

"She is a person who offers support and encouragement to others; a source if inspiration to all of us as she has demonstrated tremendous faith, hope and courage. She has been a 'point of light' and has touched our lives in a very special way."

Ansel and Elizabeth around 1967

Elizabeth was a very active community servant in the community of Morrilton. She served on the church's Administrative Board of First Methodist Church in the areas of mission and evangelism. Elizabeth was chair of the Blanket Program for the Methodist church World Hunger Ingathering emphasis.

Elizabeth was employed as a clerk/typist for 21 years with the US **Soil Conservation Service i**n Morrilton, retiring in 1982 earning at most $3500 per year. The family resided first at 101 North West Street in Morrilton. They later built a large new home (*paying cash*) in 1967 at 3 Magnolia Drive in Morrilton. Most of the money Elizabeth earned in her job with the Soil Conservation Service provided a better life for the family, like the "icing on the cake." The family had nicer furnishings in the home. The family was also able to afford nicer clothing and family vacations.

Elizabeth was a wonderful mother and wife. She spent a great deal of time sewing for her and the girls. Around 1950, Ansel challenged Elizabeth to win a sewing contest by constructing a beautiful silk 3 piece suit. She won the contest. He purchased her a brand new Singer sewing machine. This sewing machine is still working in 2024.

Elizabeth saw to it that both her daughters were given baton twirling lessons, both becoming majorettes for the Morrilton High School Band. Ansel and Elizabeth were awarded **Band Parents of the Year in 1971**.

Elizabeth Ruth Hamlet as a young girl.

The parents never missed a football game. To their credit Ansel and Elizabeth paid for both daughters to receive degrees at the University of Central Arkansas.

The Swains chaperoned many high school parties and sorority proms for their girls, often signing as responsible in the event of misuse of the country club building *(which never happened)*. They welcomed their daughter's friends into the home. They were good examples to live by, showing much love and friendship to family and friends.

During the time her girls were young, Elizabeth served in the elementary school parent teacher organization. She was also was active in community organizations. She was a 21 year volunteer for the **Conway County Commu-**

Elizabeth & Ansel Swain in the early 1990's

nity Service Advisory Board beginning in 1958. She was a member, and past president, of the **Morrilton Adelaide Club**, a service organization of women for the enhancement of the local community. Elizabeth also served as member and president of the **Town & Country Garden Club**, serving as its president. In 1990, Elizabeth joined the **Daughters of the American Revolution** *(DAR)*. She was active in the General William Lewis Chapter in Morrilton. In order to beccme a member of the DAR, one must be a descendant of a Revolutionary War soldier. Elizabeth served as a member of the **Morrilton Hospital Auxiliary**. In retirement,

Velma Hamlet

Elizabeth and Ansel took up golfing. The Swains spent winters in South Texas with friends. They were blessed with time and health for a number of years after their retirement.

Elizabeth was also a faithful daughter. She rarely missed spending a Sunday afternoon in Atkins with her parents, Velma and Turner Hamlet, as long as they lived. Elizabeth made sure Sherry and Marcia were there, too.

Turner Hamlet

As life went along, Elizabeth and Ansel had the pleasure of seeing their daughters, **Sherry** and **Marcia** become adults, marry and have children. Elizabeth and Ansel were blessed with four grandchildren, **Charles Robert** and **David Nathan Crossman** & **Bailey Erin** and **Raquel Elizabeth Borck**. **Ansel** and **Elizabeth** were blessed with many happy years as a married couple.

In her 70's, Elizabeth cared for Ansel as he died from a four year battle with cancer. During the later part of Ansel's illness, Elizabeth also developed ovarian cancer. She died ten months later in her daughter, Marcia's, home, on January 4, 1997, amid friends and family.

With tears in my eyes, I find it impossible to share more of the detailed stories of my parents lives, but will remember these in my heart. It is a blessing to have my sister, Sherry, to remember these with.

Elizabeth and Ansel are buried in **Elmwood Cemetery** in Morrilton, Arkansas. They share a memorial headstone with the words,

"No Tears."

Our mother's foot stone bears these words,

Elizabeth Ruth Hamlet Swain

January 14, 1921 to January 4, 1997

"Our Mother, Our Friend"

Marcia Swain Crossman, 2024

Elizabeth Ruth Hamlet Swain's Family Tree

Source: Ancestry.com • Marcia Swain Crossman's Family Tree, 2024

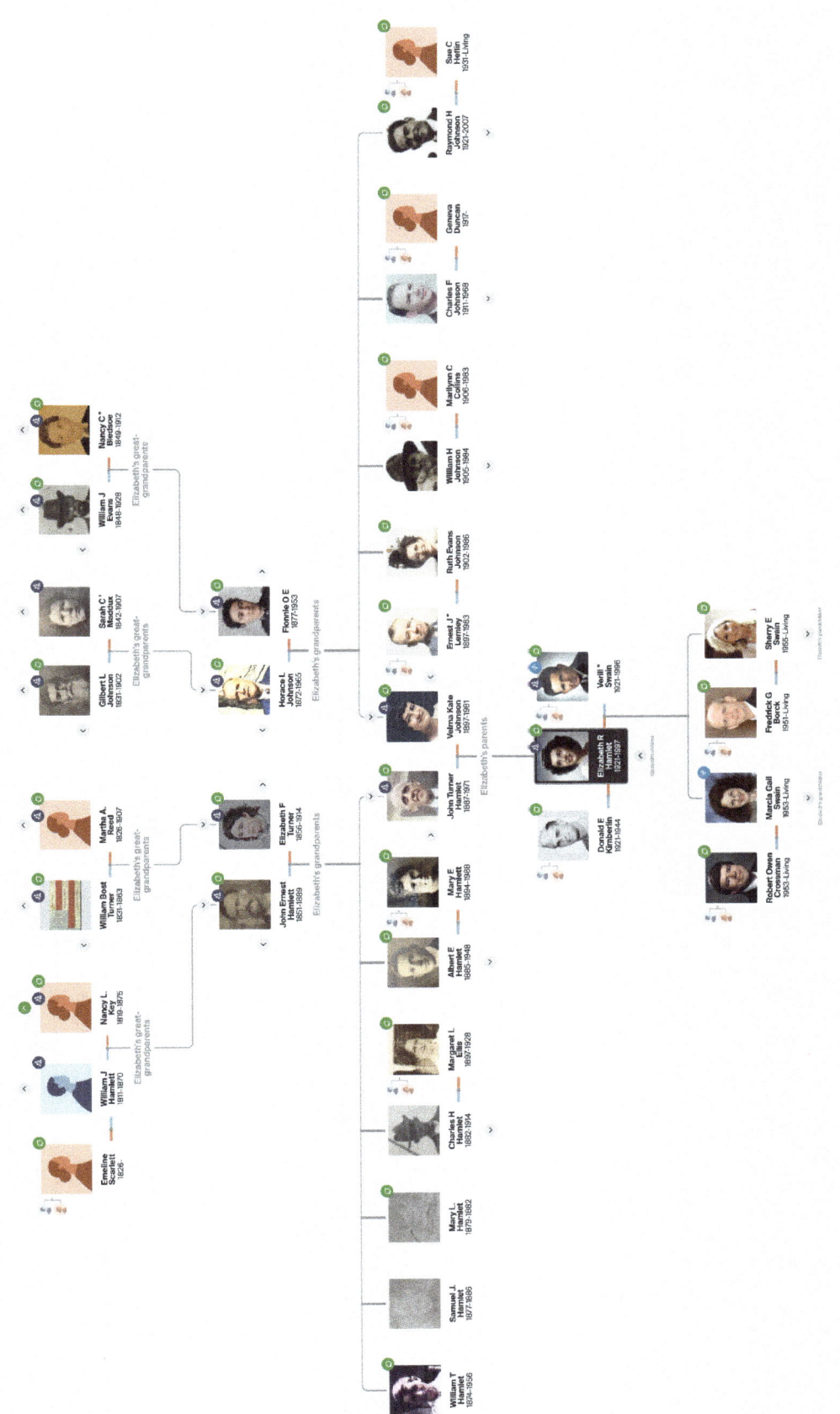

Ansel and 31 Years

at Crompton Arkansas Mills

"Manufacturing Corduroy at the Cotton Mill"

Section Eight

Ansel and 31 Years at Crompton Arkansas Mills
"Manufacturing Corduroy at the Cotton Mill" Section Eight

Ansel Swain To Be New Personnel Manager of Arkansas Cotton Mills

A **surprise development** Wednesday morning was the announcement of the resignation of Ansel Swain as County and Probate Clerk of Conway County. He was unopposed for re-election to a second term. He has accepted a position as **Personnel Manager** of the **Arkansas Cotton Mills.**

Mr. Swain succeeds Raymond Moore, who resigned last week. The unexpired term of Mr. Swain as county clerk will be filled by an appointee to be named by the governor. An **opportunity for advancement** that he would not have by remaining in a political office prompted Mr. Swain's decision to accept the new position of the Arkansas Cotton Mills. Mr. Swain has the responsibility and ability to make a difference in the lives of many people in the new position.

The Petit Jean Country Headlight

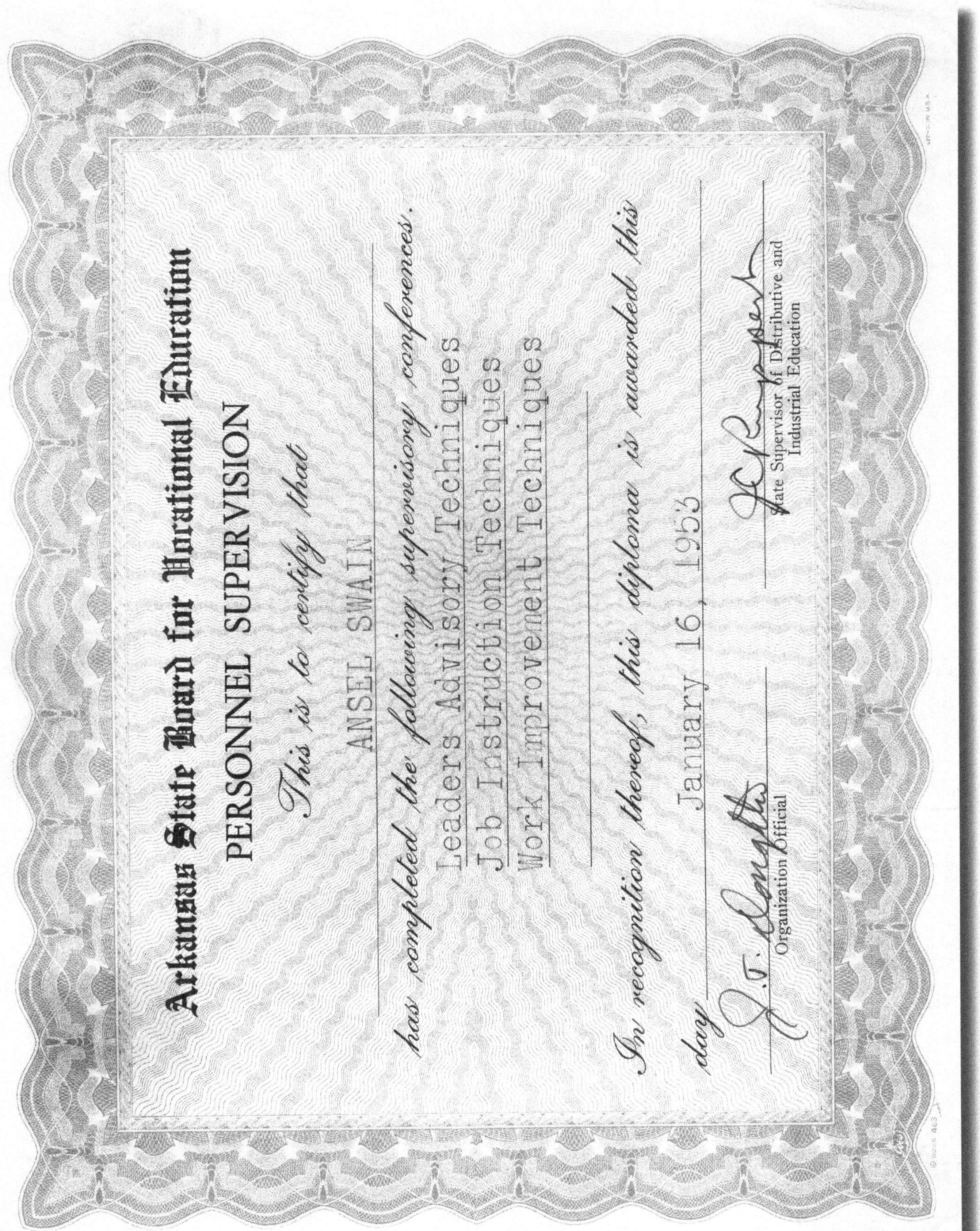

Arkansas State Board for Vocational Education

PERSONNEL SUPERVISION

This is to certify that

ANSEL SWAIN

has completed the following supervisory conferences.

Leaders Advisory Techniques

Job Instruction Techniques

Work Improvement Techniques

In recognition thereof, this diploma is awarded this

day _____ January 16, 1953

_____
Organization Official

_____
State Supervisor of Distributive and
Industrial Education

Having a Personnel Manager in the Family

Ansel Swain Inspects Yarn at Plant

Ansel and Elizabeth Swain were long term residents of Morrilton.

From his daughters,
"Our parents' lives were tied around what was happening at **'the cotton mill'** as Crompton-Arkansas Mills was affectionately called by the community. There were many people who worked there in generations and from different families. Everywhere we went in Morrilton, **folks knew "so-in-so"** from the plant. In turn, our dad knew most everybody in the area."

The most important job of the personnel manager was to **find and supply good honest laborers** who would respect the company. It seemed like **our dad knew everything about everybody** that lived in Morrilton and their reputations.

The workforce was **intergenerational**. Families who worked at the mill were proud to bring their children, nephews, nieces and grandchildren who were out of school to **see Mr. Swain for a job**. He saw people at the mill for this. To the dismay of our mother, folks also called our dad at home at nights and on weekends.

"I do believe our parents were **glad** when my sister, Sherry, and I **became young teens** who loved to talk on the phone. Back in those days, Sister and I talked on the phone a great deal of the time. Thus, the home phone was **"busy"** most nights."

From the Petit Jean Country Headlight

Wednesday, August 23, 1973

MR. SWAIN

in the Medical Department. In November **1942**, he enlisted in the **Navy**. He served as a store-keeper first class in the **64th Naval Construction Battalion** working in the payroll office. Swain was discharged in April, **1946**.

After the Navy, he attended **Arkansas Tech** in **1946** and **1947**. In **1947**, Swain built the **Swain Roller Rink** at Blackwell. During that same period, he was employed as **Conway County Draft Board clerk** in **1948** and **1949**. He was elected **Conway County clerk** in **1950**, serving in that capacity until he joined the mill.

Swain belongs to the **United Methodist Church** in Morrilton. He has been active in the church, teaching **Sunday School classes for 12 years** and is a past **chairman of the Official Board** of the church. Mr. Swain served on the **Morrilton School Board** from **1960** to **1963**. He also served as **president** of the **Morrilton Golf and Country Club**.

Mill Awards Swain 20-Year Service Pin

Ansel Swain was the recent recipient of a **20-year service pin** at Crompton-Arkansas **Mills**. He was employed **May 5, 1952**, as **personnel manager** and has held that position since that time.

Swain was born at **Cleveland** where he spent most of his childhood. He attended school at Cleveland and Wonderview until his **family moved to Blackwell** in his junior year in high school. After attending **Morrilton High School**, he graduated from **Jacksonville High School**.

Swain joined the **Civilian Conservation Corps** where he spent two years then transferred to the **Conservation Corps Base Headquarters** in Little Rock where he was employed as **chief clerk**

150th Crompton Company Anniversary Metal Coin made in 1957
In 1976, Danny Huffman, water company, found one of these while working a back hoe. Danny shined it and gave it to his father Roy, a Crompton employee.

Ansel Enjoyed Presenting Awards and Donations

Conway County public health nurse, Argie Howard accepts a check of $2,000 from **Ansel Swain**, manager of employee relations at Crompton Arkansas Mills. The donation was a result of a public effort by the **Conway County Health Department** to raise funds to construct a new office complex.

—Staff Photo by Larry Miller

Ansel Swain, *left,* manager of employee relations at Crompton Arkansas Mills presents a check in the amount of $500 to **James Anderson** for the **Morrilton Youth Association**. The plant made a donation of $150 and paying to **sponsor teams** for boys and girls for $350.

During the months of June through July, **perfect attendance awards** and **service pins** were awarded to Crompton employees. **Imelda Whitbey**, from the winding department, happily accepts a **15 year service pin** from employee relations manager, **Ansel Swain.**

"The Story of Corduroy at Crompton-Arkansas Mills"

From the Petit Jean Country Headlight

Summary
of Ansel's article . . .

Ansel Swain began, as was his style, to give Crompton **employees all credit for the success of the local company**. Also, he wanted people to become more familiar with its product. Corduroy, which was once only afforded by European luxury, had now become an item in every American home. How did the community of **Morrilton become a hub** in the manufacturer of this important fabric?

The credit of corduroy's beginning was in the **mid-1700's England and France**. It was nicknamed the *cloth of the king*. This cloth of the king went through the hands of many artisans before becoming clothing. Very few could afford it's luxury, only the wealthy.

By the **end of the 1700's**, early Americans were attempting to make cloth. During that time any idea for making corduroy was abandoned due to labor costs. As we now know, cotton became king in this country. The preparation of separating seeds and spinning thread led to the beginning of the **American Textile Industry**.

In the **early 1800's**, a group of seven men organized the sixth cotton mill in the country naming it the **Providence Manufacturing Company**. $32,000 built this plant. One of these investors and inventors was **Samuel Crompton**. The factory thrived making **calico printed fabric**. As time went on, Samuel desperately wanted the production of cloth to be sped up. As a young boy, he used the same type of simple **"Spinning Jenny"** in the plant as he did to make yarn for his family. There had to be a way. Enter his invention of the **"Spinning Mule."** The mule produced finer quality yarn. It revolutionized textile production by vastly increasing the amount of cotton that could be spun at any one time. **The plant took the name of Crompton** to honor Samuel. Within a few years, 4.6 million spinning mules were being used in textile production around the world. Samuel Crompton, however, received very little money for his invention. **He remained poor his entire life.** He died in Boston on June 26, 1827.

Continued next page . . .

Early
"Spinning Jenny"

Samuel Crompton inventor & investor

Later
"Spinning Mule"

New and improved machinery by Crompton

Continued from previous page . . .

Entering the history of fabric after the Civil War was **Howard Richmond,** whose father, George, had been a part owner of the mill with Samuel Crompton. His interactions with the plant led him to great **research in England**. There he saw bits and pieces of fabric production in many places. **Integration of the process** had to be the key. He lured workers from Europe to come back to the plant. His **love of corduroy** made the Crompron plant produce a first full yard under one roof. At this same time, all plants in Rhode Island were relocated to the South. **Two of those were located in Arkansas.**

Seeking to increase its corduroy manufacturing process, in **1948**, the Crompton Company purchased the **Morrilton Cotton Mill**. By **1950**, the plant had **350 workers**. By **1963**, its production capacity was doubled. By **1969**, the plant took on further growth reaching 2 1/2 times its original size. There were then **1000 persons gainfully employed by the plant**. The future years saw improvements in the plant, its equipment, working conditions and wages.

Company growth at Morrilton was due to **pride in workmanship**. Production of quality materials could bring prosperity to workers and the city of Morrilton. The **plant was a success** in producing unfinished corduroy sent to **Osceola,**

Arkansas for finishing and dying. **Velveteens** were also popular and successful to the plant's growth. Sales were good across the nation.

In later years, **man made fibers** were being blended into corduroy. The public was endorsing this eagerly.

The road had been long and windy in the **167 years since the start of Crompton** in the little village of Rhode Island to its success in six plants across the South, especially in Morrilton, Arkansas. Attitudes and efforts had kept the company successful.

Reflections on Morrilton:
Today we view our responsibility as being two-fold. First, striving to **uphold the tradition** of fine quality materials along with seeking our own interests will result in job security and future for the plant. Secondly, we must **feel a sense of responsibility to the community of Morrilton** and the surrounding community. Each of us have a higher standard of living and are bettered by the company's payroll. The extent to which jobs exist in the future depends on how seriously our workers view our responsibilities.

Morrilton, Arkansas, November 1975   Crompton-Arkansas Mills, Inc.

CROMPTON COMPANY MOVES TO REDUCE ENERGY CONSUMPTION

Ansel, far right front, with Crompton employees serving on Committee.

Tax Season:
As Ansel's daughters, we remember the many people from the cotton mill who came to our home and **sat at the kitchen table** where my dad helped them with tax papers. This was not in his job description. He never asked for anything in return for helping others. They were my **dad's friends**. Many would thank him for his help by giving our family food from their gardens which we enjoyed.

Employee Support, Health & Safety, plus Energy Consumption were of major importance at Crompton-Arkansas Mills, Inc.

Handing Out Checks:
When we were teens, one of our dad's jobs at the plant was to **hand out payroll checks on Fridays**. It was his responsibility to personally give checks to workers on all **three shifts**. Ansel would start in the mornings with the first shift about 4:30 a.m. and finish with the third shift around 7:00 p.m. I remember he was exhausted at night when he returned home. Ansel did not just stand at the front of a line handing out checks. **He also listened to worker's concerns, their joys and sadnesses.** It was here when workers vented about other workers or their jobs. He **cared about the people** there and this was part of his responsibilities as Personnel Manager.

Ansel, center, with other Crompton employees

Ansel's Rules on Human Relations
1) *Be thoughtful of the opinions of others.*
    There are three sides to a controversy - yours, the other fellow's and the right one.

2) *Be alert to give service. What counts most in life is what we do for others.*   *cont . . .*

Ansel Swain Editor • The Company Newsletter

November, 1973, *the year of Crompton-Arkansas Mills Twenty-Fifth Anniversary*, was the first issue of **Crompton Capers**. **Ansel** was the editor of this paper. The last issue he wrote was **June, 1983**, Volume 9, No. 3. The newsletter began as four pages. Later issues contained eight pages. The second editor of the newsletter was **Leah Dell Ward**, friend and co-worker at Crompton. Approximately 32 issues of the paper that he wrote are in a collection belonging to the Swain family.

What Did Ansel Swain Write About in the Company News?

United Way Donations • Birdtown Fire Department • College Scholarships • Contests • Stop & Swap • Funny Stories • Etc.

Celebration of the 25th Anniversary, August 1973:

Arkansas Cotton Mills began by doubling the size of the plant, a workforce that began at **300**, growing to **600** by **1963**, with a number of employees close to **900** in **1969**. Persons from 30 communities were employees of the plant. New buildings, equipment, break rooms and offices were purchased through the years. Payroll had grown to **$6,000,000**. The company and its employees participated in reaching out into the community of Morrilton and its surrounding communities. This question ended the article on growth, *" What would the company do in the next 25 years?"* The answer to future destiny would rest in our own hands.

Hobbies of Employees:

Photos with captions highlighted workers hobbies from horseshoe pitching, 34 lb. caught catfish, ladies' softball league, bowling leagues, hunting, horseback riding, Masonic involvement, Christmas parade floats, raising prize dogs, Shetland ponies, Four-H, boys' baseball teams, a pet deer and many more hobbies and human interests!

Ansel's Rules on Human Relations:

3) Speak to people. There is nothing as nice or as cheerful as a word of greeting.

4) Smile at people. It takes 72 muscles to frown and only 14 to smile. cont . . .

Honoring Employees:

Crompton was the kind of company where people, ***hung their hats,*** working in satisfying jobs for years. Every issue listed persons from different departments *(Carding, Spinning, Winding, Weaving, Shop, Cloth, and Office)* earning 5 to 20 **service year pins**. Lists were included of perfect attendance workers. **Dinners** were given for workers of 25 years and **appreciation days** for excellent workers. Some were even honored for *50 years* employment. **Photos** of employees receiving **promotions** with articles about them were featured.

Honoring Retirees and former Employees:

Photos and articles were always included about the **personal character, families, and hobbies of retirees**. Best wishes were extended along with congratulations for excellent employment records.

Annual Summer Picnics:

Around Labor Day of each fall, all workers and their **families** enjoyed a **huge picnic**. Committees were selected to finalize details. In **1974**, the ladies of Sacred Heart Church prepared and served the evening meal. A talent show for employees and families was held for entertainment. Frog races, Blue Grass Music, horse shoe pitching, volleyball, Frisbee throwing, plus snow cones were featured. Picnics were often held at the Morrilton City Park. **In 1974, more than 1500 persons were in attendance at the picnic.**

cont. next page . . .

Article Printed in Crompton Capers

EDITOR PRESENTED AWARD

Ansel Swain

Our editor, **Ansel Swain**, spends time and effort in obtaining news about employees but **little is ever said about him**. We think this is an appropriate time to put him in the news as he was **awarded a certificate** and an award in appreciation of his services toward the 4-H Clubs of Arkansas.

Together with other members of management, Ansel headed up a **tour on July 22 for a group of 4H'ers** from throughout Arkansas. At the conclusion of the tour, in appreciation for courtesies extended them during this and past visits, he was presented the certificate and award.

We might add that this is just one of the many duties he performs and deserves a **"thank you"** from all of us and a special thanks for the *Crompton Capers* which we receive each month.

Submitted by Office Personnel

cont. from previous page . . .

Christmas Parties and Celebrations:
We do want to take all of you back to some very fun times when the cotton mill had its annual Christmas parties. It was our dad's job to **purchase toys** and round up great volunteers from the mill to **wrap all those toys**. They worked at night wrapping often for an entire week! There were hundreds of toys and **no child was left out**. The Christmas parties were held at the city auditorium. By the end of the evening there was wrapping paper up to the knees of all the little kids! Were you there? *Do you remember kicking the paper?*

Some parties were held at Forrest Lanes Bowling. Children were allowed to play games. Employees were **given turkeys** and participated in **department Christmas parties**. Workers were given a bonus equal to 2% annual wages. Employees also participated in a Christmas Savings program.

Births and Deaths:
Celebrating **new babies** of employees was always a joyful time. Photos of babies were featured in every issue. Articles of parents and where they worked in the plant were included.

Representing the company when **death came to workers' families** was part of the job that Ansel was responsible for. Condolences were always published in *Crompton Capers*, the newsletter that our dad wrote. I remember when a family lost a son in Viet Nam. I had been a friend of his younger brother and asked our dad if I could go with him to the family's home during this sad time. Most of the family were cotton mill workers. Ansel **attended funerals on behalf of the company**. This was probably not his "job." He knew all the employees and would have gone to **show his own sympathy**.

Ansel's Rules on Human Relations, cont.
5) *Call people by name. The sweetest music to anyone's ears is the sound of his own name.*

6) *Be friendly and helpful. If you want friends, be helpful.*   *cont . . .*

Saying Good Bye after 31 Years with Crompton

A Farewell Message from Ansel Swain

Printed in the Crompton Capers
April, 1983

During the last two weeks of April, I have made a sincere effort to **bid goodbye to everyone** on all shifts I am certain that some were missed and I wish to take this opportunity of saying that I have enjoyed and **appreciate** to the very utmost your **individual friendships** over the years.

When the decision was made a year ago, retirement seemed so very simple and easy. Now as **April 30th** fast approaches, there are moments you may be sure that are filled with hesitation and reservations. Our thoughts now are often centered about the questionable wisdom of leaving *a job that has been so very gratifying these past 31 years*, and a job that has afforded my family the normal comforts of life, and the means of rearing and educating our children. Also, the voluntary withdrawal of oneself from the *fellowship of many fine people* is extremely difficult.

Through the nature of the work itself, there has been at all times a **deep sense of personal satisfaction** in serving you in so many ways, and as opportunities were presented to do so, we hope and trust our interests and actions revealed this fact to you.

Without any expected benefits, I could not be more pleased about **major improvements** being made in the Morrilton plant today. All are a direct indication of management's confidence in you and your fellow workers. This fact was so clearly demonstrated in earlier years during some major plant enlargements. It was true that the then existing plant lent itself well to expansion. It is also true that those **enlargements** would never have taken place without management's confidence and endorsement in the caliber of these employees here at the time. The **growth** that followed has meant much to local economy, and represents the means whereby many more people have jobs in the Morrilton area today. Whether there has been serious consideration about the matter, each of you are faced with a similar challenge to that of your predecessors, your own situation - t**o contribute and preserve the plant in such a manner that jobs for your offspring will be available 50 years hence**. I believe your interest and your concern will prevail long into the future.

In closing, I would like to add that producing and publishing the *"Capers"* and in earlier years the *"Mill Wheel"* has been a pleasure, and we hope that it has brought you equal moments of enjoyment.

Mrs. Leah Dell Ward will very capably take over this as well as other responsibilities to which I have been assigned. I am also confident you will be equally supportive to her endeavors.

For each of you, and to your families, **I wish the very best that life has to offer.**

Ansel Swain

Ansel Always Went To Work:
Our family lived on the other side of town from the cotton mill. In the winter we **always had snow**. As daughters we remember our dad rarely missed a day of work on those cold days. He would bundle up and **walk in the snow covered road**, about a mile to Hwy. 64. Someone would always stop, pick him up and **give him a lift to the mill** some five miles down the highway. He may have returned home many night in the same way.

Leah Dell Ward, Ansel & Elizabeth
Bob Culbreth, plant manager

Ansel received a new set of golf clubs
for a retirement gift from friends.

Retirement
Celebration
April 30, 1983

Play Golf!

Ansel & Elizabeth Swain

/olume 9   No.3   Morrilton, Arkansas, June, 1983   Crompton-Morrilton Pl

Ansel Swain

Article Printed in the Crompton Capers
April, 1983

This edition of the **Capers** is **dedicated to the previous editor, Ansel Swain**. With retirement becoming a reality, he plans to camp, play a lot of golf and spend more time with his two grandsons.

He **began in May, 1952**, bringing with him his familiar smile and friendly gestures. He was always available to lend an ear to every problem and constantly there **"when you needed him"** with a ready recollection of every name.

The last week, the feelings by all were shown by the many **expressions of friendship**, along with the **tears and best wishes**.

To **Ansel Swain, we salute you** for your **accomplishments** that not many can ever achieve. You have **touched our lives** in so many, many ways and we are **proud to have been associated with you**.

Ansel has been **replaced in position**, but **can never be replaced in our hearts**.

Leah Ward, Editor

Ansel's Rules on Human Relations, cont.

7) Be cordial. Speak and act
   as if everything you do is a genuine pleasure.

8) Be genuinely interested in people.
   You can like everybody if you try.

9) Be generous with praise - cautious with criticism.

10) Be considerate of the feelings of others.
    It will always be appreciated.

Dear Mr. Swain,

Just a few words that I couldn't say without crying.

I've known a "Mr. Swain" a lot longer than I've been working at the mill. I remember you visiting Daddy after he got sick and couldn't work — I was about 12 years old and didn't know what a cotton mill was. I remember seeing you at the Christmas parties Daddy use to take us to. Then when I was in high school we toured your house in our home-ec class and I thought you were so friendly.

I just want you to know I'll always remember Mr. Swain and the place won't be the same without you. Best of luck to you and many happy leisure years.

Rita

Precious note from a co-worker at the mill

Another History of Crompton Arkansas Mills

Conway County: Our Land, Our Home, Our People - Conway County Historical Society, 1992

Found at the Downtown Museum in Morrilton at the "old train depot"

Crompton Company, Morrilton Plant, operated and contributed significantly to the Conway County area's economy from August, **1948**, until October 19, **1984**. In the annals of textile history, this company is the oldest manufacturer of cotton goods in the United States, operated continuously under the same ownership from **1807** until **1984**.

First called Provident Manufacturing Company, the plant began operating near Providence, Road Island, manufacturing printed cloth. In **1823**, the company took the name Crompton in honor of Samuel Crompton inventor of the spinning mule.

In **1950**, when additional corduroy production was needed, Crompton purchased the Morrilton Cotton Mill, doubled the size of the plant to a **600-loom** capacity, and hired **350 people** to produce grey, unfinished corduroy. By **1963**, the plant had again doubled its size and production capacity, employing **600 people**. In **1969**, the plant was again enlarged, and yarn manufacturing equipment to support a **1,500-loom** operation employed **1,000 people**. Production frequently exceeded **500,000 yards** of corduroy a week. The **1,250 people** then had a chance to earn four hours pay as a weekly bonus.

In the late **1970's**, stores in the United States turned to foreign imports in greater volume, and by the early **1980's**, Crompton found it could no longer compete in the manufacture and sale of corduroys. Although the company carried out a **$3.5 million modernization** of the Morrilton plant, intending to produce the finest quality corduroy in an attempt to capture the fashion designer market, the necessary sales volume proved unattainable and led to the **close of Crompton's three remaining plants in 1984**.

In **1988**, the huge plant stood deserted, a memorial to owners with good intentions and the **dedicated efforts of many workers in the Morrilton area**. Business leaders and workers hoped that another occupant would be found for the plant.

This history was copied by the author of this book in 2024. By this time the plant has been completely torn down. Nothing is left except the train tracks behind the plant that brought in raw cotton from growers. The Elmwood Cemetery is directly across the highway from where the plant once stood.

From the book, "Conway County: Our Land, Our Home, Our People" hardcover, found at the Conway County Historical Museum at the Old Depot in Downtown Morrilton, published, 1992.

Crompton plant at Morrilton, Arkansas - as it looked in its day.

Ansel's

Christian and Civic Commitments

"Serving Others in the Community"

Section Nine

Ansel's Christian and Civic Commitments

"Serving Others in the Community" Section Nine

First United Methodist Church MORRILTON

Ansel Swain *served as Church School Superintendent in 1959-1960.*

Ansel Swain, board chair, speaking for the congregation of First United Methodist Church, Morrilton *welcomed the Conway District Conference* to that church on ***January 9, 1969***. Also, seen are Rev. Harold Spence, host pastor, Rev. Roy Poyner, conference secretary and Rev. Ben Jordan, district superintendent.

Ansel Swain served the First United Methodist Church in many ways, among them ...
Chair of Administrative Board • Church School Superintendent •
Sunday School Teacher • United Methodist Men

Ansel Swain, chair of the Morrilton First United Methodist Church Administrative Board *welcomed Phillip Mains*, Little Rock firefighter, as leader of the three day local **"Lay Witness Mission"** that was ***December 12-14, 1969***. Mains led missions all over the world saying, This is not a Methodist-oriented activity alone. *It is a Christ-oriented activity.*

Ansel became a member of the Methodist Episcopal Church South when he married Elizabeth in 1950.

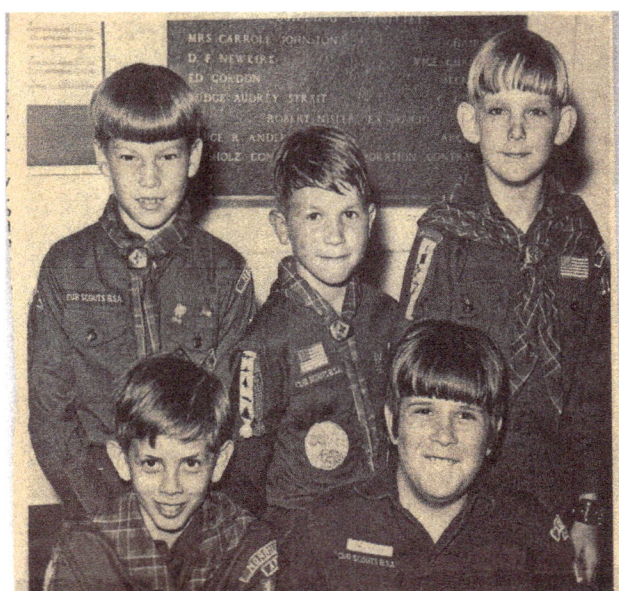

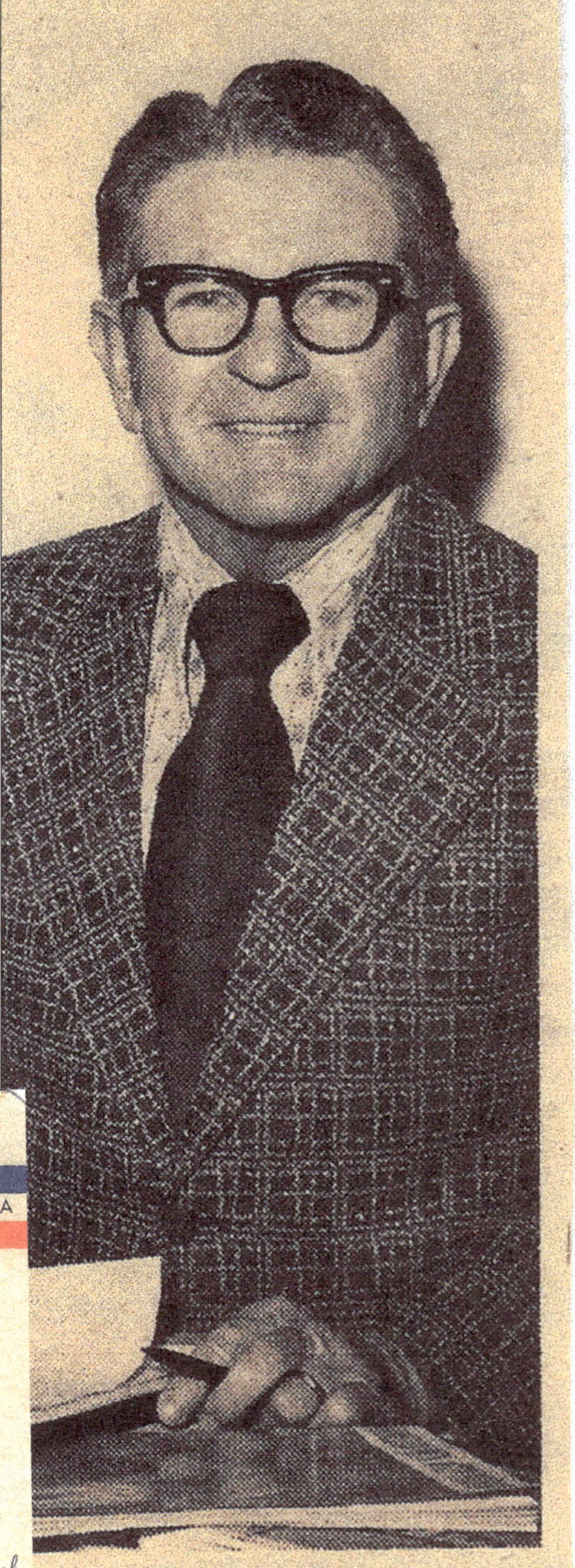

Five members of **Cub Scout Pack 184** were named ***"Recipients of Light"*** Cub Scout's highest honor. Held at First United Methodist Church in Morrilton, **Ansel Swain was the speaker for the event**.

In 1952, Ansel served as District Chairman Quapaw Area Council of the Boys Scouts of America.
In 1959, Ansel Swain was Chairman of Troup 173 in Morrilton.

BOY SCOUTS OF AMERICA

ANSEL SWAIN
HAS DULY QUALIFIED AND IS REGISTERED WITH THE BOY SCOUTS OF AMERICA

CHAIRMAN
TROOP 173
MORRILTON ARK
TO THE LAST DAY OF

JULY 1959
IN ACCORDANCE WITH THE CONSTITUTION AND BYLAWS OF THE BOY SCOUTS OF AMERICA, IN WITNESS WHEREOF ITS SEAL IS HERETO AFFIXED

PRESIDENT — CHIEF SCOUT EXECUTIVE

BOY SCOUTS OF AMERICA

Ansel Swain
HAS DULY QUALIFIED AND IS REGISTERED WITH THE BOY SCOUTS OF AMERICA FOR ONE YEAR AS

District Chairman
Quapaw Area Council

IN ACCORDANCE WITH THE CONSTITUTION AND BY-LAWS OF THE BOY SCOUTS OF AMERICA, IN WITNESS WHEREOF ITS SEAL IS HERETO AFFIXED

DATED December 31, 1952
18

PRESIDENT — CHIEF SCOUT EXECUTIVE

—Staff Photos by Larry Miller

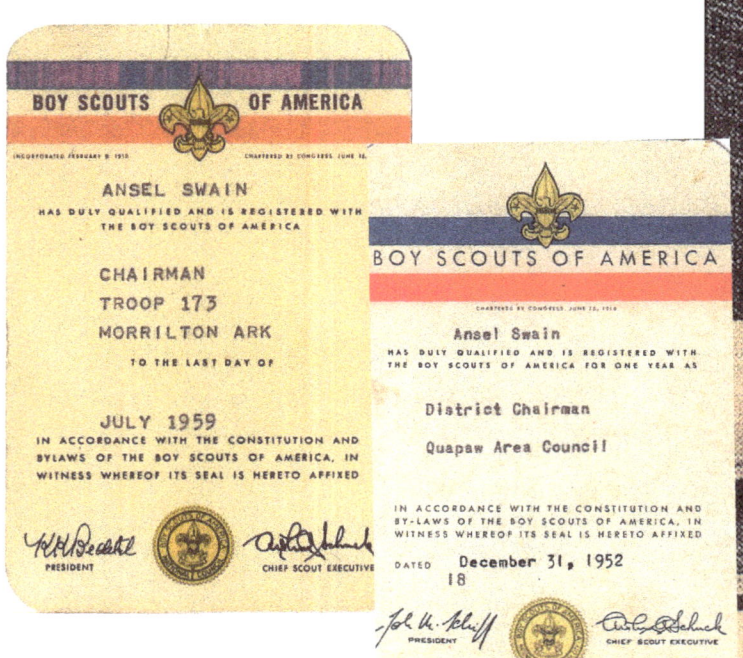

MR. SWAIN

From the Petit Jean Country Headlight . . .

"**A hotly contested campaign** for two vacancies of the Board of Directors of the Morrilton Board of Education brought a record of voters in the annual election of the school district.

The **unusually large vote**, was attributed to the opposition for the school directors for the first time in a quarter of a century.

Ansel Swain and **Jack Bland** were elected as the two new members of the School Board for a term of three years each. Swain received 1,106 votes and Bland received 849 votes.

In the same election a $350,000 bond issue was also passed for additions to North Side Elementary School which was to absorb children from the old Central Ward Elementary School."

In **1960**, the **key to the new school was passed from the architect to Ansel Swain**, President of Board.

In **1960**, at the **graduation** ceremonies for the Morrilton High School, **Ansel Swain presented the diplomas** to 106 members of the **Class of 1960**.

Ansel Swain President
Morrilton Board of Education
1959-1961

A set of photographs of all serving Presidents of the Morrilton School Board of Education were displayed for many years in the school administration building. A few years ago all the photographs were given to families in honor / memory of their loved one's service.

MORRILTON DEMOCRA

COVERS THE PETIT JEAN COUNTRY LIKE THE SUNSHINE

Swain Elected President Morrilton Golf and Country Club in 1970

From the Morrilton Democrat . . .

"**Ansel Swain**, Personnel Director at Crompton Arkansas Mills, has been elected **1970 President of the Morrilton Golf and Country Club**. He succeeds Edward Lee Eddy. Swain served the club as **Vice President in 1969**."

From the Petit Jean Country Headlight . . .

September 7, 1971

"**Ansel Swain**, certainly enjoyed his afternoons and weekends on the golf course. Here he is shown with Aaron Oliger and Larry Zimmerman winners of **First Flight in an annual club tournament**."

Ansel Swain
Serving the United Way Fund

Ansel served the **Conway County United Way**, assisting in annual drives to raise gifts from employees at Crompton Arkansas Mills to the United Way.

The fund supported 15 charitable organizations in the county from the Red Cross, boys baseball, boys and girls scouting, the local Cerebral Palsy Day Care Center and others.

Ansel was awarded a **plaque for work with the United Way**.

It said,
"In grateful Appreciation for helping the people of our Community, from the United Way." (no date on plaque)

In 1984, **Ansel** was awarded a **plaque for work with the Conway County Library Board**.

It said,
"Certificate of Appreciation presented to Mr. Ansel Swain for outstanding and dedicated service to the Morrilton-Conway County Library." (1984)

—Staff Photo by Stewart Nelson

Ansel Swain is shown here accepting a check from the Levi Strauss plant to the United Way on behalf of chairman Bunk Allison reaching a goal of **$32,000 goal in 1977**.

Ansel Swain
Served on the
Conway County Library Board

The Conway County Library in Morrilton was established in 1916 as a Carnegie Library.

Ansel Swain served on the
Conway County Industrial Committee

The Conway County Industrial Commission was established by the Arkansas State Legislature Act #404 in **1955**. Elected March of **1978**, **Ansel Swain served on the Board of Directors** for four years. This organization acquires land and made available spaces for development, securing payment for property.

Certificate of Appreciation

Presented to

Answel Swain

in recognition of your address before the

KIWANIS CLUB OF MORRILTON, ARKANSAS

Your contribution to our Club is deeply appreciated. We hope this certificate will serve as a lasting memento of this pleasant occasion.

Billy J. Roper
PRESIDENT

[signature]
PROGRAM CHAIRMAN

5-12-77
Date

Ansel Swain, personnel manager at Crompton Arkansas Mills spoke on *"Changes in Personnel Practices"* at the meeting of the **Morrilton Optimist Club**.

Ansel Swain was the speaker at the annual Dinner and Meeting in 1977.
"Your contributions to our Club are deeply appreciated. We hope this Certificate will serve as a lasting memento of this pleasant occasion."

Ansel Swain, Member and Speaker
Annual Kiwanis Club of Morrilton

Ansel Attended Morrilton High School 50 Year Graduation Reunion

Class of 1939 • October 25, 1939

Ansel actually received his high school diploma in 1940 at Jacksonville, Arkansas High School while in the Civilian Conservation Corps. But, his friends at Morrilton High, where he attended before he went to Jacksonville, knew he should have graduated with them in 1939.

A dinner was held at the Morrilton Country Club on October 7 and picnic was held at the J.H. Scroggin home. Class members traveled from as far as San Diego. A scholarship was given in the rewards at the banquet.

Old Morrilton High School

Find Out More About Morrilton, Arkansas

Introduction

For those interested in the **history of the Morrilton area** from it's earliest beginnings, I have included parts of a paper by **Mary Ellen Guffey Brents** from Morrilton, Arkansas, **Encyclopedia of Arkansas** and revised, **2022**, and by **David Sesser, Henderson State University**. Information from **Rachel Silva**, employed by the **Arkansas Historic Preservation Program** wrote, *"Walks through History: A History of Morrilton"* in **2014**. Other information came from the book, *"Butterfield Overland Mail Through Conway and Pope Counties in Arkansas"* by author **Bob Crossman** published in **2024**. *Thanks so much to all of these educators for their research and writing that informs us today. I hope you enjoy this!* **Edited by Marcia Swain Crossman, 2024.**

The Geography of Conway County

Located in the Arkansas River Valley, Conway County's geography ranges from the ridges of the Ozark foothills, in the extreme northwest, to the rich lowlands near the Arkansas River — a quite varied topography. The **Arkansas River divides the county into two unequal parts**, the largest being to the north. To the south is Petit Jean Mountain *(elevation 1,207 feet)*, the county's highest summit.

Pre-European Exploration

Spears and darts dating from very early periods have been found at the **Travis Moreland Site**, which was perhaps a camp for the butchering of animals. Other sites dating from more recent prehistoric periods have been located in Conway County, including the **Alexander Site**, which some archaeologists believe was a satellite community for the larger **Toltec Mounds Site** in Lonoke County. More than 700 pictographs are located on or near Petit Jean Mountain. Ancestors of the **Quapaw Indians** may have lived in the county.

Louisiana Purchase through Early Statehood

Conway County's early settlers came by way of the **Arkansas River** and included **trappers, traders, and fugitives**. Most of the earliest settlements were along the **Arkansas River** and in the valley of **Cadron Creek**, which forms part of the county's east boundary. The county was under **French and Spanish** rule before the **Louisiana Purchase** put it under American control, though there were no permanent French or Spanish settlements in the area. A few Americans had settled in the area before the Louisiana Purchase, such as the family of **Benjamin Standlee**, who lived above the mouth of Cadron Creek from **1777** to **1780**.

The Trail of Tears

From **1817** to **1828**, the **Western Cherokee occupied a reservation in Arkansas** that included a great deal of Conway County. In **1828**, the **Cherokee in Arkansas** signed a treaty swapping this reservation for lands west of the territorial border. *This coincided with the 1820's and 1830's removal of Cherokee and other Indians from the southeast United States to Indian Territory (present-day Oklahoma) on what is known as "The Trail of Tears."* The **Arkansas River** was a much-used water route for **Indian removal**, with **Point Remove** in **Conway County** being a stop along the route. The **Via Dolorosa** road was built from the east of the White River and west through **Springfield** to transport these Indian refugees.

Creation of Conway County

Conway County was **created by the Arkansas General Assembly on October 20, 1825** from land taken from Pulaski County. It was **named for Henry Wharton Conway**, from of the Arkansas Territory's delegation to Congress. *At the time, it comprised 2,500 square miles and included most of the present Conway, Faulkner, Van Buren, White, Cleburne, and Perry counties and part of Yell Count, all tiny compared to today's population.*

The town of **Cadron**, which was then located centrally in **Conway County,** was made a temporary county seat. In **1829**, the territorial legislature moved the county seat to **Harrisburg** *(then the house of Stephen Harris in Welborne Township).* In **1831**, the county seat moved again after Dr. Nimrod Menifee donated a plot of land in **Lewisburg** for the building of a courthouse. **Lewisburg** remained the county seat until **1850.**

Note: On December 11, 1840, when **Lewisburg** was still the county seat, a steamboat named **"Cherokee" exploded** after leaving the dock from Lewisburg. The incident led to the deaths of at least twenty people.

The county seat then moved to **Springfield** because of that town's more central location. The **first post office** for the county was at **Peconery**, an early settlement on the Arkansas River between **Lewisburg** and **Cadron.**

Secession of Arkansas and The Civil War

Dr. S. J. Stallings went to the **Secession Convention** held in Little Rock *(Pulaski County)* in **March, 1861** with instructions to **vote against Arkansas leaving the Union**. After the **firing upon Fort Sumter,** the following month, most **Conway County citizens supported secession.** *(Note: Stallings owned six enslaved people at the time of the 1860 census).* The county recorded **5,895 white residents in 1860** and **802 enslaved persons**, showing that about **twelve percent of the population was held in bondage.** The county produced 3,181 bales of **cotton** in **1860** and almost 35,000 pounds of **tobacco.**

The **first Confederate Civil War company** in the county was organized by **Robert W. Harper** of **Lewisburg**. Other companies were subsequently raised at **Lewisburg** and **Springfield. About 900 men from Conway County fought in the Civil War, primarily in Arkansas but also in Tennessee and Kentucky; only 200 men returned home from the war. *There were no major* *actions fought in Conway County, although numerous minor engagements took place.*

The Third Arkansas Cavalry, *from the Union side*, was partially **recruited in Conway County. They patrolled from a base in Lewisburg**. Operations in the county included scouts to locate Confederate cavalry in June **1864** and anti-guerrilla operations in August **1864**, and an expedition into Johnson County in November **1864**. A skirmish fought at **Lewisburg on February 12, 1865, saw the end of most military operations in the Conway County**.

Note: Some of these war solders are buried at the Lewisburg Missionary Baptist Church Cemetery and others at the Elmwood Cemetery in Morrilton. In 2024, a new Internet home page was created for the Elmwood Cemetery population which includes Civil War solders buried there.

Conway County Seat was moved to Morrilton

In 1873, the county seat was returned to **Lewisburg** from **Springfield**. In **1883**, it again was taken from Lewisburg and established at **Morrilton**, where it remains to this day. It's original parent county was **Pulaski**. The current courthouse was constructed in **1929**.

Transportation In the Mid 1800's

In its early days, beginning in **1828**, the Conway County area thrived due to its **location on the Arkansas River.** Travel on the river was the best transportation for crops and business. In that day **Lewisburg**, on the Arkansas River, boasted over **80 businesses**, including two sawmills, two gristmills, a flour mill, cotton gin, hotels, two newspapers, saloons and numerous stores. The location of the county seat which, was at **Lewisburg** for many years, brought this commerce there.

Before the railroad in the **1870's**, **stagecoach** and **horse drawn** vehicles were the main means of travel by the people of the area. **Persons** and the **United States Mail** were delivered by the **Butterfield Overland Mail Company**, a popular but slow line of travel. **Steamboats** also carried mail and people across the state. When the **railroad tracks** were laid through Conway County, it quickly became the major mode of transportation.

In **1867**, surveyors for the **coming of the Little Rock and Fort Smith Railroad** were looking at land outside of **Lewisburg**. The progress of the railroad was interrupted by the Civil War.

About **1870,** actual construction of the railroad began after the war. The railroad company invited the residents of **Lewisburg** to provide $3,000 to defray costs. The residents of **Lewisburg declined the invitation**.

Edward Henry Morrill and **James Miles Moose** were forward thinking businessmen in the area. They **donated land for railroad track to run through their property about a mile north of Lewisburg.** *The area along the tracks grew quickly.* The twenty-four miles of **Missouri Pacific Railroad** tracks were completed through the county. In **1872**. *Residents of Conway County could see that the area around the new track was better for business.* ***Many Lewisburg residents disassembled their houses and***

businesses and moved these one mile north to be near the new tracks. *Note: James Miles Moose bought* **Lewisburg's Markham Tavern** *and moved it to* **Morrilton** *as his new home.*

The **first bona fide rail depot** in that area was established in **1873**. The land for the depot was given by **E. H. Morrill**. The first station agent, was **Capt. J.W. Boot**. With a **flip of a coin, between Morrill** and **Moose, choose the town to be named after Mr. Morrill. Morrilton** was first spelled with two "l's" like its namesake. The population of the **Lewisburg area slowly moved to Morrilton**. The new town of **Morrilton** was incorporated in **1835** with a **population of 800**.

Note: In **1874**, the **Springfield-Des Arc Bridge was completed**, spanning the north fork of Cadron Creek connecting Conway County with the newly created Faulkner County. *It is now on the National Register of Historic Places.*

Newspapers in the Town of Morrilton

The **earliest newspaper** to be published in Conway County was the *Wide Awake*, established in **Lewisburg** in January **1872**. In May of that year, the *Western Empire* also began publication in **Lewisburg**. Neither paper lasted more than a few years. A number of papers have been based in Conway County since that time, but the only one surviving today is the *Petit Jean Country Headlight*, which was **founded on April 8, 1874**, by the **Reverend W. C. Stout**, an Episcopalian minister, as the *Weekly State*.

In the News:
In **1889**, Conway County attracted national attention when **John Middleton Clayton**, brother of former governor Powell Clayton, was **assassinated** at **Plumerville** *(Conway County)*. John Clayton ran as a Republican candidate in the **1888** congressional election against Democratic incumbent **Clifton Rhodes Breckinridge**, losing narrowly in what was one of the most **fraudulent elections** in Arkansas history. **Clayton had the support of black Republican voters**, and **in Conway County, four white masked men armed with guns had stolen a ballot box at a predominately black precinct**. Clayton contested the election and came to Plumerville to investigate missing votes.

On January 29, **1889, Clayton** was **shot through the window** of his boarding house and died instantly. The **murderer was never brought to justice**, probably due in some part to a great antipathy in the county to the **Republican Party and their black allies**. One man who offered to turn state's evidence in the case was murdered by his brother, though the **coroner ruled the death an accident**. In **1893**, a man named **Hickey** was tried for Clayton's murder, but though he admitted his guilt in the Conway County court, the jury deliberated for only a few minutes before returning a **not guilty verdict**. Clayton's murder was only one incident of violence that was perpetrated in the county from 1886 to 1892 **related to politics**, with the period being known as the **Plumerville Conflict of 1886–1892**.

The newspapers reported **multiple incidents of racial violence within the county**, with at least four African American men lynched from the late nineteenth to the early twentieth centuries. At least three **lynchings** followed the alleged murder of law enforcement officials. The body of **William Rice** was discovered hanging near Plumerville on November 7, **1891**. **Flanigan Thornton**, accused of killing a constable, was lynched on April 19, **1893**. A crowd lynched **John Williams** on July 4, **1912**, for the alleged killing of a citizen serving as a temporary deputy. The most recent lynching took place on

December 9, **1922**, when **Less Smith** was lynched for the alleged killing of a deputy.

Later in the news: Conway County **sheriff, Marlin Hawkins,** played an out sized role in the **politics of the state** in the **1950-60's**. Local newspaper **publisher Gene Wirges** helped expose **corruption in the county**.

Agriculture and Economic Life

Agriculture has long been a mainstay of Conway County's economic life. Many farmers cleared land to plant **cotton**. In the **1930**s, local farmers, like those throughout the South, were trying to plant more cotton to offset their losses due to the perpetually low price for cotton.

Many people became concerned with the number of **acres left abandoned** after the demise of cotton farming and sought ways to put abandoned acres back into production. Eventually, the **Central Valley Soil Conservation District** — *comprising Conway, Faulkner, and Van Buren counties, as well as parts of Pope and Cleburne counties* — was formed to encourage soil and water conservation. This was one of the first districts in Arkansas; it was granted a state charter on February 16, **1938**.

As time went on, the county's native **hardwood and pine forests** have been a resource for the timber and recreation industries. **Cotton** had been grown in the early days of the county, but now the dominant agriculture products became **soybeans and hay**, as well as **poultry** and **livestock**. In modern days, Conway County's northwest corner became the site of **natural gas deposits** deep underground.

Two Civilian Conservation Corps (CCC) camps operated in Conway County during the **Depression years. Company 1781** was active at **Petit Jean Mountain,** from **1933** to **1938**. They built and maintained the facilities at what was Arkansas' first state park. **Company 3789** carried out work such as terracing and sodding pastures under the supervision of the **Soil Conservation District**. The camp was closed in **1937**.

Despite its rural nature, Conway County did have some **limited industry** in the **early twentieth century**. The **Morrilton Cotton Mill** was built in **1901** and operated for more than **forty years It later becoming Crompton-Arkansas Mills. John B. Richard** started a **soda bottling company** in Morrilton in **1919**. In **1929**, the **Coca-Cola Company** established a bottling plant in the same town. Other smaller industries were also present, most of them concentrated in Morrilton. The first **hospital in Conway County** opened in **1920**.

Conway County's most famous resident, **Winthrop Rockefeller** of the famous Rockefeller family, bought a large amount of land on Petit Jean Mountain in the early **1950's**. He established a showplace home there. In **1964**, he founded the **Museum of Automobiles** atop the mountain. In **1966, Rockefeller became the first Republican elected governor since Reconstruction**. *He served two terms and was widely recognized as the standard bearer of a new progressive* **Spirit in Arkansas**.

World War II and Korea

Many Conway County men served in World War II. Lieutenant Nathan Gordon of Morrilton received the **Medal of Honor** in **1944** for using his Catalina patrol plane to rescue personnel shot down in combat over Kavieng Harbor on February 15, **1944**. *Gordon would go on to serve as lieutenant governor from 1947 to 1967, the longest tenure of anyone to hold the office in Arkansas' history.* Plumerville native **John Yancey** received a battlefield commission as a second lieutenant in the Marine Corps along with the **Navy Cross** during the **Battle of Guadalcanal**. During the **Korean War**, Yancey received a **second Navy Cross** for his actions at the Battle of **Chosin Reservoir**.

Education Prospered

The first recorded school in Conway County was a **small log house at Lewisburg** sometime before **1836**. In **1867, the Male and Female Academy** was operating at **Lewisburg**. Morrilton's first public **school for white children** appeared in **1881**. Its first **school for black children** was built in **1895**. Soon, every community had a small school, many of only one room. The **Springfield Male and Female Collegiate Institute** operated for a number of years in the late nineteenth century.

In **1889**, Morrilton founded the **Male and Female College**, which lasted until the late **1890's.** It later became part of the public school system. **Arkansas Christan College** was established in Morrilton in **1922**. Two years later, it merged with a college in Harper, Kansas, and changed its name to **Galloway Female College** in Searcy, Arkansas later becoming **Harding College**.

On May 26, **1965**, the **Morrilton School Board abolished the black Sullivan High School**, transferring the black students to the city's predominately white junior and senior high schools. At the present time, **Conway County has four high schools and five elementary schools**. It is also the home of the **University of Arkansas Community College in Morrilton**.

Modern Era

In the **1960's**, Conway County became home to **four of Arkansas's eighteen Titan II Missile silos**. *The Titan II was an intercontinental ballistic missile (ICBM) placed in five Arkansas counties, as well as sites in Arizona and Kansas. The program was decommissioned in the early* **1980's**. Launch Complex 374-1 **near Blackwell** was **deactivated** on August 19, **1985**; 374-3 near **St. Vincent** on August 6, **1986**; 374-4 near **Springfield** on August 28, **1986**; and 374-2 near **Plumerville** on September 16, **1986**.

In **1968, Interstate 40 was completed**, creating a main thoroughfare through previously rural Conway County. *Some will remember that the Morrilton High School Band performed in the middle of the Interstate the day it was officially opened.* In **1966**, construction began southwest of Morrilton on **Lock and Dam No. 9**, part of the McClellan-Kerr Arkansas River Navigation System. Finished in **1969**, it was renamed the **Arthur V. Ormond Lock and Dam** at a dedication ceremony on November 17, **1986**. The dam has aided transportation and flood control on the Arkansas River.

Modern-day Conway County has twenty-one townships and three incorporated cities, as well as one incorporated town. Today, the **county seat of Conway, County is Morrilton**. It was established October 20, **1825**. The population in **2020** was **20,715**. That census also showed the area to be **551.92** square miles.

Attractions

One point of interest in Conway County is the state park on **Petit Jean Mountain**; it was the **first state park in Arkansas** and is the most visited. Petit Jean State Park holds many attractions for tourists such as the **Museum of Automobiles, Cedar Falls** *(one of the highest waterfalls in the South)*, and many hiking trails with scenic vistas of the river valley and mountains beyond. The **Winthrop Rockefeller Institute** is also located on Petit Jean Mountain. The Arkansas Sky Observatories operate two sites on the mountain.

The **Depot Museum in Morrilton** opened in **1981** and houses a collection of Conway County memorabilia. An old **Missouri Pacific depot** that closed in **1954**, it was later purchased by the **Conway County Historical Preservation Society** and remodeled. Another attraction in the area is the **Conway County Library**, one of the few Carnegie Libraries remaining in the state. **The Great Arkansas Pig Out**, a two-day festival, is held in Morrilton each August. Also, the downtown **Rialto Theatre**, closed for many years, has been refreshed and opens for plays and special events.

Downtown Morrilton looking west down West Broadway Street.

Downtown Morrilton looking east down East Broadway Street.

Ansel and Elizabeth's

Daughters and Grandchildren

Marcia Gail Swain
1953

Sherry Elizabeth Swain
1955

"Legacy Carried On Through Descendants"

Section Ten

Ansel and Elizabeth's Daughters and Grandchildren
"Legacy Carried On Through Descendants" Section Ten

Ansel & Elizabeth Swain
were parents of two daughters,
Marcia Gail Swain, born April 26, 1953 &
Sherry Elizabeth Swain, born May 6, 1955.

The family photo (above) is
Sherry, Elizabeth, Marcia & Ansel, taken for
a church directory, was make around 1968.

The family make their home in Morrilton,
Arkansas where the daughters graduated from
Morrilton High School.

The studio photo (to right) of *Marcia &
Sherry* was made around 1957.

Sherry & **Marcia,** as little girls, growing up on North West Street in Morrilton.

Left:
This is the Swain home at 101 North West Street in Morrilton. The family lived there until around 1966.

Below:
The Swains moved into a new home in 1967 located at **3 Magnolia Drive in Morrilton**. Ansel & Elizabeth lived the remainder of their lives in this home.

Sherry & Marcia had a
set of photos taken at Olan Mills, as a surprise
Christmas gift, for Ansel & Elizabeth,
around 1980.

Sherry & Marcia in Manhattan, Kansas on a
family visit, around 1983.

Marcia & Sherry,
together for a photo, at Bailey
& Cole Bachamp's wedding,
June 2013.

Bailey is Sherry's older daughter.

Marcia G. Swain Married Robert O. Crossman
February 9, 1973 in Morrilton, Arkansas

**Marcia & Bob Crossman
have been married for 51 years in 2024.**

They have lived in Conway, Arkansas, since 1988,
near their sons & grandchildren.

Marcia Gail Swain Crossman
b. April 26, 1953

Marcia and Bob at their Wedding Reception
in 1973 at Morrilton Arkansas's
First United Methodist Church.

Robert Owen Crossman
b. February 24, 1953

The Sons of Marcia and Robert Crossman

Charles Robert Crossman, born August 1, 1978
& David Nathan Crossman, born November 2, 1981

Right:
Brothers
Charlie (left) &
David (right),
around 2020.

Below:
Charlie (left) &
David (right)
on a fishing trip with their
dad, **Bob Crossman,**
around 2020.

The Family of Charles and Jessica Crossman

Charles Robert Crossman & Jessica Wenzell became the parents of twin sons
Blake Winfield & Grayson Robert on September 16, 2008.

Left:
Grayson
2018

Right:
Grayson
&
Blake,
high school
2023

Left:
Blake
2018

The Family of David Nathan Crossman

David Nathan Crossman & Holly Lynn Elliott became the parents of three children.
Marlie Grace Crossman was born on April 21, 2009.
Owen Elliott Crossman was born on October 17, 2011.
Cooper Maddox Crossman was born on December 20, 2013.

Left:
Marlie Grace Crossman (left back),
Owen Elliott Crossman (right back)
Cooper Maddox Crossman (front),
about 2023.

Above: Marlie, David & Owen, about 2023.

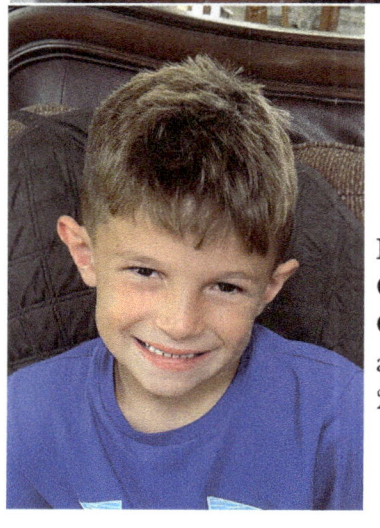

Left:
Cooper Crossman, about 2023.

Above: Owen and **Cooper Crossman** (front row)
David & Marlie Crossman (back row), about 2022.

Thanksgiving Photo: Cooper, Owen, Marlie, Grayson & Blake Crossman (front row) Charlie & David Crossman (back row) standing on the bridge at Marcia & Bob's home in Conway, about 2019.

Christmas Photo Below: Bob, Blake, Grayson, Cooper, Owen, Marlie & Marcia Crossman standing in front of the fire place at Bob & Marcia's home, around 2023.

Sherry E. Swain Married Frederick G. Borck

July 11, 1987 in Blue Rapids, Kansas

**Sherry & Fred have
been married for 37 years in 2024.**
Their home is in Manhattan, Kansas.

Sherry Elizabeth Swain Borck
b. May 6, 1955

Sherry and Fred on their Wedding Day
in 1987 at at the home of Fred's parents,
Marge and Harold Borck.

Fredrick George Borck
b. September 20, 1951

The Daughters of Sherry and Fred Borck

Bailey Erin Borck Bachamp, born March 3, 1989
& Raquel Elizabeth Borck, born April 4, 1994

Left:
Sisters
Raquel (left) &
Bailey (right),
around 2020.

Below:
Bailey (left) &
Raquel (right).

Bailey and Cole Bachamp and Sons

Bailey Erin Borck & Cole Ryan Bachamp became the parents of twin sons
Dylan Gray & Brooks Ryan on May 13, 2021

**Cole
Ryan
Bachamp**
b. July 29, 1988.

Bailey and Cole Bachamp
on their wedding day, June 22, 2013.

Above:
Cole and Bailey sharing ultrasound
photos of the twins.

Right:
Twin Brothers,
Dylan (left) & **Brooks** (right), age 2.

Raquel Elizabeth Borck and Family

Right:
Raquel Elizabeth Borck
b. April 4, 1994
high school graduation.

Left:
Raquel Borck (front)
Bailey Borck & **Sherry Borck**
(middle) with
Fred Borck (right),
about 2007.

Right:
Raquel Borck (center)
Cole Bachamp &
Sherry Borck (left)
with
Bailey Bachamp &
Fred Borck (right),
about 2018.

Other Photos

Our Wedding
February 9, 1973
First United Methodist Church
Morrilton, Arkansas

Marcia Swain & Bob Crossman

Announce the Happiness of Their
GOLDEN WEDDING ANNIVERSARY
February 9, 2023

The Wedding Party: Marty Forbes Luebker, Pat Farish Smith, Brigitte Swain Brent, Sherry Swain Borck, Marcia Swain Crossman, Reverend Clyde T. Parsons, Robert Crossman, Ansel Swain, Paul Crossman, Randal Oates, Barry Swain, Jim Bob Humphrey & Bill Swain.

Charlie, Bob, Marcia & David

Left: 50th Anniversary for **Marcia & Bob Crossman.**

Above: Ansel Swain (left) with **Sherry Borck** (right). Sherry is wearing her mother's, **Elizabeth Swain's, wedding dress**, around 1987.

What a surprise it would have been for our parents, Ansel & Elizabeth Swain, to learn they had two sets of **twin greatgrandsons**! The older set is **Grayson Crossman** (left) & **Blake Crossman** (right). The younger set is **Brooks Bachamp** (left) & **Dylan Bachamp** (right), *second cousins and great grandchildren*. Photo at Sherry's home, around 2023.

One Last Photo:
The **Crossman Cousins** together: Owen, Grayson, Marlie, Cooper & Blake, around 2016.

Ansel and the Lessons
He Taught His Daughters

"Words of Wisdom at the Right Moment"

Section Eleven

Ansel and the Lessons He Taught His Daughters

"Words of Wisdom at the Right Moment" Section Eleven

"Cornbread and Milk"

Our Dad always told us girls he grew up on cornbread and milk. My sister and I always said we grew up on ice cream and hamburgers.

Our Dad gives a lot of himself to work hard and give a good life for us. We are grateful he did because we sure liked ice cream!

"Work Ethic"

Our Father very rarely missed a day of work in all the years he worked at the Cotton Mill. We remember the times he would walk to work in the snow down to the highway. He would catch a ride on to the plant with someone driving that way. It taught us that earning your living honestly was the right thing to do in life.

"Be Practical"

Live moderately and live within your means. This advice became ours from our Father. Find happiness in moderation. Happiness is more important than riches and fame. In the end who you are is much more important than what you are and what you have.

I wanted to do something special for our dad for Father's Day.

I came up with the idea of writing little stories about the lessons he taught us about life.

There are many lessons we are grateful for. This collection was not the total.

I bought a Father's Day coffee cup and tied a little note on it.

I asked our dad to read one every day to know what he had taught us.

After he died, I got this little collection back. I read it often.

"I Have A Coat"

Words that we will never forget. We were driving home from Little Rock. Sherry proudly stated the number and types of coats she had. I replied by telling her the same about me. Then came words of wisdom that I never forgot. Our Dad said to us, "I have a coat."

"Last to Leave the Church"

"Where is he? Is he still talking to everyone?" said the two girls sitting in the car after church was over. Our Dad never met a person he couldn't make friends with or talk to. He spoke and waved to everyone. He taught us to make friends. He once said, Talk to the other person about himself. This is the way to make friends."

"Get Your Education"

One of the most valuable lessons our Father taught us was to get educated. He said, "It's something that no one can take away from you. He was right. It did make a difference in our lives.

"Get With the Program"
Never put off doing the things you don't want to do. It's better to go ahead and do them.

"A Community Leader"
We are proud of the contributions our Father gave to the community of Morrilton. We humorously recall when our dad served as president of the Morrilton school board that we actually told some kids, "If you are not nice, our dad will kick you out of school. What a silly bluff!"

"No, I Don't Know That Family"
Wow! One boy that our Dad didn't know him or his family. And, I married him. Dads are good at watching out for our good.

We are bound to our parents in the passage of time.

Yet, we cannot look into their eyes, or touch them, or hear their voices.

We honor the history of our parents.

We will cherish their memories.

We will remember them.

We hope to pass the llegacy of our parents to our children.

"A Church Leader"
We are proud of the contributions our Dad gave to the Methodist people in Morrilton. He served on just about ever committee and board of the church. He was even a Sunday School teacher. He was a Christian example to us.

"Always Loved!"
My Dad is always near in my heart. I knew he loved me even as a teenager and young adult. I must have tried his patience many times. His capacity for forgiveness is now a part of who I am. Thanks Dad!

"It's A Girl"
The set of Dick Tracy guns was a neat Christmas present to a little girl. But the rifle melted in the sun in the back of our dad's old Studebaker.

"A Picture to Recall"
This is a photograph I keep in my heart. Our Father with a Bible tucked under his arm, holding the hand of a little girl on their way to church. That little girl was me!

"Look deeply into the palm of your hands.

You will see your parents and all the generations of your ancestors.

All of them are alive within you this moment.

Each is present within you.

You are the continuation of each of these people."

"Make Friends With Everyone"

In the eighth grade I ran for vice president of the student council. My dad told me to go up and ask everyone, both black and white, for their vote. I won the office by 10 votes and learned a valuable lesson about

"Charlie Was Coming"

A present for our Dad one time was a box of baby disposable diapers. Dad got the message quickly taking to the floor and rolling around in joy--the coming of his first grandchild had been announced.

"The Pockets Were Empty"

At the end of the wedding photograph album is a favorite photo of our Dad. His pockets were pulled inside out. He had walked his little girl down the isle. The wedding was over. His empty pockets paid for the big day. What a wonderful day to walk down the isle holding the arm of a wonderful Dad. I was so proud.

"His Surgery"

In his 60's our Dad faced a very scary and threatening brain surgery. His great courage kept us going throughout day and time following. Thank God for good doctors and nurses. They gave us back our Dad so we could spend many more years with him.

"The Middle of the Night!"

The baby slept all night? No, not really. Dad had gotten up in the middle of the night and fetched him when he cried. Early in the morning I would find him sitting in his favorite chair with Charlie or David and the two of them asleep after a long night. Thanks, Dad, for the sleep!

"We Cried"

When our Dad was facing death in the hospital at Morrilton, we touched him and cried. His last words to his girls was, "No tears."

"There are two lasting bequests we can give our children.

One is roots and the other is wings."

Final Memories of Ansel and Elizabeth

"No Tears"

Section Twelve

ℱinal ℳemories of 𝒜nsel 𝑎𝑛𝑑 𝓔lizabeth
"No Tears" Section Twelve

THE DEATH OF ANSEL SWAIN

In the final days of my parent's lives, both were very ill and suffering from cancer. Each spent time with the other as life grew shorter in hospital beds.

Ansel had been ill for several years with prostate cancer that had spread elsewhere before his death. He would not take chemotherapy as he did not want to lose his beautiful white hair.

Many friends stopped by the St. Vincent hospital in Morrilton to wish him "Good Luck." Some were brave enough to say, "Good Bye." It required all the strength he had to visit with each, shaking their hands, and speaking if he could.

Our mother, also very ill and weak with cancer, sat quietly in a chair in the corner of the room. Her health did not allow her to do anything else. My sister, Sherry, and I, off and on, held our father's hand and whispered, **"We love you, Daddy."**

Once, our dad looked at both my sister and I to say, **"No tears."** This was later inscribed on our parents monument. Ansel was telling us that he had no regrets about how he lived his life. He was telling us not be sorry he was going away. We knew and he knew his time was almost over. We are not meant to know when death will come to our door.

Our mother, Sherry and I were exhausted after days in the hospital. My father's youngest brother, **Dallas Swain** and **Nealia Jane Swain** were there with us. On March 10, 1996, with their encouragement, of calling us "if anything happens," our mother was taken home to rest. Mother, Sherry and I went to sleep.

Very early in the morning, the phone rang. It was the hospital saying Ansel had died. We were so happy that our dear Aunt Nealia and Uncle Dallas were with him when he died. They described his passing like *a tire that lost air a little at a time until it was flat*. They told us it was a **peaceful, good death**, one that Ansel would have liked to have.

Ansel had asked that his funeral be at the **First United Methodist Church in Morrilton**. Many people came to the funeral, friends from all walks of his life.

The **Petit Jean Country Headlight** carried a beautiful obituary on the front page of the March 13, 1996 newspaper with the title, *"Ansel Swain Local Leader, Dies at 74,"* along with a photograph. The **Arkansas Democrat Gazette** also carried the same article with a photograph.

Ansel Swain's Obituary

V. Ansel Swain, 74, of Morrilton, a **long-time civic, business, and church leader died Sunday** after a lengthy battle with cancer.

He was born **April 13, 1921 in Cleveland**, a son of Sherman Norton Swain and Stella Trimble Swain.

He retired in 1983 from **Crompton Arkansas Mills** after 24 years service, first as personnel manager and later manager of employee relations.

He was a member of **First United Methodist Church** of Morrilton where he served in many capacities including chairman of the administrative board and as a Sunday school teacher. He also worked with the **United Methodist Men**.

He served as president of the **Morrilton School Board**, president of the board of the **Morrilton Golf and Country Club**, member of the **Conway County Library Board**, **Conway County Industrial Development Corp.**, **Morrilton Lions Club**, **Morrilton Optimist Club**, co-chairman of the **United Way** and on the advisory council of the **Boy Scouts**.

As a member of the **Civilian Conservation Corps** at Jacksonville, he was promoted to hospital attendant and then to a civilian job as clerk for the Medical Department Base Headquarters, CCC, in Little Rock.

During World War II, he served 3 1/2 years with the **64th Naval Construction Battalion Seabees** and rose to the rank of storekeeper first class in disbursing. He returned to civilian life in 1946 and attended Arkansas Tech University and the University of Central Arkansas. Between 1947 and 1957, Ansel operated a **skating rink** at Blackwell. From 1943 through 1957 he served as clerk of **Conway County Draft Board**. In 1950, Ansel was elected **Conway County Clerk** and probate clerk, serving one term.

Survivors include his wife, Elizabeth Ruth Hamlet Swain, two daughters, Marcia Swain Crossman of Conway Arkansas and Sherry Elizabeth Borck of Manhattan, Kansas, a brother, Dallas Swain of Atkins, two sisters, Allene Smirl of Morrilton and Shirley Teddar of Merced California, and four grand children. Funeral services were 11 a.m., Tuesday, at **First United Methodist Church** by Dr. Robert O. Crossman. Burial was at **Elmwood Cemetery** by Harris Funeral Home. **Pallbearers** were nephew Joe Smirl, grandsons Charlie and David Crossman, and nephews Bill Sam, Barry and Brian Swain. Honorary pallbearers were Wade Oates, Earl Ward, Earl Maxwell, Rupert Sanderson, Al Barth, J.H. Allison, Charlie Owens, Joe Duvall, Johnny Moll, George Hubbard and members of the Wesleyan Sunday school class. Memorials may be made to the First United Methodist Church of Morrilton or to the building fund of Grace United Methodist Church of Conway.

Petit Jean Country Headlight & Arkansas Democrat Gazette, March 13, 1996

THE DEATH OF ELIZABETH SWAIN

Ansel had passed away on **March 10, 1996**. Elizabeth's life was never the same without him. She would live only ten months after his death. Our mother had come through a major abdominal surgery to remove ovarian cancer. She had suffered with this cancer for several years before Ansel's death. She bravely faced chemotherapy. Elizabeth did her best to continue her membership in the **Daughters of the American Revolution** and her unit of **United Methodist Women**. With the assistance of Ansel's sister, **Allene Swain Smirl**, and employed helpers, she managed day by day. In October of 1996, Marcia and husband, Bob began to see that our mother's care needed to be around the clock. We invited her to come and eat dinner in Conway at Western Sizzlin. We urged her to stay and visit with us for a few days. She did stay the remainder of her life in our home in **Scherman Oaks** in Conway.

During this time, Bob was working to begin a new **United Methodist Church** in the area of Conway where we lived. Our new home became the church office. People were in and out of our home at all hours of the day doing the business of the church. The **church secretary** used an **upstairs bedroom** as an office. All of these people, in and out of our home, were a great blessing to our mother and to our family. They spent time visiting with her on their way in and out. For me, this was a great help because the print shop downtown also needed my constant attention.

One special church member, **Debbie**, was employed to be with Elizabeth during the day. She often brought our mother **soup or pie** from Bob's Grill, downtown. Bob and I took care of her at night. On Sundays after church, our **family physician**, a church member, would stop by to see how she was doing. Charlie and David, our sons in their late teens, were in and out of the house. *All of this coming and going helped our mother pass the time.*

When **December of 1996** arrived, we could see our mother was really going downhill. She became frail, would not eat much and required a hospital bed to be brought into the home. We placed her hospital bed in the family room so she could continue to be with everyone. **Hospice**, out of Morrilton, began to come once or twice a day. I remember crying at her bedside saying, *I wish I knew how to stop this thing.*" She very gently slipped her hand onto the skin of my back. We both sat in silence.

My sister, Sherry, came to be with us around Christmas time of 1996. Sherry's visit passed very quickly. On **January 4, 1997**, it was time for her to fly back home to Manhattan, Kansas. By this time, our mother was in and out of sleeping most of the time. Sherry and I drove to the airport in Little Rock. She boarded her plane.

It is true that dying people often leave this world, in a way, that keeps family from suffering. Elizabeth waited **until Sherry and I were gone to die**. By her side, in our home, was our church friend, **Debbie**, and **Charlie**, our oldest son. She was not alone. Thankfully, Bob's brother, **Paul**, who had worked in the airline industry, knew how to get Sherry off of the plane. We drove back to Conway, together. It was a great moment of sadness. Sherry and I stayed in Morrilton, in our parents home, for over a week, taking care of our parent's final business.

Elizabeth Swain's Obituary

Morrilton: Elizabeth Ruth Hamlet Swain, age 75, of Morrilton, died Saturday, January 4, 1997 at the home of her daughter in Conway, after a lengthy battle with cancer. She was the widow of V. Ansel Swain who died on March 10 of last year. They were married September 3, 1950 in Atkins. She was born January 14, 1921 at Atkins, Arkansas, daughter of John Turner Hamlet and Velma Kate Johnson. Elizabeth attended Arkansas Tech in Russellville following her graduation from Atkins High School in 1939.

Elizabeth retired from the **Soil Conservation Service**, Watershed Division, Morrilton where she worked for 21 years as a clerk-typist. She previously worked for the Veterans Administration in Russellville and Little Rock. During WWII, she worked with the Office of Price Administration at Russellville and in California with the War Department.

Elizabeth was a member of the Conway County **Community Service Board** for 21 years. In her retirement she continued as a 35 year member and past president of the **Morrilton Adelaide Club**. She served as president of the **Town and Country Garden Club**, and a member of the **Morrilton Hospital Auxiliary**.

Elizabeth was a member of **Morrilton's First United Methodist Church** serving as a member of the choir and unit and circle chairperson of **United Methodist Women** for two years. Upon receiving her Life Membership Award, the announcement read, *"She is a person who offers support and encouragement to others; a source of inspiration to all of us as she has demonstrated tremendous faith, hope and courage. She touched our lives in a very special way."* Her church work was also in the area of **evangelism and missions**, served as chair of the blanket program for **world hunger** for a number of years. Elizabeth also served on the **administrative board**.

In 1990, Elizabeth joined the **Daughters of the American Revolution**, General William Lewis Chapter in Morrilton. She served one year as vice regent and was serving in her third year as regent when she died. *Elizabeth's Revolutionary War ancestor was Moses Powell, Jr. of Georgia.*

Survivors include two daughters, Marcia Gail Swain Crossman of Conway, and Sherry Elizabeth Swain Borck of Manhattan, Kansas. She had four grandchildren. Family visitation will be 5-6 p.m. today at the Harris Funeral Home in Morrilton. Funeral services will be at 2 p.m. at the Morrilton United Methodist Church by Reverend Russell Moore, with burial to follow at Elmwood Cemetery. **Pallbearers** will be grandsons David and Charles Crossman, Bob Crossman, son-in-law, Paul Crossman and Louis Lefebvre, close family friends, and nephew, Joe Smirl.

Memorials may be made to the building fund of First United Methodist Church of Morrilton or to the building fund of Grace United Methodist Church of Conway.

Petit Jean Country Headlight & Arkansas Democrat Gazette, January 6, 1997

A VERY PERSONAL EXPERIENCE

Many people believe that when loved ones pass away, we still encounter them in odd and very personal ways. Some people believe deceased family looks in on us from time to time, keeping up with our lives. Others believe our deceased love ones send messages to us. In my lifetime, I have had only one encounter of this sort.

Late in September of 1997, just a few months after my mother died, is when my encounter occurred. Our father had died just ten months before our mother. I was driving alone in my Safari van on Oak Street in Conway going west. The encounter happened just before I went through the intersection of Harkrider and Oak Streets. My car was moving. It never came to a stop. This vision was short, perhaps lasting only a millisecond.

Becoming an observer, I saw three people I knew quite well. Clouds surrounded their knees. Nothing else except the people and the clouds were in the vision. My father, Ansel, was standing. He was wearing a horizontal striped golf shirt tucked into his pants. The stripes were crooked as they always were when he dressed in a golf shirt. My mother was standing next to him. She had on a sport shirt with kakai pants, pleated at the waistline. With them stood my Uncle Dallas Swain, my dad's youngest brother, who had died earlier that month after a prolonger battle with stroke. I knew their faces. There was no question in my mind of who they were.

My dad, talking to Dallas said, "Dallas how did you get here?" There was no response. My dad then said, "You don't mean it. You don't mean it!" It was the typical way he spoke to most people when he was surprised. This was the end of my encounter, my vision. It was over, yet I remember it like it was yesterday. I still see it today exactly like it was some 27 years ago.

A STORY MY HUSBAND, BOB CROSSMAN, HAS TOLD AT MANY FUNERALS

As a ship leaves the dock, family and friends gather to wave,
　　shed a tear, and wish a fond farewell to their loved ones.

They watch the ship slowly disappear past the horizon.
　　Yet, we know that the ship is not gone.

It still exists.
　　Its hull and mast are still the same size, and still strong for the journey.
　　　　For we know and believe, that there on that distant shore,
　　　　　　is a cloud of witnesses waving and shouting a fond welcome
　　　　　　　　to their loved ones who are about to arrive.

So it is now, as we lay our loved ones to their eternal rest.
　　Trusting that our Heavenly Father, is waiting and anxiously welcoming them to
　　　　their heavenly and eternal home.

Appendices

A Genealogy of The Swain Family Descendants of Jesse Abner Swain, 1987

The Life & Times of John Turner Hamlet Atkins, Arkansas Merchant Early 1900's, 2022

Lucinda Elizabeth Norman & John Mason Liner Grandparents of Stella Trimble Swain Great Great Grandparents of This Generation of Swains, 2024

Appendix One:

"A Genealogy Of The Swain Family:

Descendants Of

Jesse Abner Swain"

Research by

Verill Ansel Swain & Robert O. Crossman

who contacted living relatives for all included stories & information.
Photos were borrowed from living family and returned.

Robert O. Crossman &
Marcia Swain Crossman
compiled & published this book.
Copyright & First Printing in 1987

by Battlefield Printing & *Copies*, Prairie Grove, Arkansas
Marcia Swain Crossman

This volume is included for family
who want to learn more about the ancestors of
Verill Ansel Swain and his siblings.

A
GENEALOGY
OF
THE SWAIN FAMILY

DESCENDANTS
OF
JESSE ABNER SWAIN

COMPILED BY

MARCIA GAIL SWAIN CROSSMAN
AND
ROBERT OWEN CROSSMAN

Jesse Abner Swain - Updated Information

A NOTE FROM MARCIA SWAIN CROSSMAN IN 2024

Additional Information on **Jesse Abner Swain** was found in 2022-24, many years after "The Descendants of Jesse Abner Swain" was compiled. Little was found about **great great grandfather, Jesse Abner Swaim(n),** when information was researched and recorded for this book in 1987 by his great grandson, Verill Ansel Swain. The modern invention of the Internet has opened doors for family genealogists. **I could not print this appendix without corrected and additional information on Jesse Abner Swaim. Jesse and Sarah Caroline Anderson (3rd wife) are the ancestors of all the Swains I am related to.** I continue searching for more *"treasures of the heart"* on Jesse and Sarah Anderson. I come to a close on this collection on the Swain family history. I found it to be exciting to find information and a joy to share it with family and others interested in the Swains.

EVERYTHING I KNOW ABOUT JESSE ABNER SWAIN IN 2024

Jesse Abner Swaim was born June 22, 1819 to **Henry Swaim** *(April 23, 1795 - October 14, 1824)* and **Elizabeth Rogers Swaim** *(1793–1853)* in **Guilford, North Carolina**. Henry and Elizabeth were parents to at least three children: **Caroline**, born in 1818, **Jesse Abner**, born in 1819, and **Deborah** born in 1824. Jesse's father, Henry, died in Henry, Indiana, at the age of 29 on when Jesse was only 5 years old. Jesse's youngest sister was born the year their father died, We do not know of the family's financial situation. The family were farmers. Elizabeth Swain, mother, was surely left with a heavy workload after Henry Swain died. It appears that Jesse was also a farmer his entire life.

> **NOTE:** Some of Jesse's grandchildren changed their name to **"Swain,"** around the time of WWI, after soldiers called them **"Swim."** *(Grandfather Sherman Norton Swain was among these soldiers.)* We often see Jesse Abner as "Swaim" in today's research. This was correct, in his time, to call him, **"Swaim."** I have seen it spelled both ways in my family search. **Through the end of this addition, I will refer to all of the family as "Swain."**

Jesse Abner Swain was married to THREE Sarahs: Sarah FAIN, Sarah Elizabeth BRUMMIT, and Sarah Caroline ANDERSON. He became the parent of five sons and five daughters with his first and third wives.

Jesse married first wife, **SARAH FAIN**, *(1823 - 1956)* on Aug 29, 1842 in Johnson Co., Illinois, when she was 19 years old. Her first child was born, after a year of marriage, when she was 20. Each child came 2-3 years after. Her children were:

- **Mary C.** *(1843 - 1882)*
- **Elizabeth** *(1845 - 1849) Not seen in census records. Several family trees have her death as 1849.*
- **Celia Ann** *(1847 - 1940) I remember my parents talking about her. Ansel Swain would have been 19 years old when she died.*
- **Eliza** *(1849 -)*
- **Charles** *(1852 -)*
- **William Riley** *(1855–1925) Ansel Swain would have been four years old when he died.)*

1

> *The 1850 US CENSUS records that seven people lived in the household. Jesse Abner, age 31, head of household; first wife Sarah Fain, age 26; three children, Mary C. age 7; Celia Ann age 3; and Eliza E. age 1. Two adult males with the last name of Fain, both age 21, also lived in the household. They were Louis C. Fain and Jesse M. Fain. Perhaps they were younger twin brothers of first wife, Sarah Fain.* Unanswered questions: Where was second daughter Elizabeth??? One family record in Ancestry notes she died the same year she was born. Not proven yet. Could this Sarah really have four children by the time she was 26??? Do the math. It sure looks like this.

Jesse married his second wife, **SARAH BRUMMIT,** on June 20, 1858, in Illinois, two years after the death of his first wife. Jesse had no children with her. Perhaps Sarah Brummit and a baby and died in childbirth.

> *The 1860 US CENSUS records Jesse Abner as head of household at age 39. They lived in Johnson Co., Illinois. Four children live with in the home of Jesse. This includes: Mary, age 16, Celia Ann, age 13, Eliza, age 11, and William Riley, age 5.* There is no second marriage wife, Sarah Brummit, or young daughter, Elizabeth, from the first marriage. Question: Why did the Sarah Brummit die so early in life???

Jesse married his third wife, **SARAH CAROLINE ANDERSON**, in 1862. Sarah was born in 1843 in Tennessee. Her father, John Anderson, was 37, and her mother, "Fanny" or Mary Anderson, was 38. Sarah Anderson was much younger than Jesse Abner Swain. She was about **24 years old when they married**.

SARAH CAROLINE ANDERSON BECAME THE
GREAT GREAT GRANDMOTHER TO ALL THE PERSONS IN OUR FAMILY TREE.

> *The 1870 US CENSUS records Sarah had four children with Jesse Abner Swain. By this time the family had moved to Liberty Township, Van Buren Co., Arkansas. Living with them were John Abner, Frances, George and Perry.* Her last child was born in 1869 giving her a seven year period of childbearing. She gave birth to:

• **John Abner Swain** *(1863 - 1910)*, was born first to Sarah Caroline Swain, one year after her marriage to Jesse. John Abner was the **great grandfather** in our family tree of Swains.

> *John Abner was the father of* **Sherman Norton Swain**, **grandfather** *to my generation.* **Mystery solved!** *When Sherman Swain was a boy, some of his siblings, (maybe him, too?), found their father, John Abner Swain,* **hanging in the barn, deceased.** *I had heard of this suicide all of my life, but neither my sister or first cousins could confirm this. I was finally able to* **confirm this from the granddaughter of Molly Swain, Sherman's sister.** She would be a second cousin to our generation.

The last three children born to Jesse and Sarah Anderson seem virtually hidden from history.

2

Other family descendants,*(found on Ancestry.com)*, have little or nothing to say about these thee persons. I am still searching for them and their descendants.

- **Frances Swain** *(female, 1865 -)*
- **George Swain** *(1867 -)*
- **Perry Swain** *(1869 -)*

NOTE: Have you noticed that Jesse became the father of a new child about every two years between 1843 and 1869 in a 26 year period. He married very young women of childbearing age. There was the possibility of another infant not surviving after the 6th child was born to the second Sarah. How did Jesse afford to have all those children back then? As **farmers**, like most people of the day, they had a life of constant labor and housework.

I have yet to locate records about the death of Jesse Abner Swain.

However, I did locate a Civil War record from Illinois on a Jesse Swain. *The Thirteenth Congressional District of the State of Illinois, called a Jesse Swain from Illinois to duty on August 31, 1863. As of now, I cannot confirm this was our Jesse. At that time, our Jesse would have been around 44 years old.*

What happened to our great great grandmother, the third Sarah, after Jesse died? Sarah Caroline Anderson Swain was **married twice** after Jesse died. Sarah was married after Jesse Abner to **Adam Cariker** on January 30, 1873. She had another child, **James Cariker**, with **Adam.** The couple was married only a short time. Adam was killed in a horse accident just three years after they married. Adam was a veteran of the War of 1812. *The War of 1812 was fought with Great Britain, much like a second Revolutionary War, to reinforce our independence from that country.*

The 1880 US CENSUS records Sarah living in Liberty Township, Van Buren Co., Arkansas. (We are familiar with this area as our grandparents Sam and Stella Swain are buried there.) Sarah was about 40 years old, and, married to Adam Cariker, head of household. They are living with three children, Frances, George, and Perry Swain. Older son, John Abner Swain, is married to Catherine "Catie or Cate" Costley, both age 18, living separately in a home next to Sarah and Adam. The child of Sarah and Adam, James Cariker was not listed in this census.

After **Sarah Anderson Swain** became the widow of **Adam Cariker,** she married **Argyle Fletcher McCoy** in 1888. The marriage lasted less that one year as Argyle died the same year as their marriage.

The 1870 US CENSUS tells us what Argyle McCoy was doing before he married Sarah Cariker. Argyle was head of household living first wife, Susan Williams (who died before 1880). The couple were parents to seven children. The family lived on Lick Mountain, Conway, Co. Arkansas. He was a Civil War soldier from Alabama. Argyle and Susan were the owners of 170 acres of land, acquired in 1862, in Conway, Co. Arkansas from the US Land Office. Notice both Sarah and Argyle lived in adjoining counties when their spouses died.

3

Sarah Anderson is thought to have died in Liberty, Van Buren Co., AR. *(Not too far from Conway Co., Arkansas where I live.)* My Swain family sources say her death was in 1893 when she was around 53 years old. Ancestry sites say she died in 1899 around age 60.

Nothing is confirmed concerning the death of Sarah Anderson Swain Cariker McCoy. No burial place is yet to be found in 2024. No birth or death certificates have been found, yet, for Sarah Anderson. Many of the Swain family are buried in the Old Liberty Cemetery near Scotland and some are buried in Pleasant Grove Cemetery. I have not found Sarah listed in cemetery population records. Her son, **John Abner Swain** and wife **Catherine Costley Swain** are buried at *Old Liberty in Scotland, Arkansas*. Jesse and Sarah Swain's grandson, **Sherman Norton Swain**, is buried a Old Liberty.

Photo on Left: Catherine "Cate or Catie" Costley Swain was the spouse of John Abner Swain, son of Jesse Abner Swaon.

Sherman Norton Swain, is standing behind Catherine Costley Swain (his mother) who was the great grandmother to our generation.

*Catherine was the mother of eleven children: Joseph, Jesse Abner (named after his grandfather), **Thomas, Sarah, Minnie, John, Mollie, Sherman Norton** (our grandfather), **Pearle, Ann and William**. She died in 1920, ten years after her husband, John Abner died in 1910.*

possibly one of the oldest photos available

Additional information or corrections on any Swain would be gratefully received.

Marcia Swain Crossman's contact information in 2024:
mcrossman@conwaycorp.net
8 Sternwheel Drive, Conway, Arkansas 72034
501-908-8180

Marcia Swain Crossman, born on April 26, 1953, is the gggranddaughter of Jesse Abner Swain, the ggranddaughter of John Abner Swaim, the granddaughter of Sherman Norton Swain, and the daughter of Verill Ansel Swain.

4

A
GENEALOGY
OF
THE SWAIN FAMILY

Descendants
of
Jesse Abner Swain

compiled by

Marcia Gail Swain Crossman
&
Robert Owen Crossman

Crossman Printing and Press

First Printing

This is copy number

Additions and corrections should be sent to the author's address on page 3.

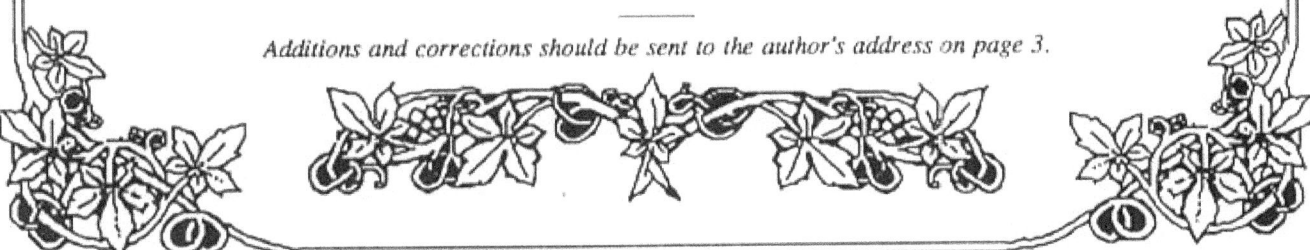

TABLE OF CONTENTS

This family history
is
dedicated to our children:

**CHARLES ROBERT CROSSMAN
&
DAVID NATHAN CROSSMAN**

PREFACE

We have compiled this book but we are not professional genealogists. We are aware that the records of the descendants of Jesse Abner Swain are incomplete, yet genealogical records are constantly in need of revision to reflect the most recent births, deaths, and records recently discovered. We will always be searching for more information, continually adding birth and death dates for generations to come. Perhaps we will always be searching for the parentage of Jesse Abner Swain. Though this record is incomplete, we believe that the material available needs to be distributed before it is lost or forgotten.

If the record of your family is incomplete or inaccurate, please accept our apologies. Also, some of the photographs did not reproduce well due to the particular qualities of the originals provided to us. We will gladly receive additions and corrections or duplicates of additional photographs to be used in a revised GENEALOGY OF THE SWAIN FAMILY when enough material has been compiled to warrant such a revision.

We have footnoted names, dates, and biographical material as much as possible so that future Swain family historians can retrace the sources used in this collection of family history.

Each person in direct descent from Jesse Abner Swain is assigned a generation number. For example, "Verill Ansel-4 Swain" would indicate that he is a fourth generation descendant of Jesse Abner Swain. To give Verill Ansel Swain's complete ancestry, a list would be given: (Verill Ansel-4, Sherman Norton-3, John Abner-2, Jesse Abner-1). We have tried to follow this pattern throughout.

Perhaps some day the parents of Jesse Abner Swain will be found in a will, Bible record, or in city vital statistics, but for now we must be content to have the record as complete as it is, and celebrate the distant cousins we may discover through this genealogy.

Additional material or corrections may be sent to:

Marcia Swain Crossman	or	Ansel Swain
First United Methodist Church		#3 Magnolia Drive
Post Office Box 216		Morrilton, AR
Prairie Grove, AR 72753-0216		72110

Copies of this genealogy are available from either of these addresses.

Marcia Gail Swain & Robert Owen Crossman

ACKNOWLEDGEMENTS

We want to give a special thanks to V. Ansel Swain, Marcia's father, for his research that resulted in the basic collection of material enclosed in this genealogy. We must also acknowledge the work of Bill Swain, Dale Swain, John Dunsworth, "Sissy" Ovaline Harris and Nina Swain for providing large amounts of original research and records of Swain family history.

REFERENCE FOOTNOTES

We have attempted to provide reference footnotes after each date, or in some cases at the bottom of the pages so that future Swain genealogists could retrace our sources for the names, dates, and notes in this family history. The following abbreviations were used in the reference footnotes:

(DS)   This material was provided by Dale Swain, son of Joseph Swain. Dale lives at 808 N. Oak Street, Morrilton, Arkansas 72110.

(GR)   This material was provided by Gladys Rhoades of Scotland, Arkansas 72141.

(HV)   This material was provided by Hazel Veatch (Mrs. Richard Veatch) 1921 Shamrock Ave., Lee's Summit, MO 64063.

(JD)   This material was provided by John Dunsworth of Scotland, Arkansas 72141.

(NS)   This material was provided by Nina Swain (Mrs. James LeRoy Swain). Copy of this material was given to me from SOH and directly from Nina. Nina Swain lives at Rt. 1, Branch, Arkansas 72928.

(ROC)   This material was provided by Robert Owen Crossman, son-in-law of Ansel Swain. Bob is the compiler of this Swain Family History, and lives (1986) at Prairie Grove, Arkansas.

(SOH)   This material was provided by "Sissy" Ovaline Harris (Mrs. Gene Harris) of Rt. 2, Box 2073 Selah, Washington 98942.

(STS)   This material was provided by Stella Trimble Swain, widow of Sherman Norton Swain. She lives (1986) in Blackwell, Arkansas.

(VAS)   This material was provided by V. Ansel Swain, son of Sherman Norton Swain. Ansel lives (1986) at #3 Magnolia Drive, Morrilton, AR 72110.

(WSS)   This material was provided by William "Bill" Swain, grandson of Sherman Norton Swain. Bill lives (1986) in Atkins {P.O. Box 3000 Russellville, AR 72801}.

Additional material was obtained from cemetery headstones at Cleveland, Arkansas and from the Conway County Courthouse.

LIST OF ABBREVIATIONS

b.   Date of Birth
d.   Date of Death
m.   Date of Marriage
m.(2nd) Date of Second Marriage
_____   Date unknown. example: m. _____ John Doe.
_____   Name unknown. example: m. _____ John _____.

Our

First

Generation

JESSE ABNER-1 SWAIN (John Abner-1)
- b. June 22, 1819 in Illinois (SOH); or "Jessie Abner Swaim" (NS) born in North Carolina (NS);
- d. no record (ROC);
- m.(1st) Sarah Fain on Aug. 18, 1842 (NS), she was born on Nov. 25, 1823 (SOH);
- m.(2nd) Sarah E. Brumit, licensed granted on June 8, married on June 20, 1858 (NS);
- m.(3rd) Sarah Anderson who died in 1893 (DS).

CHILDREN: [by Sarah Fain his first wife]
MARY C.-2 SWAIN, b. Nov. 10, 1843 (SOH) and (NS);
- d. June 10, 1882 (NS);   children ?
- m. 1864, William Hahs (NS).

ELIZABETH-2 SWAIN, b. Aug. 14, 1845 (SOH); children ?

see page 9   CELIA ANN-2 SWAIN, b. Oct. 30, 1847 in either Vienna or Cairo, Illinois (SOH);
- d. Oct. 8, 1940 Scotland, Arkansas (SOH);
- m. 1869 (NS) Wiley Bost (STS), or Wylie Wilson Bost (SOH) possibly in Illinois (SOH) or Wiley Boss (NS); spelled 'Boss' in Illinois census and 'Bost' on marriage license(NS).

ELIZA-2 SWAIN, b. Jan. 12, 1849 (SOH), or called "Elisa"(NS);
- m. Jim Short (NS); children ?

CHARLES-2 SWAIN, b. Jan. 23, 1852 (SOH); children ?

see page 15   WILLIAM RILEY-2 SWAIN, b. Sept. 6,1856 (SOH), or 1855 (NS);
- d. April 30, 1925 (NS);
- m. _____ Morris (STS), or m. Lucenda Riley who was born March 4, 1857 and who died March 5, 1923 (NS).

CHILDREN: [by Sarah Brumit his second wife]
see page 16   JOHN ABNER-2 SWAIN, b. April 20, 1863 at Scotland, Arkansas (STS)(SOH);
- d. 1910 at Cleveland, Arkansas (STS)(SOH);
- m. Catherine Costley (STS) who died in 1929 (NS).

FRANCIS-2 SWAIN, b. 1865 (NS).
GEORGE-2 SWAIN, b. 1867 (NS).
PERRY-2 SWAIN, b. March 1, 1869 (NS); d. May 28, 1875 (NS).

"No record has yet been found to indicate the parentage of Jesse Abner-1 Swain. Stella Thomas (Trimble) Swain remembers hearing that he came from Alabama, to Tennessee, to Illinois, to Arkansas. Perhaps a land deed, will, Bible record, or birth record will be found to lead us back into Jesse's past." (ROC)

"Jesse Abner Swain, born June 22, 1819. I was told he was born in Illinois, and we think for sure Celia Swain Bost was born in either Vienna or Cairo, Illinois. I was also told by Aunt Minnie Summers Singleton, Etta Summer's daughter, that Celia's mother was Sarah Fain. Maybe Sarah Anderson was Sarah Fain. Also I have, she was born Nov. 25, 1823." (SOH).

"The children were as follows. This also came from Etta Summer's papers. Mary Swain, born Nov. 10, 1843; Elizabeth Swain, born Aug. 14, 1845; Celia Swain, born Oct. 30, 1847; Eliza Swain, born Jan. 12, 1849; Charles Swain, born Jan. 23, 1852; William B. Swain, born Sept. 6, 1856; John Abner Swain, born April 20, 1863." (SOH)

Jesse Abner Swain didn't come to Arkansas until after he married Sarah Brumit, his second wife, June 8, 1858. All the family moved with him except Mary and William. William came to Arkansas with Wiley and Celia Bost Oct. 25, 1869. Mary, the oldest child, stayed in Illinois. (NS)

"The story goes Jessie & Sarah moved to Van Buren Co. next year after William came with Celia and Wiley, but left the children in Ill. and went back later after them. I found in 1870 census for Van Buren Co. in Arkansas the only child living with Jessie & Sarah was William. ... I believe the name was SWAIM since in all the research it's spelled SWAIM or SWIM so in trying to pronounce it with the 'm' they were leaving the 'a' out. I'm glad they started spelling it SWAIN - the way it's pronounced." (NS)

****

Land Deed
January 15, 1859
Sanders & Eliza Brown to Jesse Swim
Johnson County, Illinois

"This Indenture made this tenth day of January in the year of our Lord Eighteen hundred and fifty Nine Between Sanders Brown and Eliza Brown his wife of the county of Johnson and State of Illinois of the first part and Jesse Swim of the county of Johnson and State of Illinois of the second part. Witnesseth that the said party of the first part for and in consideration of the Sum of five hundred and fifty Dollars to them paid the receipt whereof is hereby acknowledged, do grant bargain sell convey and confirm unto the said party of the Second part and to his heirs and assigns a certain tract or parcel of Land, with the appurtenances lying and being in the county of Johnson and State of Illinois Described as follows to wit. The South West Quarter of Section No. 110) Five in Township No(15), thirteen South Range No. 2, Thor. East Containing one hundred and Sixty acres more or less — To have and to hold the above granted premises to the Said party of the Second part his heirs and assigns to his use and behoof forever. Provided Nevertheless that if the Said party of the first part their heirs Executors or Administrators, shall pay or cause to be paid to the party of the second part his heirs Executors Administrators or assigns shall pay or cause to be paid to the party of the Second part his Executors Administrators or assigns five promissory Notes given by Said Sanders Brown on the 10th day of January 1857, to the Said party of the Second part, to wit, four for the Sum of one hundred Dollars each and one for the

Continued on Next Page

[Handwritten land deed — cursive manuscript]

Sums of one hundred and fifty Dollars due in one. Two. Three four & Five years from date, Together with the Interest thereon in manner Specified in Said notes, then this Indenture to be null and void. otherwise to remain in full force and effect, On Witness whereof the Said party of the first part have hereunto set their hands and Seals the Day and year first above written. Signed Sealed and delivered in the presence of

Sanders Brown (Seal)
Eliza her mark Brown (Seal)

J. S. Toler. Jesse Swaim

State of Illinois } I. J. S. Toler a justice of the Peace in and for Said Johnson County County do hereby certify that the above named Sanders Brown and Eliza Brown who are personally known to me to be the persons whose names is subscribed to the foregoing deed as having executed the Same, this day in their proper person came before me and acknowledged that they Signed Sealed and delivered the Said deed for the uses and purposes therein Mentioned And the Said Eliza Brown wife of the said Sanders Brown having been by me made fully acquainted with the contents of Said deed and by me Examined Seperate and apart from her Said husband declared that She Signed and acknowledged Said deed and relinquished her Dower in and to the Said lands conveyed freely Voluntarily and without Compulsion of her Said husband. Intestimony whereof I have hereunto Set my hand and — Seal this 21 day of January 1853

J. S. Toler (Seal)

[Margin note]: Recorded Feb. 11th 1859. S. Copeland Clk & Reg.

Land Deed transcribed as accurately as possible from previous pages...

"This indenture made this fourth day of January in the year of our Lord, Eighteen hundred and fifty Nine, Between Sanders Brown and Eliza Brown his wife fo the county of Johnson, State of Illinois of the first part and Jesse Swaim of the county of Jahnson and State of Illinois of the second part. _____ that the Said party of the first part for and in consideration of the Sum of five hundred and fifty Dollars to them paid the reciept whereof is hereby acknowledged do grant bargains, Sell convey and confirm unto the Said party of the Second part and to his heirs and ___ a certain tract or parcel of Land, with the appertenances lying and being in the County of Johnson and State of Illinois Described as follows _____. The South West Quarter of Section No. 110 In the Township No 13 thirteen Sough Range No. 2, Two East containing one hundred and Sixty acres more or less. To have and to hold the above granted primises to the Said Party of the Second Part his heirs and ___ to his use and hold of forever. Provided even the ___ that if the Said party of the first part their heirs Executors or Administrators shall pay or cause to ___ paid to the party of the Second part his heirs Executors Administrators of ___ shall pay or cause to be paid to the party of the Second part his Executors Administrators or ____ five promissory notes given by Said Sanders Brown on the 10th Day of January 1839 to the Said party of the Second part, for the Sum of one hundred Dollars each and one for the sum of one hundred and fifty Dollars due in one Two Three Fourths Five years from date. Together with the Interest thereon in monies sufficient in said notes, then this Indenture to be null and void, otherwise to remain in full force and effect. On _____ whereof the Said party of the first part have hereunto let this hand and Seal the Day and year first above written.
Signed.....Sanders Brown and Eliza Brown. Eliza marked with an "x", J. S. Toler, and Jessee Swaim.
J. S. Toler, a justice of the Peace in and for Said Johnson County do hereby certify that the above maned Sanders Brown and Eliza Brown who are personally known to me to be the persons whose names is subscribed to the foregoing deed as having executed the Same, this day in their proper person came before me and acknowledged that they Signed, Sealed and delivered the Said deed for the uses and purposes therein mentioned and the Said Eliza Brown wife of the said Sanders Brown having been by me made fully acquainted with the contents of Said deed and by me Examined Seperate and apart from her Said husband declared that She Signed and acknowledged Said deed and relinquished her Dower in and to the Said lands conveyed freely voluntarily and without compulsion of her Said husband.
Intertimonily whereof I have here unto let my hand and Seal this 21 Day of January 1839. J. S. Tolet."

Jesee Swim

Sarah Fair

Marriage Certificate
Jesee Swim & Sarah Fain
August 18, 1842

State of Illinois
Johnson County

I hereby Certify that the Rights of Matrimony was duly performed by Joining together according to Law the in then named Jesee Swim and Sarah Fain on the 18th day of August 1842

John Oliver J P

Recorded 29th day of August
WD 1842
Attest

J. Copland
Clk

Marriage Certificate
Jesee Swim & Sarah E. Brummmit
June 20, 1858

STATE OF ILLINOIS,
_____ County. } ss.

THE PEOPLE OF THE STATE OF ILLINOIS,
To all who shall see these Presents,---GREETING:

Know Ye, That license and permission has been granted to any Minister of the Gospel authorized by the church or society to which he belongs; any Justice of the Supreme Court, of any Inferior Court, or Justice of the Peace, to celebrate and certify the marriage of—

Jesse Swain & Miss S. E. Brumit

of this County, according to the usual custom and laws of the State of Illinois.

In Witness, W. B. Gibbs Clerk of the County Court in and for the County of Johnson and the Seal of said Court hereunto affixed at _____ this 8 day of June A. D. 1858.

June 25
1858

W. T. Gibbs CLERK.

STATE OF ILLINOIS,
_____ County. } ss.

I Hereby Certify, That on the 20 day June A. D. 1858 I joined in the Holy State of Matrimony

Jesee Swain & Miss S. E. Brummit

S. E. Sarah

2nd marriage

Our

Second

Generation

CELIA ANN-2 SWAIN (Celia Ann-2, Jesse Abner-1)
  b. Oct. 30, 1847 at Cairo, Illinois in Alexander County or Vienna, Illinois in Pulaski County (SOH);
  d. Oct. 8, 1940 at Scotland, Arkansas, buried in Old Liberty cemetery (SOH);
  m. about 1870 Wylie Wilson Bost (SOH), they married on a Sunday and left for Arkansas on Tuesday. They were probably married in Illinois (SOH). He was born May 28, 1837 probably at Mount Pleasant, North Carolina in Cabarus County (SOH). He died Nov. 1, 1911 at Scotland, Arkansas (SOH).

CHILDREN: (of Celia and Wylie)
JOHN D.-3 BOST, b. April 7, 1871 at Scotland, Arkansas (SOH);
  d. Oct. 2, 1954 at Scotland, Arkansas Old Liberty Cemetery (SOH);
  m. March 4, 1907, Sadie or Zadz Hartsell at Scotland, Arkansas (SOH).

  CHILDREN: (of John and Zadz):
  CROSBY-4 BOST, b._____ "Scotland, Arkansas" "deceased" (SOH).
  ESTHER-4 BOST, b._____ "Mapleton, Oregon" (SOH).
  ALVIS-4 BOST, b. _____ "Scotland, Arkansas" (SOH).
  CARNA-4 BOST, m. _____ Arnold Emmerson (SOH); "Eugene, Oregon" (SOH).
  ZENA-4 BOST, m. _____ Weldon Stroud (SOH); "Mapleton, Oregon" (SOH).
  CELIA-4 BOST, m. _____ Goodson (SOH); "El Dorado, Arkansas" (SOH).
  IMOGENE-4 BOST, m. _____ Black (SOH); "Scotland, Arkansas" (SOH).

MARY EVALINE-3 BOST, b. Aug. 22, 1873 at Scotland, Arkansas (SOH), children ?

CHARLES-3 BOST, b. Jan. 20, 1878 (STS) at Scotland, Arkansas (SOH);
  d. April 16, 1955 (STS);
  m. December 1900 (STS) Lula Trimble at Scotland, Arkansas (SOH); she was born Jan. 20, 1878 (STS); she died June 14, 1969 (STS).

  CHILDREN: (of Charles & Lula)
  GERTIE MAE-4 BOST, b. Oct. 5, 1901 (STS);
    m. 1921 Albert Deroy Koone who was born June 25, 1898 (STS).

    CHILDREN: (of Gertie and Albert)
    CARL-5 KOONE, b. _____ (SOH).
    HAROLD-5 KOONE, b. _____ (SOH).
    NELMA-5 KOONE, b. _____ (VAS); or "Naomi Faye" (SOH).

  BESSIE PARALEE-4 BOST, b. March 28, 1905 (STS);
    m. Dec. 29, 1932 Charles Bowls who was born Dept. 27, 1903 (STS).

    CHILDREN: (of Bessie and Charles)
    GERALDINE-5 BOWLS, b. _____ (VAS).

  DEWEY-4 BOST, b. _____ (SOH).

  HUEY-4 BOST, b. _____ (SOH).

FRANK-3 BOST, b. _____ at Scotland, Arkansas (SOH);
  m. _____ Etta Gosslin (SOH).

  CHILDREN: (of Frank and Etta)
  WEADOR-4 BOST, b. _____ (SOH).
  CLAUDE-4 BOST, b. _____ (SOH).
  JEWEL-4 BOST, b. _____ (SOH).

this family continued on next page...

BERTIE-4 BOST, b. _____ (SOH), who m. _____ Will Halbrook (SOH).
MINNIE "Betty"-4 BOST, b. _____ (SOH).
SYBLE-4 BOST, b. _____ (SOH).
EDGAR-4 BOST, b. _____ (SOH).
ARNOLD-4 BOST, b. _____ (SOH).
GLADYS-4 BOST, b. _____ (SOH).
JOHN ORVILLE-4 BOST, b. _____ (SOH).

see   LOU ETTA-3 BOST, b. March 12, 1880 at Scotland, Arkansas (SOH);
page   d. June 16, 1976 at Lawton, Oklahoma (SOH);
19   m. Jan. 5, 1899 William T. Summers at Scotland, Arkansas (SOH).

NORA-3 BOST, b. at Scotland, Arkansas (SOH);
    m. Matthew Stroud (SOH).

    CHILDREN: (of Nora and Matthew)
    ELVA-4 STROUD, b. _____ (SOH).
    LOUIS-4 STROUD, b. _____ (SOH).
    MARVIN-4 STROUD, b. _____ (SOH).
    LLOYD-4 STROUD, b. _____ (SOH).
    DOROTHY-4 STROUD, b. _____ (SOH).
    PAULINE-4 STROUD, b. _____ (SOH).

MARATHA-3 BOST, b. Oct. 20, 1887 at Scotland, Arkansas (SOH);
    d. Nov. 30, 1967 at Morrilton, Arkansas Robertson Cemetery (SOH);
    m. Keltner Stroud (SOH).

    CHILDREN: (of Maratha and Keltner)
    FILMORE-4 STROUD, b. _____ (SOH) of Morrilton, Arkansas;
    WILLARD-4 STROUD, b. _____ (SOH). of Jerusalem, Arkansas;
    IVA-4 STROUD, b. _____ (SOH).
        m. _____ Warren, Jerusalem, Arkansas (SOH).

All information concerning this family marked with (SOH) has come from: "Sissy" Ovaline Harris (Mrs. Gene Harris) of Route 2, Box 2073 Selah, Washington 98942.

****

Marriage Certificate
W.W. Bost to Seala Ann Swaim

STATE OF ILLINOIS.
JOHNSON COUNTY. } ss.

I HEREBY CERTIFY, That on the____24ᵗʰ____day

of____Oct____A. D. 1869 I joined in the Holy State of Matrimony_____

W W Bost & miss Seala Swaim

according to the usual custom and laws of Illinois.

Given under my hand and seal this____24____day of____Oct____A. D. 1869

Gabret Nelly M. G.

Wiley & Celia Bost and family
sitting: Wiley & Celia Ann (Swain) Bost
between parents: Nora (Bost) Stroud
standing by mother: Martha (Bost) Stroud
left to right: Charles, Etta Lou (Bost) Summers, Frank Bost

JOHN & ZADA (Hartsell) BOST
"Wedding Day", March 4, 1907
[top row, left to right]
John & Zeda (Hartsell) Bost, Martha (Bost)
Stroud, Lula (Trimble) & Charles Bost {Charles is
holding Bessie}, Nora (Bost) & Mathew Stroud
{Matthew is holding Elva}
[middle row, left to right]
Lou Etta (Bost) {holding Melvin} & William T.
Summers, Wiley & Celia (Swain) Bost, Gertie
(Bost) Koone is between Wiley & Celia, Frank
Bost {holding Jewel Bost}, standing, Bertie
(Bost) Halbrook, Etta (Gosslin) Bost.
[bottom row, left to right]
Charlie, Luther and Pearl (Summers).

Pictured At Left:
John & Zada (Hartsell) Bost
taken 1950

Mathew & Nora Bost Stroud

Martha (Bost) Stroud

Frank & Etta (Gosslin) Bost

[Back row. left to right]
Gertie (Bost) Koone
Bessie (Bost) Bowles

[Front row, left to right]
Dewey
Charles Bost
Lula (Trimble) Bost
Huey

Charles & Lula (Trimble) Bost

WILLIAM RILEY-2 SWAIN (William-2, Jessie Abner-1)
b. Sept. 6, 1856 (SOH), or 1855 in Illinois (NS) .
d. April 30, 1925 (NS);
m. Aug. 6, 1878 at Van Buren Co. Ark. Lucenda Riley who was born March 4, 1857 and
who died March 5, 1923, daughter of Hugh Riley of Van Buren Co. Ark. (NS), or m.
_____ Morris (STS).

"William Riley Swaim ... came to Van Buren Co. Ark with his sister Celia (Swain) Bost and
husband Wiley (Boss) Bost. {spelled 'Boss' in Illinois census and 'Bost' on marriage license}...
William {known as Will Swaim} at the age of 14 years wished to live with his sister since his
father had married again after his mother's death.
William (Will) Swaim told his son James Albert many stories about how good his sister was
to him. William Swaim married Lucenda Riley, daughter of Hugh Riley who lived in Van Buren
Co. Ark. They lived as neighbors when he was 15 and she 13..." (NS)

CHILDREN: (of William and Lucenda)
see   CHARLES DUDLEY-3 SWAIN, b. June 1879 (NS);
page   d. April 11, 1944 (NS);
23   m. Rella Morris who was born January 1878 (NS).

see   CELCE ELIZABETH-3 SWAIN, b. March 3, 1882 (NS);
page   d. 1906 (NS);
24   m. July 20, 1899 Sam Hankins who was born May 23, 1872 (NS).

       WILEY ANDREW-3 SWAIN, b. 1885 (NS);
            d. 1907 (NS);
            m. Millie Plank (NS).

see   RUTHIE JANE-3 SWAIN, b. April 3, 1887 (NS);
page   d. 1923 (NS);
25   m. Nov. 14, 1909 Wess Horn who was born April 25, 1883 (NS).

       PERRY EDWARD-3 SWAIM, b. March 1889 (NS);
            d. 1943 (NS);
            m. Oma Bell (NS).

            CHILDREN: (of Perry and Oma)
            ESKELL-4 Swaim, b. Aug. 4, 1915 (NS);
                m. June 1971 Rella Langdon (NS).

see   JAMES ALBERT-3 SWAIN, b. Feb. 22, 1895 (NS);
page   d. Nov. 20, 1984 (NS);
26   m. July 1, 1917 Amanda Luvenia Nelson who was born Feb. 11, 1894 and died March 7,
            1963 (NS).

see   WILLIAM JESS-3 SWAIN, b. Oct. 13, 1898 (NS);
page   d. 1977 (NS);
27   m. Oct. 13, 1920 Eva Cherry who was born Dec. 27, 1898 (NS).

****

JOHN ABNER-2 SWAIN (John Abner-2, Jesse Abner-1)
  b. April 20, 1863 (SOH), Scotland, Arkansas (STS); middle initial "N" (NS);
  d. 1910 at Cleveland, Arkansas (STS);
  m. 1879 (NS) Catherine Costley (STS), she was born Feb. 27, 1863 and died in 1920 (NS), daughter of Joseph Oscar Costley and Elizabeth Woods (VAS).

CHILDREN:

see page 28 JOSEPH OSCAR-3 SWAIN, b. Dec. 11, 1880 (STS);
    d. Jan. 29, 1958 (STS), buried at Pleasant Grove near Scotland, Arkansas (VAS);
    m. Gertie Dunsworth (STS) she died May 11, 1982, buried at Pleasant Grove near Scotland, Arkansas (JD).

see page 31 JESSE ABNER-3 SWAIN, b. Sept. 27, 1882 (STS);
    d. Feb. 25, 1955, buried at Liberty Cemetery at Cleveland, Arkansas (STS);
    m. Ola Martin, she was born Jan. 24, 1887 and died April 30, 1943 and was buried at Liberty Cemetery at Cleveland, Arkansas (STS).

see page 32 THOMAS EDISON-3 SWAIN, b. Aug. 9, 1884 (NS);
    d. July 2, 1945 (NS), buried at Fort Smith, Arkansas (STS);
    m. Elisa Meeler (STS).

ELIZABETH or LIZZY-3 SWAIN, b. Aug. 4, 1886 (NS); first name "Sarah Elizabeth"(NS);
    d. "Clifton, Colorado in 1979" (STS); or Jan. 11, 1984 (NS);
    m. (   ) Luther Hillis (STS).

see page 33 MINNIE-3 SWAIN, b. Jan. 5, 1889 (NS) at Cleveland, Arkansas (STS);
    d._____
    m. Thomas Dunsworth (STS).

see page 35 JOHN WESLEY-3 SWAIN, b. Nov. 15, 1890 (NS);
    d. April 21, 1953, see Probate Court Record Book Q, p. 12 Conway County AR (ROC), buried at Old Liberty Cemetery, Cleveland, Arkansas (VAS);
    m. Dec. 1, 1912 Naomi Brents (STS), by M.A. Blue J.P., she was born March 17, 1893, Conway County, Arkansas Book S (ROC).

see page 36 MOLLY MAY-3 SWAIN, b. Nov. 21, 1892 (NS) at Cleveland, Arkansas (STS);
    m.(1) Harvey Lancaster (STS);
    m.(2) Phillip Henry (NS) (STS).

see page 37 SHERMAN NORTON-3 SWAIN, b. Oct. 18, 1894 at Cleveland, Arkansas (STS);
    d. Aug. 23, 1959 at Blackwell, Arkansas buried at Old Liberty Cemetery (STS);
    m. May 6, 1917 Stella Thomas Trimble (STS).

PEARLIE-3 SWAIN, b. Dec. 2, 1896 (NS); middle name "Idell" (NS);
    d. died in Oklahoma City, OK in 1985, she is buried near Ashland, Oklahoma (JD);
    m. John Bailey (STS) buried near Ashland, Oklahoma (JD).

    CHILDREN: (of Pearlie and John)
    BASIL-4 BAILEY, b. _____ (STS).
    PETE-4 BAILEY, b. _____ (STS).

ANNIE-3 SWAIN, b. Mar. 27, 1898 (NS); middle name "Martha Ann" (NS)
    m. (   ) Elbert Lentz (STS); "lives on Jefferson Street in Idabell, OK in 1979 " (STS); this family continued on next page...

CHILDREN: (of Annie and Elbert)
STANLEY-4 LENTZ, b._____ (STS).
LENTZ-4, LENTZ, b. _____ (STS).

see <u>WILLIAM THEODORE-3 SWAIN</u>, b. May 11, 1902 (STS);
page   d. Nov. 4, 1928 (STS);
40   m. Opal O'Neal (STS).

****

Gravel Hill String Band: members, left to right:
W.B. Halbrook, Lum Halbrook, Clay Hogan, **Jess Swain,**
Lando Halbrook, **Tom Swain**, Oscar Halbrook, and **Joe Swain**.
{Original photo in the posession of Dale Swain}

From left to right:
Pearl, Joe, Bill, Tom, Sam, Annie, Elbert Lentz.
{Original photo in the possession of Bessie Henry}

Catherine Costley Swain, widow
of John Abner Swain
is shown seated at front,
together with her four youngest
children.
From left to right:
Annie, William "Bill",
Sherman "Sam", and Pearl

Our

Third

Generation

LOU ETTA-3 BOST (Lou Etta-3, Celia Ann-2, Jesse Abner-1)
  b. March 12, 1880 at Scotland, Arkansas in Van Buren County (SOH);
  d. June 16,1976 at Lawton, Oklahoma, buried in Old Liberty Cemetery, Cleveland, AR (SOH);
  m. Jan. 5, 1899 William T. Summers at Scotland, Arkansas (SOH); he was born Sept. 17, 1875 at Karnak, Illinois in Pulaski County, he died Dec. 3, 1944 at Scotland, Arkansas and is buried at the Old Liberty Cemetary in Cleveland, Arkansas; he was the son of David Summers who is buried in the Old Liberty Cemetery and Mary Lentz Summers (SOH);

CHILDREN:

see page 41 PEARL ANN-4 SUMMERS, b. Oct. 31, 1899 at Scotland, Arkansas (SOH);
    d. April 1, 1980 at Yakima, Washington in Yakima County (SOH);
    m. Aug. 5, 1922 Charlie W. Kincannon at Scotland, AR in Van Buren County (SOH).

see page 43 CHARLIE OWENS-4 SUMMERS, b. Jan. 8, 1901 at Scotland, Arkansas in Van Buren
      County (SOH);
    d. Jan. 1962 in California (SOH);
    m. Icylona Bishop at Scotland, Arkansas in Van Buren County (SOH).

LUTHER WILSON-4 SUMMERS, b. March 26, 1903 at Scotland, Arkansas (SOH);
    m. (1st) Gertie Burnett at Cleveland, Arkansas (SOH);
    m. (2nd) Elena (SOH) "lived in Mississippi in 1985" "no children" (SOH).

see page 44 MELVIN RAY-4 SUMMERS, b. Jan. 24, 1907 at Scotland, Arkansas (SOH);
    m. (1st) Vida Newton at Scotland, Arkansas (SOH);
    m. (2nd) Mary Esterely Seadore; she was born April 8, 1918 (SOH).

see page 45 DESSA MAE-4 SUMMERS, b. March 28, 1909 at Scotland, Arkansas (SOH);
    m. Jan. 28, 1928 Larkin Osborne at Scotland, Arkansas (SOH); he died Aug.
       29, 1977 (SOH).

OTTO WILLIAM-4 SUMMERS, b. May 4, 1911 at Scotland, Arkansas (SOH);
    m. June 30, 1973 Beatrice Henderson at Scotland, Arkansas (SOH); lived at Rt. 3, Box
       138 Clinton, AR in 1986 (SOH); "no children" (SOH)

see page 46 DOVIE BELL-4 SUMMERS, b. March 29, 1913 at Scotland, Arkansas (SOH);
    d. Aug. 24, 1983 at Gilcrest, Oregon and was buried at Lapine, Oregon (SOH);
    m. Aug. 29, 1929 Barney D. Newton at Scotland, Arkansas (SOH).

see page 47 MINNIE-4 SUMMERS, b. Oct. 5, 1914 (twin) at Scotland, Arkansas (SOH);
    m. Ed Singleton at Russellville, Arkansas; they live at 804 Sullivan Drive, Lawton, OK
       73701 in 1986 (SOH).

LENNIE-4 SUMMERS, b. Oct. 5, 1914 (twin) at Scotland, Arkansas (SOH);
    d. Sept. 14, 1917 at Scotland, Arkansas (SOH).

HANCEL WOODROW-4 SUMMERS, b. July 12, 1917 at Scotland, Arkansas (SOH);
    m. Cora Wells at Cleveland, Arkansas. (SOH)
       "Lived in Cleveland, AR, 1985 (SOH).

    CHILDREN: (of Hancel and Cora)
    CLEO-5 SUMMERS, b. (SOH)

All information concerning this family marked with (SOH) has come from: "Sissy" Ovalene Harris (Mrs. Gene Harris) of Route 2, Box 2073 Selah, Washington 98942.

****

Sitting:
William T. Summers
Lou Etta (Bost) Summers
Dovie (on mother's lap)

Standing between parents:
Otto

Left to right:
Dessa
Charlie
Pearl
Melvin
Luther

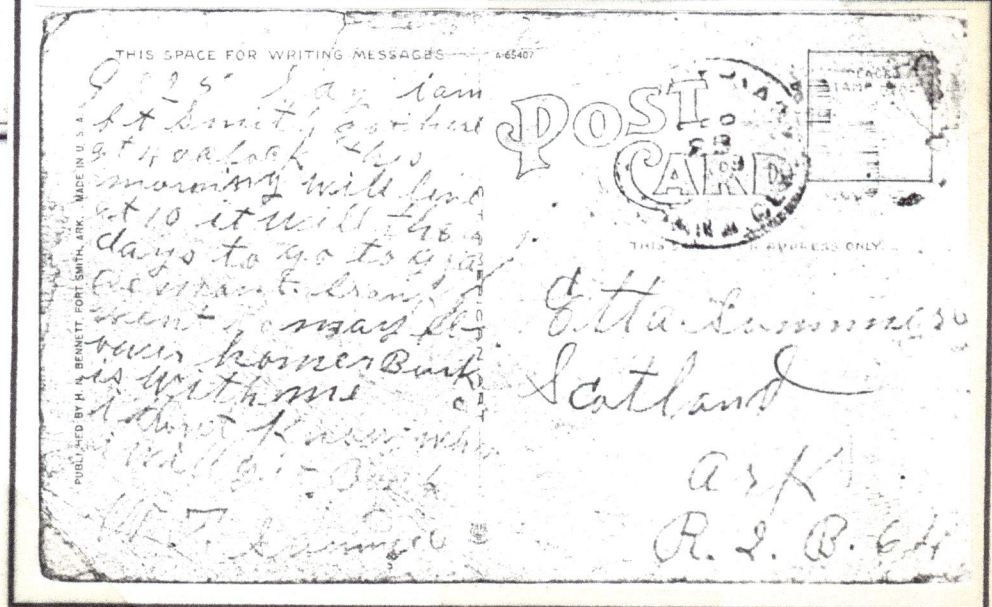

W.T. Summers mailed this card while on his way to look for work in Gracemont, Oklahoma in 1925.

see page 15

page 21

The Summers Family, December 4, 1944:

The Summers Family, Dec. 4, 1944:
(Back row, left to right)
Charlie
Otto
Melvin
Hancel
Luther
(Front row, left to right)
Dovie Newton
Pearle Kincannon
Dessa Osborne
Etta Lou Summers
Minnie Singleton

see page 15 page 22

Etta & Will Summers, taken at Rock Garden in Oregon

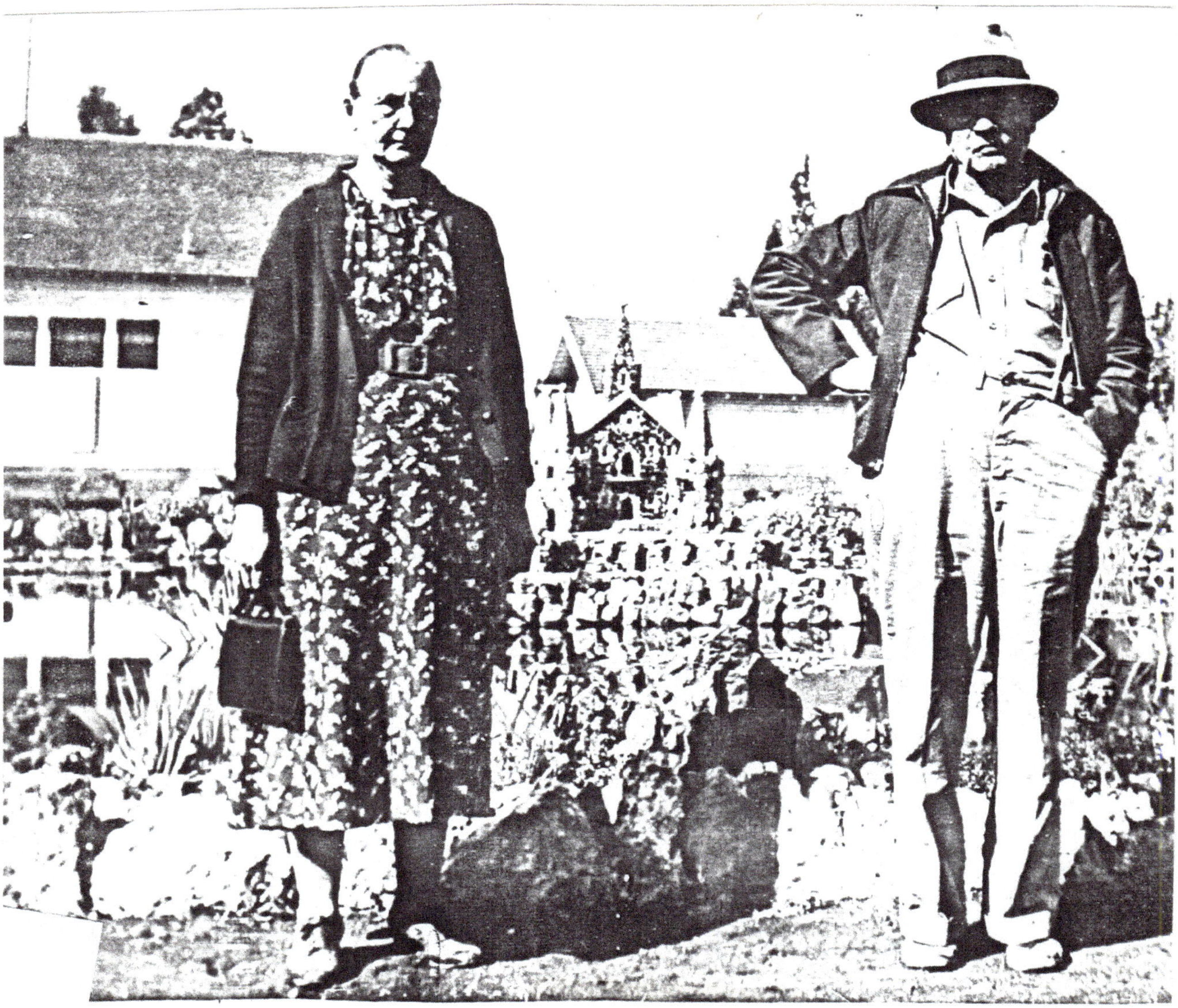

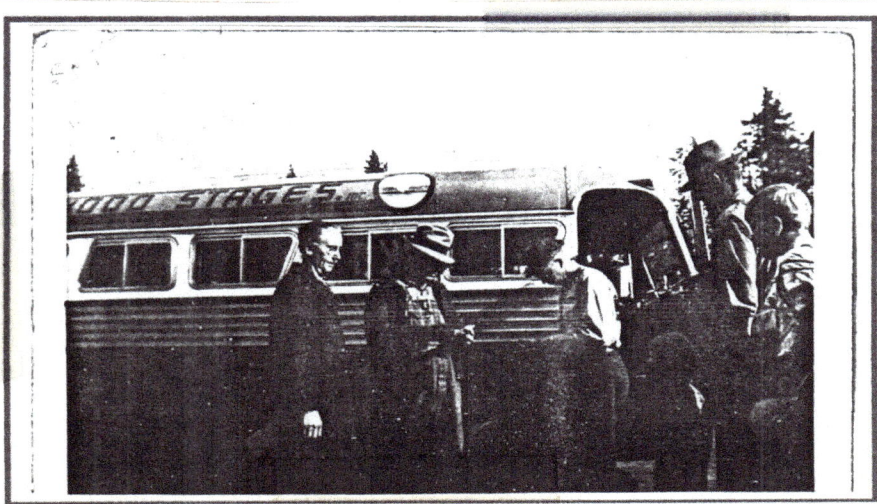

Etta & Will Summers
leaving Lapine, Oregon
for Scotland, Arkansas in 1943

CHARLES DUDLEY-3 SWAIN (Charles Dudley-3, William-2, Jessie-1)
    b. June 1879 (NS);
    d. April 11, 1944 (NS);
    m. (1st) Rella Morris who was born January 1878 (NS).
    m. (2nd) Janie Low (NS).

    CHILDREN: (of Charles and Rella)
    JOHN W.-4 SWAIN, b. Feb. 1900 (NS);
        d. "infant" (NS).

see MARY ELIZABETH-4 SWAIN, b. March 1, 1902 (NS);
page   m. Nov. 29, 1920 Bill Wyrick (NS).
48

    MARVIN C.-4 SWAIN, b. Feb. 5, 1905 (NS);
        d. May 9, 1943 (NS);
        m. Ada Lee Gilbert (NS).

        CHILDREN: (of Marvin and Ada)
        MARY SUE-5 SWAIN, b. _____ (NS);
            m. Boyd Stanford (NS).

            CHILDREN: (of Mary & Boyd)
            VIRGINIA-6 STANFORD, b. _____ (NS).
            CHARLES-6 STANFORD, b. _____ (NS).

    CHILDREN: (of Charles and Janie)
    LULA-4 SWAIN, b. Nov. 19, 1914 (NS);
        m. Charles Gilbert (NS).

      CHILDREN: (of Lula & Charles)
      ROBERT-5 GILBERT, b. July 16, 1948 (NS);
        m. Christal Clements (NS).

        CHILDREN: (of Robert & Christal)
        SANDRA MICHELLE-6 GILBERT, b. Oct. 2, 1968 (NS).

CELCE ELIZABETH-3 SWAIN (Celce Elizabeth-3, William-2, Jessie-1)
  b. March 3, 1882 (NS);
  d. 1906 (NS);
  m. July 20, 1899 Sam Hankins who was born May 23, 1872 (NS).

CHILDREN: (of Celce and Sam)
GOTHIE MICHAEL-4 HANKINS, b. May 26, 1900 (NS);
  d. Sept. 6, 1904 (NS).

FRANCIS LUCINDA-4 HANKINS, b. Aug. 11, 1902 (NS);
  m. Feb. 11, 1928 Cris Bradley (NS).

  CHILDREN: (of Francis & Cris)
    G. C.-5 BRADLEY, b. Oct. 13, 1928 (NS).

    VIRGINIA DALE-5 BRADLEY, b. April 11, 1930 (NS).

    MADLINE-5 BRADLEY, b. March 26, 1933 (NS);
      m. July 24, 1953 John M. Jones. (NS).

    ALICE ANN-5 BRADLEY, b. Feb. 23, 1937 (NS);
      m. Oct. 21, 1960 Allen Looney who was born Dec. 25, 1937 (NS).

      CHILDREN: (of Alice & Allen)
      CELLIA-6 LOONEY, b._____(NS).

      ALAN-6 LOONEY, Jr., b._____(NS).

      LORI ANN-6 LOONEY, b._____(NS).

CLARA SLAINE-4 HANKINS, b. May 29, 1905 (NS);
  m. Lawrence Pendergrass (NS).

  CHILDREN: (of Clara & Larence)
  PAUL-5 PENDERGRASS, b. (NS);
    m. _____

    CHILDREN: (of Paul & _____)
    PAUL HADEN-6 PENDERGRASS, b. (NS).

RUTHIE JANE-3 SWAIN (Ruthie Jane-3, William-2, Jessie-1)
b. April 3, 1887 (NS);
d. 1923 (NS);
m. Nov. 14, 1909 Wess Horn who was born April 25, 1883 (NS).

CHILDREN: (of Ruthie & Wess)
<u>OTIS-4 HORN</u>, b. Aug. 17, 1910 (NS);
page   m. Aug. 3, 1935 Bernice Cravens who was born Oct. 9, 1918 (NS).
49

<u>ORIE ELIZABETH-4 HORN</u>, b. Dec. 31, 1911 (NS);
page   m. Arch Varnill (NS).
50

<u>GERTRUDE-4 HORN</u>, b. Dec. 9, 1913 (NS);
page   m. March 4, 1933 Tom Sparkman who was born Jan. 3, 1908 (NS).
51

BOYCE-4 HORN, b. JAN. 29, 1916 (NS);
    m. Correnia Cain (NS).

LOYD-4 HORN, b. Nov. 17, 1920 (NS);
    m. Katie Mae Webb (NS).

<u>THOMAS McRAY-4 HORN</u>, b. Oct. 17, 1922 (NS);
    m. April 3, 1946 Betty Sanders who was born July 30, 1929 (NS)

    CHILDREN: (of Thomas & Betty)
<u>DANNY RAY-5 HORN</u>, b. Feb. 7, 1947 (NS);
    m. (1st) June 1966 Helen George (NS);
    m. (2nd) Feb. 6, 1982 Betsey Draper (NS).

    CHILDREN: (of Danny & Helen)
DARRELL BRUCE-6 HORN, b. Feb. 4, 1967 (NS).

<u>HOWARD DALE-5 HORN</u>, b. Aug. 11, 1950 (NS);
    m. Dec. 22, 1979 Donna Gale Loyd who was born June 23, 1951 (NS).

    CHILDREN: (of Howard & Donna)
HEATHER DAWN-6 HORN, b. Jan. 31, 1982 (NS).

<u>CHARLES GLEN-5 HORN</u>, b. Jan. 31, 1952 (NS);
    m. Feb. 12, 1976 Vickie Zemel who was born Oct. 19, 1954 (NS).

    CHILDREN: (of Charles & Vickie)
AMY MICHELE-6 HORN, b. July 13, 1979 (NS).
WENDY JOY-6 HORN, b. Oct. 23, 1982 (NS).

PHILLIP LEE-5 HORN, b. Sept. 30, 1953 (NS);
    m. Dec. 12, 1981 Jane _____ who was born Sept. 15, 1956 (NS).

JAMES ALBERT-3 SWAIN (James-3, William-2, Jessie-1)
    b. Feb. 22, 1895 (NS);
    d. Nov. 20, 1984 (NS);
    m. July 1, 1917 Amanda Luevena Nelson, b. Feb. 11, 1894 and died March 7, 1963 (NS).

CHILDREN: (of James and Amanda)
JAMES LeROY-4 SWAIN, b. Sept. 11, 1918 (NS); known as "Roy" (NS);
    m. Oct. 24, 1936 Nina Norene Beason, she was born April 11, 1918; Nina contributed all
        the information with the initials (NS), and lives at Rt. 1 Branch, Arkansas 72928.

CHILDREN: (of "Roy" and Nina):
see
page
89
JAMES WILLIAM-5 SWAIN, b. Aug. 31, 1937 (NS);
    m. Jan. 5, 1957 Georgia Raye Ragsdale; she was born Oct. 9, 1939 (NS).

BARBARA SUE-5 SWAIN, b. June 3, 1939 (NS);
    m. Jan. 1, 1959 Tommy Ratterree; he was born May 28, 1939 (NS).

    CHILDREN: (of Barbara and Tommy)
    SHERRY DALE-6 RATTERREE, b. April 11, 1960 (NS);
        m. Sept. 26, 1981 Henry "Hank" Fram; he was born July 14, 1961 (NS).

    DANIEL LEROY-6 RATTERREE, b. June 25, 1961 (NS);
        m. March 28, 1980 Mary Florene Carmen; she was born Oct. 8, 1964 (NS).

        CHILDREN: (of Daniel and Mary)
        HEATHER DENISE-7 RATTERREE, b. Oct. 18, 1980 (NS).

    LORI SUZANNE-6 RATTERREE, b. Aug. 3, 1962 (NS);
        m. Sept. 25, 1982 Paul Shannon Moore; he was born June 19, 1963 (NS).

MELVIN LEROY-5 SWAIN, b. Aug. 24, 1941 (NS);
    m. (1st) Oct. 7, 1960 Donna Jean Lee; she was born March 25, 1943 (NS);
    m. (2nd) Oct. 2, 1970 Anna Vee Johnson; she was born Dec. 24, 1950 (NS).

    CHILDREN: (of Melvin and Donna)
    RALPH LEROY-6 SWAIN, b. July 21, 1962 (NS); died same day (NS).
    LISA JEAN-6 SWAIN, b. Sept. 6, 1963 (NS).
    RANDALL LEROY-6 SWAIN, b. Jan. 22, 1965 (NS);
        m. Jan. 7, 1984 Sheila DuVall (NS).
    RONNIE MARK-6 SWAIN, b. Aug. 6, 1966 (NS).

    CHILDREN: (of Melvin and Anna)
    MELINDA ANN-6 SWAIN, b. April 24, 1973 (NS).

CARROLL WILLIE-5 SWAIN, b. June 26, 1946 (NS);
    m. Oct. 22, 1964 Nelda Rue Grubb; she was born Nov. 5, 1947 (NS).

    CHILDREN: (of Carroll and Nelda)
    LEROY SAMUEL-6 SWAIN, b. May 8, 1965 (NS).
    CURTIS RAY-6 SWAIN, b. Jan. 20, 1968 (NS).

****

WILLIAM JESS-3 SWAIM (William-3,William-2, Jessie-1)
> b. Oct. 13, 1898 (NS); spelled last name 'Swaim' (NS);
> d. 1977 (NS);
> m. Oct. 13, 1920 Eva Cherry who was born Dec. 27, 1898 (NS).

CHILDREN: (of William and Eva)

page 52
PAULINE-4 SWAIM, b. April 6, 1922 (NS);
> m. Oct. 30, 1945 Norman Greenfield; he was born Sept. 16, 1923 (NS).

page 53
IRENE-4 SWAIM, b. Sept. 25, 1923 (NS);
> m. Nov. 25, 1942 Glen Chambers (NS).

page 55
WILLIAM JOHN "Billy"-4 SWAIM, b. Aug. 1, 1925 (NS)
> m. Sept. 1943 Audrey Hill; she was born Nov. 11, 1923 (NS).

CURMIT-4 SWAIM, b. Dec. 27, 1930 (NS);
> m. _____ Sally Bennett (NS).

> **CHILDREN:** (of Curmit and Sally)
> JANET-5 SWAIM, b. _____ (NS).
> SHIRLEY-5 SWAIM, b. _____ (NS).

page 56
OZELL-4 SWAIM, b. Jan. 23, 1933 (NS);
> m. Nov. 18, 1948 Joe Apple (NS).

MAGGIE SUE-4 SWAIM, b. Oct. 17, 1935 (NS);
> m. Feb. 1, 1953 Robert Chambers (NS).

> **CHILDREN:** (of Maggie and Robert)
> BOBBY-5 CHAMBERS, b. _____ (NS);
> > m. Sept. 15, 1977 Elizabeth Long (NS).

> > **CHILDREN:** (of Bobby and Elizabeth)
> > BRENT-6 CHAMBERS, b. March 8, 1978 (NS).

> DAVID-5 CHAMBERS, (NS);
> > m. Jan. 19, 1977 Rita Treadwell (NS).

> > **CHILDREN:** (of David and Rita)
> > BRYON-6 CHAMBERS, b. Jan. 20, 1978 (NS).

> ROGER-5 CHAMBERS, b. (NS);
> > m. July 31, 1982 Merry Means (NS).

> > **CHILDREN:** (of Roger and Merry)
> > BRAD-6 CHAMBERS, b. Feb. 9, 1983 (NS).

JOSEPH OSCAR-3 SWAIN (Joseph Oscar-3, John Abner-2, JesseAbner-1)
b. Dec. 11, 1880 (STS);
d. Jan. 29, 1958 (STS) buried at Pleasant Grove Cemetery at Scotland, Arkansas (JD);
m. Gertie Dunsworth (STS); she was born Jan. 6, 1890; and she died May 9, 1982, buried at Pleasant Grove Cemetery at Scotland, Arkansas (JD).

CHILDREN:

see
page
57 VIRGIL-4 SWAIN, b. Oct. 22, 1906, (from cemetery headstone);
d. June 3, 1972 buried at Pleasant Grove Cemetery near Scotland, AR (JD);
m.(1st) Lela Guinn (STS); she is buried in Michigan (JD).
m.(2nd) Mable Lefler (STS).

SON-4 SWAIN, b. Dec. 6, 1908 (STS) and (JD);
d. May 16, 1909, buried at Liberty Cemetery at Cleveland, AR (STS) and (JD).

see
page
58 FAYE-4 SWAIN, b. Sept. 4, 1910 (JD); resides at Scotland, AR (JD); first name "Letha" (NS);
m. Ellis Ward (STS); he was born Aug. 5, 1910 and died Sept. 3, 1968; he is buried at St. Mary's Cemetery at Mt. Vernon, Arkansas (JD).

see
page
60 RAY THOMAS-4 SWAIN, b. Sept. 26, 1915 (from cemetery headstone);
d. July 31, 1954 buried at Pleasant Grove Cemetery near Scotland, AR (JD);
m. Dorothy Dunsworth (STS).

see
page
61 DALE-4 SWAIN, b. July 5, 1925 (JD); resides in Morrilton, AR (JD);
middle name "Draper" (NS);
m. Feb. 13, 1943 Mildred Stracner who was born July 5, 1923 (VAS).

"Joe was the oldest son of John and Katherine Costley Swain. He homesteaded 56 acres of land when just a young person. Joe and Gertie lived on the place all their married life. They never moved. All of the children were born there: Virgil, Ray, Faye and Dale." written by daughter Faye Swain Ward Feb. 23, 1986 (ROC)

"Joseph Oscar "Joe" Swain was born in the Gravel Hill Community near Scotland, Arkansas where he spent his entire life.

It would be a reasonable contention of all those who knew him and definitely the conviction of this writer (VAS) that at an early age Joe came to feel a sense of responsibility in setting good and proper examples for five younger brothers to follow.

It would also well be a correct assumption and conjecture that the younger brothers did profit from his exemplary conduct and behavior, and credit should be given not only to the parents but to Joe Swain as well for the responsible citizens that each of these men became.

Looking at the kind of life he led it can be said that Joe was attracted to only that which was good and honorable. For example, as a young man he learned to play the violin and probably influenced two of his younger brothers, Jess and Tom, to also become members of the Gravel Hill String Band where they played for a number of years at most of the local community programs.

That he was serious and well-intentioned is evidenced by the fact that he worked hard and long as a young man in already buying and paying for a farm and a log cabin home to which he could take his young bride and life-long companion, Gertie Dunsworth, also of the Gravel Hill Community. The log cabin home, where Virgil, the eldest child was born, was later replaced by a more modern, bungalow-type home.

Nephews can recall pleasurable visits to his home where this kind, gentle and caring man could easily be persuaded to play remembered tunes on that same treasured fiddle still in his possession, and that he was sure to take them across a highway from his home to a well-kept orchard and would pluck for them some of the best apples from a tree. Also, there were well-remembered trips in the hot summer time to an almost air-conditioned like storm cellar, planned and built large enough to provide a haven of protection from tornadoes for nearby neighbors as well.

A brother once made this tribute, a most deserving one we believe, to his memory. "Joe Swain lived a life-time in complete peace and harmony with his family, his neighbors, and his friends."

He was an Elder in the New Liberty Church of Christ where he and Gertie were members for many years.

His descendants can be rightfully proud to share in such a heritage." (VAS)

****

Joe Swain

From left to right: taken January, 1956
Lela, Virgil, Mildred, Dale

From left to right: taken January, 1956
{photo in the possession of Dale Swain}
Standing: **Virgil, Gertie, Lela,
Fay Ward, Mildred, Joe, Dale**
Sitting: _____, **Alma Sue**

Joe & Gertie, made 1929

Joe & Gertie, made in 1922

Last picture made of **Joseph Oscar Swain.**
Made at Faye Swain Ward's home, Dec. 1957

From left to right:
Joe, Virgil, Faye, Gertie
taken about 1914
(original photograph belongs
to Faye Swain Ward)

see page 16

page 31

JESSE ABNER-3 SWAIN (Jesse Abner-3,John Abner-2, Jesse Abner-1)
  b. Sept. 27, 1882 (STS);
  d. Feb. 25, 1955, buried at Old Liberty Cemetery at Cleveland, Arkansas (STS);
  m. Ola Martin, she was born Jan. 24, 1886 and died April 30, 1943 and was buried at Old
     Liberty Cemetery at Cleveland, Arkansas (STS).

CHILDREN:
GLADYS-4 SWAIN, b. Jan. 15, 1907 (STS);
page
62   m. Aug. 1922 Floice Rhoads (NS).

THOMAS EDISON-4 SWAIN, b. July 8, 1921 (STS);
page
64   m. Jan. 16, 1951 Alma J. Harlin at Durant, Oklahoma (STS).

"Jesse Abner "Jess" Swain resided near Scotland, Arkansas in the Gravel Hill community and taught school there in his younger years. For several years he was employed by the U.S. Government in verifying cotton and corn acreages, a program that is no longer existent. Throughout most of his working years, he was a farmer, blacksmith, and a carpenter.

For many years, he was a Justice of the Peace, and as a J.P. he performed marriage rituals for numerous young couples who sought him out for this purpose, and in this capacity, he also presided over the Justice of the Peace Court in settling local, controversal issues.

Jess was a member of the Masonic Lodge, an organization that he supported and loved very much, and he was also a Royal Arch Mason." (VAS)

Photo of **Jesse Abner Swain**, and his daughter **Gladys Swain Rhoads** taken in 1943

****

see page 16

THOMAS ELMORE-3 SWAIN (Thomas Elmore-3,John Abner-2, Jesse Abner-1)
- b. August 9, 1884 at Cleveland, Arkansas (HV) (NS) middle name is 'Elmore' not 'Edison'(HV);
- d. July 2, 1945 buried at National Cemetery in Fort Smith, Arkansas (HV);
- m. March 24, 1901 Elisa Meeler (HV).

"Thomas E. 'Tom' Swain entered upon a military career at an early age and served with distinction and honor for a period of 30 years including overseas duty with the American Expeditionary Forces of World War I.

In his early years as an enlisted man he became noted for his outstanding ability as a rifle marksman, and when on military leave at home near the rural community of Scotland, Arkansas people came from several miles distance, on foot, on horseback, in wagons and buggies, on a day set aside solely for the purpose of witnessing his expert marksmanship.

He received a Bachelor of Laws degree from LaSalle University on June 22, 1931, for which he had studied for some years.

A Master Sergeant at the onset of WWI, he immediately went on active duty as a Captain and was retired on July 31, 1935. He also had a commission in the reserve as a Lieutenant Colonel. He was active as a Mason and Shriner.

Following military retirement, he took a course on operation of Military Cemeteries at Arlington National Cemetery in Washington, D.C. He then served as Superintendent of the National Cemetery at Baton Rouge, Louisiana, and then at Alexandria, Louisiana, and last at Ft. Smith, Arkansas. His gravesite and that of his beloved wife, Elisa, are there alongside that of Colonel William E. 'Bill' Darby, one of Arkansas' heroes of WWII." (HV)

CHILDREN:
see page 65
HERVEY-4 SWAIN, b. Feb. 22, 1904 at Cleveland, Arkansas (HV); m. July 23, 1928 Marguerite Haguewood (HV).

see page 66
HAZEL-4 SWAIN, (STS);
b. Sept. 30, 1908 at Ft. Leavenworth, Kansas (HV);
m. Dec. 25, 1931 Richard A.Veatch at Ft. Leavenworth, Kansas (HV);
they reside at 1921 Shamrock Ave., Lee's Summit, MO 64063 (HV).

****

Thomas E. Swain
&
Elisa Swain
probably around 1940

MINNIE-3 SWAIN (Minnie-3, John Abner-2, Jesse Abner-1)
b. Jan. 5, 1889 (JD) at Cleveland, Arkansas (STS); resides at Scotland, Arkansas, 1985 (JD)
m. Tommy Dunsworth, he was born Dec. 24, 1887 and died July 11, 1927, buried at Pleasant
Grove Cemetery at Scotland, Arkansas. (JD).

CHILDREN:
OLLIN A.-4 DUNSWORTH, b. Oct. 13, 1907 (JD);
d. Oct. 6, 1931 buried Pleasant Grove Cemetery at Scotland, AR (JD).

see   EUEL N.-4 DUNSWORTH, b. Nov. 16, 1909 (JD);
page   d. Jan. 1981 buried at Pleasant Grove Cemetery at Scotland, Arkansas (JD);
68   m. Wade Hiland, and resided in Cleveland, Ohio 1985 (JD).

see   BRANNON-4 DUNSWORTH, b. June 7, 1912 (JD); resides in Scotland, AR (JD);
page   m. Winnie Underwood (STS).
69
see   JERRELL-4 DUNSWORTH, b. Oct. 13, 1914 (JD); resides at N. Hollywood, California,
page   1985 (JD);
70   m. Geneva Hall (STS) and (JD).

see   JOHN THOMAS-4 DUNSWORTH, b. June 19, 1921 (JD);
page   m. Norma Dale McCoslin (STS); she died Sept. 15, 1961, buried at Pleasant Grove
71   Cemetery in Cleveland, Arkansas (JD).

"Providing insight and history about this sturdy, honest, and hardworking American family
and the kind of people they really were can best be illustrated by relating something of the
hardships earlier generations endured and conquered, much of which was done with one objective
in mind: in order that those who were to follow would have a better way of life.

None would be more representative than Aunt Minnie Dunsworth, the hardships she faced, the
manner in which she dealt with these hardships, can only endear others to this truly remarkable
woman, and could do no other than cause a feeling of pride that there were those like her in their
family background.

The loss due to the death of her husband and helpmate came at a time when there were 5 young
sons to raise, and there were no social or welfare programs to which to turn, and there were no
family members financially able to help.

It is said that Aunt Minnie sewed, washed and ironed clothes, sold milk, butter, and garden
vegetables, and in essence did anything whereby she might honorably earn in providing for and
rearing her sons.

The incredible thing throughout her years is that she has been an ever-smiling, pleasant, and
uncomplaining person, and seemingly always more concerned about others than herself.

A niece, Faye Ward, voicing what many others have said, states that she has never heard this
lady utter an unkind word about anyone in her entire life.

Her ever-pleasant and cheerful attitude throughout the years endeared neighbors and
acquaintances to her and their love for her has been demonstrated in so many ways. For example,
folks from throughout the community on any Sunday afternoon drop by in surprising numbers to
pay their respects with this continuing to this date. The same is true of former residents. A return
home is to include for sure, a visit to Aunt Minnie's.

Now 97 years of age and long since confined to a wheel chair, she continues to recognize her
visitors and has a smile and a kind word for them." (VAS)

Photograph of MINNIE, JOHN AND JOHN JR.

"This picture was made Dec. 24, 1961 at Faye Swain Ward's in Cleveland, Arkansas. Minnie Dunsworth, her son John Thomas Dunsworth Sr. better known as (Jack) Dunsworth, and his son John Tommie Dunsworth Jr. Minnie Swain Dunsworth is 97 years old Jan. 5, 1986. She lives at Scotland, Ark. Aunt Minnie to me is one of the best. She never speaks evil of anybody. In her younder years she was always ready to help people. She is among one of the best Christian mothers, friends and neighbors."
Written by Faye Swain Ward on Feb. 23, 1986.

Minnie Dunsworth, taken July, 1961

Aunt Minnie Dunsworth and four of her five sons.
From left to right:
Euel, Brannon, Jerrell, and John.
Ollin is not shown.

JOHN WESLEY-3 SWAIN (John Wesley-3,John Abner-2, Jesse Abner-1)
  b. Nov. 15, 1890 (NS) (STS);
  d. April 21, 1953, see Probate Court Record Book Q, p.12 Conway County, AR (ROC);
  m. Dec. 1, 1912 Naomi Brents (STS), by M.A. Blue J.P., she was born March 17, 1893, see Conway County, Arkansas Book S (ROC).

CHILDREN:
BESSIE MILDRED-4 SWAIN, b. May 4, 1914 (STS);
  d. Aug. 9, 1914 (STS).

see
page
72 GRADY LAYDUS-4 SWAIN, b. Dec. 4, 1915 (ROC) at Cleveland, Arkansas (STS);
  d. Dec. 17, 1975 (ROC);
  m. Dec. 24, 1939 Mary Ruth Wright, by Geo. M. Powell, (STS)
    Mary was born April 13, 1920 (ROC).

CLYDE-4 SWAIN, b. Oct. 27, 1918 (STS);
  d. March 11, 1923 (STS).

"Among the several children born to John Abner and Catherine Swain, John Wesley presents, perhaps, the most interesting case study of all. This statement is made, in part, due to the fact that the writer, through a close association with him over a period of years, came to better know him and the kind of man he was.

While most of the brothers and sisters were more kind and gentle in nature, in contrast, 'Wes' as he was best known had a more fiery disposition, quick to voice his own interpretations and beliefs on any controversial or political issue, and if sufficiently pushed, was never known to walk or run away from a fist fight, particularily when he felt his position was a just one.

He was a loyal and staunch supporter of the Republican Party and one of his greatest enjoyments came in open and often-time heated debate in defending the policies and platform of the party he loved.

As a young man and well into mid-years he played on the local baseball team at Cleveland, Arkansas and was remembered as a scrappy and always enthusiastic player. Perhaps it was because of such characteristics that in early years he was nick-named 'Rooster'.

Nonetheless, he was considered a just and honest man.

Most of his working years were spent at public jobs in the Cleveland, Arkansas area where he resided, and for a great many years he served as a substitute U.S. Mail Carrier. During WWI he worked at Shipbuilding in San Francisco, California. Following WWII, he moved to Blackwell, Arkansas and worked until his death in 1963 in the grocery store belonging to his brother, Sam, and also working at a skating rink belonging to his nephew, Ansel." (VAS)

****

MOLLY MAY-3 SWAIN (Molly-3,John Abner-2,Jesse Abner-1)
  b. Nov. 24, 1892 (ROC) or on the 21st (JD) at Cleveland, Arkansas (STS); "now lives at 614 West Harrison, McAlester, Oklahoma in 1986" "in a nursing home" (ROC)
  m.(1st) Harvey Lancaster (STS);
  m.(2nd) Phillip Henry (JD) (NS);

CHILDREN: (of Molly and Harvey)
<u>BESSIE-4 LANCASTER</u>, b. Aug. 29, 1911(ROC),
  lives at 24 W. Miami in McAlester, OK 74501 in 1986 (ROC)
  m. 1925 Emmett Henry (ROC).

  CHILDREN:
  EUGENE-5 HENRY, b. 1927 (ROC); "deceased" (ROC);
  RICHARD K.-5 HENRY b. 1932 (ROC); "lives in Sherman, Texas retired from US Air Force"; "has four children" (ROC)

FRED-4 LANCASTER, b. Aug. 14, 1913 (ROC), "now deceased" "retired from Army" "Fred has one child" (ROC)

BOB "Babe"-4 LANCASTER, b. Oct. 7, 1915 (ROC), "no children""lives in Citrus Heights, California" (ROC).

WILLIE ERMA -4 LANCASTER, b. 1917 "has two children" "lives in Port Richey, Florida" (ROC);
  m. Charles W. Dando (ROC).

CHILDREN: (of Molly and Phillip)
I.D.-4 HENRY, b. about 1923, "63 years old" in 1986, "retired teacher lives in Okmulgee, Oklahoma" "has two boys" (ROC).

PHYLLIS MAE-4 HENRY, b. about 1925, "61 years old" in 1986, "lives in Tulsa, Oklahoma" "had two children, one deceased" (ROC);
  m. Bill Tallman (ROC).

JUNE-4 HENRY, b. about 1927, "59 years old" in 1986, lives in McAlester, Oklahoma" "has two children, 1 boy, 1 girl" (ROC);
  m. Bob Loar (ROC).

JOY-4 HENRY, b. about 1929, "57 years old" in 1986, "has four children" "lives in Naperville, Illinois"(ROC);
  m. James Fitzgerald (ROC)

Information on this page marked with (ROC) was sent to Robert O. Crossman by Bessie Henry of 24 W. Miami in McAlester, Oklahoma 74501 on January 23, 1986.

Photo of sisters:
{left to right}
Molly Henry,
Minnie Dunsworth,
and Pearl Bailey

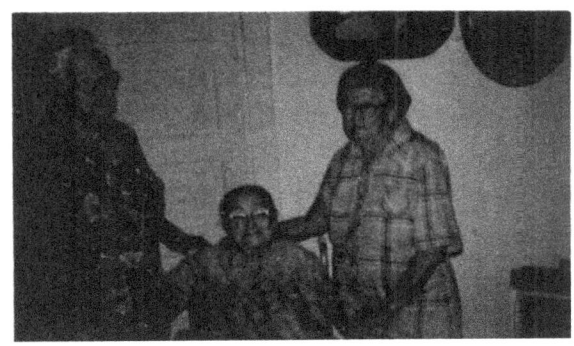

see page 16

SHERMAN NORTON-3 SWAIN (Sherman Norton-3, John Abner-2, Jesse Abner-1)
- b. Oct. 18, 1894 at Cleveland, Arkansas (STS);
- d. Aug. 23, 1959 at Blackwell, Arkansas (STS);
- m. May 6, 1917 Stella Thomas Trimble (STS), daughter of Thomas Milton Trimble and Teresa Mason Liner; Stella was born on Dec. 30, 1896 at Scotland, Arkansas (STS); Stella is a sixth generation descendant of James & Grace Trimble (James-1 Trimble & Grace; Moses-2 Trimble & Catherine Lewis; John Haddon-3 Trimble & Elizabeth Evans; Milton Conyers-4 Trimble & Elizabeth Susan Copeland; Thomas Milton-5 Trimble & Teresa Liner; Stella Thomas-6 Trimble) as recorded in "American Beginnings" by David B. Trimble, copyright 1974, San Antonio, Texas. Sherman & Stella were married by J.G. Leavell, see Conway County Arkansas Book U, page 483 (ROC).

CHILDREN:

see <u>EUNICE ALLINE-4 SWAIN</u>, b. April 22, 1918 at Cleveland, Arkansas (STS);
page "Alline & Oliver live in Blackwell, Arkansas in 1986" (ROC).
73   m. July 27, 1938 Oliver Daniel Smirl (STS) by Geo. M. Rowell, see Conway County Arkansas Book 35, page 630 (ROC); Oliver was born Jan. 18, 1914 at Blackwell, Arkansas, the son of Lyndon Biggs Smirl and Hettie Roberta Oliver (STS).

see <u>VERILL ANSEL-4 SWAIN</u>, b. April 13, 1921 at Cleveland, Arkansas (STS);
page "Ansel & Elizabeth live in Morrilton, Arkansas in 1986" (ROC).
74   m. September 3, 1950 Elizabeth Ruth (Hamlet) Kimberlin (STS), at Atkins, Arkansas by Rev. H.C. Minnis, Elizabeth was born Jan. 14, 1921 at Atkins, Arkansas, widow of Donald Kimberlin, she is the daughter of John Turner Hamlet and Velma Kate Johnson.

see <u>DOYLE THERON-4 SWAIN</u>, b. March 24, 1925 at Cleveland, Arkansas (STS);
page d. June 14, 1980 buried at Fort Smith, Arkansas, National Cemetery (ROC);
78   m. Aug. 19, 1947 Mary Alice Cranford (STS), by Clarence Dawson, see Conway County Arkansas Book 36 page 57 (ROC); Mary was born Aug. 10, 1926 at Perryville, Arkansas, daughter of Gil Cranford and Lillie May Beard (STS).

see <u>DALLAS LYNN-4 SWAIN</u>, b. Oct. 15, 1930 at Cleveland, Arkansas (STS);
page "Dallas & Nealia Jane live at 505 North Church St., Atkins, AR 72823 in 1986" (ROC).
83   m. April 18, 1951 Nealia Jane Fry in Atkins, Arkansas. Nealia Jane was born Feb. 11, 1931 in Atkins, the daughter of William Clinton Fry Jr. and Ocie Smith (WSS).

see <u>SHIRLEY ANN-4 SWAIN</u>, b. May 10, 1934 at Cleveland, Arkansas (STS);
page "lives at 1253 W. 20th Street, Merced, California 95340 in 1979" (ROC).
85   m. Donald G. Tedder on April 10, 1954, Donald was born Aug. 28, 1933, son of John Tedder (STS).

"Sherman Norton 'Sam' Swain's formal education was abruptly ended at about the age of 15 years due to the untimely death of his father, necessitating his taking over the responsibility of the family farm, his mother, some older sisters and a younger brother, all yet members of the family household. Under such conditions his was one of undoubtedly maturing early in life, and probably accounted for the fact that he was considered by those who knew him as a deep thinker, and a keenly intellectual and knowledgeable person, considerably advanced beyond many of those of this time.

At the end of WWI Sherman Norton 'Sam' Swain returned from duty in France and was discharged as a Sergeant First Class. Arising out of interest for others, he began to help WWI veterans who came from as far as 50 miles away in establishing pensions and obtaining medical benefits, with this leading to a full-time job for a period of time with the then organization known as the Arkansas Veteran's Bureau in Little Rock, Arkansas.

continued on next page...

In his younger years as a talented singer of gospel music he attended and graduated from th Hartford School of Music and later taught singing schools in a great many Arkansas communit

In 1928, he opened a general mercantile store in Cleveland, Arkansas. Later, in 1937, he purchased a similar business at Blackwell, Arkansas and soon thereafter was appointed to the postmastership where he continued to serve in conjunction with operating the store until ill heal forced his retirement in 1955.

Maintaining a life-long interest in Masonry, he reached the 7th degree level, that of a Royal Arch Mason, and was a certified lecturer, teaching candidates as they sought to memorize the lengthy masonic rituals.

A lasting tribute to his memory --the fact that throughout his lifetime, he stood instantly rea to assist those in need, serving as councelor, advisor, and benefactor to those who sought his assistance, and many persons did." (VAS)

"**STELLA TRIMBLE SWAIN** was born and reared in the Claude Community near Scotland, Arkansas and was the last of five children born to Thomas and Teresa Liner Trimble.

Her father died at the age of 37 years, two months before her birth, and the family endured considerable hardships as her mother sought to rear her young family.

Through necessity Stella learned to sew and make her own clothes at a young age, a talent ; her marriage that was to benefit her own family of five children, especially during the lean depression years of the 30's when she would completely remake a worn out suit or dress of an adult into a usable garment for one of the children. Numerous young, expectant mothers, unab sew themselves, sought her aid in making needed items for a soon to arrive infant.

The family budget was benefited for many years also with the excellent gardens Stella and children produced. The size and the quality of the sweet potatoes, pumpkins, and other vegetab she grew was a frequent topic of conversation in the Cleveland community where they once resided.

Also in providing for the needs of her family, Stella assisted in the operation of a family ov grocery store over a period of 30 years.

She is now a resident of Morrilton Manor at 1212 W. Childress, Morrilton, AR 72110, following a broken hip which she incurred in April of 1986, and which restricts her activities somewhat. In December of 1986, she observed her 90th birthday." (VAS)

photo of Sherman "Sam" Swain in his store at Blackwell, Arkansas.

Sherman "Sam" Swain

Sherman "Sam" and Stella

Sherman "Sam" Swain

WILLIAM THEODORE-3 SWAIN (William Theodore-3, John Abner-2, Jesse Abner-1)
- b. May 11, 1902 (STS); called "Bill" (NS);
- d. Nov. 4, 1928 (STS);
- m. Aug. 28, 1926 Opal O'Neal at Scotland, Arkansas (STS);
     she lives at Rt. 1, Box 86 Okemah, Oklahoma 74859 in 1986;
     she married Wallen Franks in 1970 (VAS).

"William 'Bill' Swain entered the U.S. Army shortly before the end of World War I as a very young man. With the intentions of making a career of military service as did an older brother, Tom, he had served a three year term of enlistment and had re-enlisted for a similar period when it was discovered that he had tuberculosis and was discharged because of physical disability.

On August 28, 1926 he was married to Opal O'Neal of Scotland, Arkansas and to this union one child, William O'Neal, was born.

The disease which Bill had contracted in military service took his life at the early age of 26 years. He was a Mason and a Christian.

Opal moved to Bowlegs, Oklahoma soon afterward to life near her parents and continued to live there for many years. In 1970 she was married to Reverend Wallen Franks, a Baptist minister, who retired in 1986 after 50 years of active ministry. The Franks currently reside at Rt. 1, Box 86, Okemah, Oklahoma." (VAS)

CHILDREN: (of William & Opal)

see
page
87 WILLIAM O'NEAL-4 SWAIN, b. May 22, 1928 (STS);
m. Dixie Yadon, Seminole, Oklahoma (VAS).

Photo of
Bill-3 Swain
taken about 1926
(original photo belongs to
Opal O'Neal Swain Franks)

****

Our

Fourth

Generation

see page 19

PEARL ANN-4 SUMMERS (Pearl Ann-4, Lou Etta-3,Celia Ann-2, Jesse Abner-1)
b. Oct. 31, 1899 at Scotland, Arkansas in Van Buren County (SOH);
d. April 1, 1980 at Yakima, Washington in Yakima County (SOH), she was buried at Terrace Heights Memorial Park in Yakima (SOH);
m. Aug. 5, 1922 Charlie W. Kincannon at Scotland, Arkansas in Van Buren County (SOH); he was born Jan. 30, 1904 at Scotland, Arkansas, and he died on May 7, 1978 at Yakima, Washington, he was the son of William Jackson Kincannon and Margaret Ann Campbell Comstock Kincannon (SOH).

CHILDREN:

see p.90
IRENE-5 KINCANNON, b. Feb. 11, 1923 at Scotland, Arkansas (SOH);
m. Sept. 4, 1943 William Campbell (SOH).

see p.91
ARNOLD-5 KINCANNON, b. March 19, 1924 at Scotland, Arkansas (SOH);
m. (1st) April 1942 Moatte Dodd (SOH);
m. (2nd) Sept. 1957 Pauline Oberlander (SOH);
m. (3rd) June 12, 1976 Joyce Barker Weston (SOH).

see p.92
REBA OVALENE "SISSY" -5 KINCANNON, b. March 26, 1925 at Scotland, AR (SOH);
m. March 26, 1946 Eugene Delbert Harris (SOH).

see p.93
CARLELL-5 KINCANNON, b. Nov. 8, 1928 at Scotland, Arkansas (SOH);
m. May 5, 1947 Mary Wales at Scotland, Arkansas, "divorced" (SOH).

see p.94
CARMEL E.-5 KINCANNON, b. April 30, 1932 at Scotland, Arkansas (SOH);
m. (1st) Oct. 8, 1947 Gerald Whorton (SOH);
m. (2nd) Jan. 14, 1971 James Trimm (SOH).

All information concerning this family marked with (SOH) has come from: Reba "Sissy" Ovalene Harris (Mrs. Gene Harris) of Route 2, Box 2073 Selah, Washington 98942.

****

THE KINCANNON'S
sitting:
Charlie & Pearl
50th Wedding Anniversary, August 5, 1972
Their Children:
{left to right}
Carmel, Arnold, Ovalene, Carl, Irene

see page 19

CHARLIE OWENS-4 SUMMERS (Charlie Owens-4, Lou Etta-3, Celia Ann-2, Jesse
Abner-1)
    b. Jan. 8, 1901 at Scotland, Arkansas in Van Buren County (SOH);
    d. Jan. 1962 in California (SOH);
    m. Icylona Bishop at Scotland, Arkansas in Van Buren County (SOH).
       She lived in California in 1984 (SOH).

CHILDREN:
GERALD-5 SUMMERS, b. at Scotland, Arkansas in Van Buren County (SOH).
LAUDINE-5 SUMMERS, b. at Scotland, Arkansas in Van Buren County (SOH).
LINDEN-5 SUMMERS, b._____ (SOH).
CAROL-5 SUMMERS, b._____ (SOH).
LYLE-5 SUMMERS, b._____ (SOH).
KYLE-5 SUMMERS, b._____ (SOH).

All information concerning this family marked with (SOH) has come from: Reba "Sissy
Ovalene Harris (Mrs. Gene Harris) of Route 2, Box 2073 Selah, Washington 98942.

****

see page 19

MELVIN RAY-4 SUMMERS, (Melvin Ray-4, Lou Etta-3, Celia Ann-2, Jesse Abner-1)
    b. Jan. 24, 1907 at Scotland, Arkansas (SOH);
    m. (1st) Aug. 1929 Vida Newton at Scotland, Arkansas the daughter of Jesse Logan
       Newton and Maggie Gertrude Miller; Vida died March 3, 1960 at Scio, Oregon (SOH).
    m. (2nd) Feb. 24, 1961 Mary Esterly Seadore; she was born April 8, 1918 (SOH).

    CHILDREN: (of Melvin and Vida)
    IMOGENE-5 SUMMERS, b. May 31, 1932 at Scotland, Arkansas (SOH).
      "single" (SOH)

    CAROLYN-5 SUMMERS, b. May 29, 1943 at Bend, Oregon (SOH);
      m. April 20, 1961 Glenn Clark at Lebanon, Oregon (SOH).

      CHILDREN: (of Carolyn and Glenn)
      JASON DEAN-6 CLARK, b. June 12, 1964 at Lebanon, Oregon (SOH).
      JERRED-6 CLARK, b. Feb. 5, 1970 at Lebanon, Oregon (SOH).

All information concerning this family marked with (SOH) has come from: Reba "Sissy" Ovalene Harris (Mrs. Gene Harris) of Route 2, Box 2073 Selah, Washington 98942.

****

see page 19

DESSA MAE-4 SUMMERS (Dessa Mae-4, Lou Etta-3, Celia Ann-2, Jesse Abner-1)
   b. March 28, 1909 at Scotland, Arkansas (SOH);
   m. Jan. 28, 1928 Larkin Osborne at Scotland, Arkansas (SOH), who died Aug. 29,1977, buried at Lane Memorial Garden, Eugene Oregon; Larkin is the son of John and Helah Osborne (SOH).

CHILDREN: (of Dessa Mae and Larkin)
ETTA MAE-5 OSBORNE, b. May 6, 1929 (SOH);
   m. Elmore McCaslin; "lives in Mapleton, Oregon " (SOH).

   CHILDREN: (of Etta Mae and Elmore)
   DIANA-6 McCASLIN, b. Aug. 15, 1950 (SOH);
     m. (1st) June 9, 1973 John Tack, now divorced (SOH);
     m. (2nd) Aug. 7, 1982 Marvin Huet (SOH).

     CHILDREN: (of Diana and Marvin)
     STEPHEN DOUGLAS-7 HUET, b. Dec. 9, 1985 (SOH).

see p.95 TILLMAN-5 OSBORNE, b. Aug. 30, 1930 (SOH);
   m. June 13, 1953 Ellen Louise Dujardin, "lived in Stanwood, Washington " (SOH).

RALPH-5 OSBORNE, b. Sept. 30, 1935 (SOH);
   m. (1st) Wanda Holman (SOH); they had 3 children (SOH);
   m. (2nd) Betty Childress (SOH); no children (SOH).

   CHILDREN: (of Ralph and Wanda)
   DWAYNE-6 OSBORNE, b._____ "lives in Roseburg, Oregon" (SOH);
     m. Joy _____ (SOH).

     CHILDREN: (of Dwayne and Joy)
     JAMIE DOYLE-7 OSBORNE, b._____ (SOH).
     SHAWN-7 OSBORNE, b._____ (SOH).

   MARK-6 OSBORNE, b._____ (SOH).

   WARREN-6 OSBORNE, b. _____(SOH).

All information concerning this family marked with (SOH) has come from: Reba "Sissy" Ovalene Harris (Mrs. Gene Harris) of Route 2, Box 2073 Selah, Washington 98942.

****

page 46

see page 19

DOVIE BELL-4 SUMMERS (Dovie Bell-4, Lou Etta-3, Celia Ann-2, Jesse Abner-1)
  b. March 29, 1913 at Scotland, Arkansas (SOH);
  d. Aug. 24, 1983 at Gilcrest, Oregon and was buried at Lapinem, Oregon (SOH);
  m. Aug. 29, 1929 Barney D. Newton at Scotland, Arkansas the son of Jesse Logan Newton
    and Maggie Gertrude Miller and grandson of Ephraniaus D. Newton (SOH). "Barney lived
    in Gilcrest, Oregon, 1985" (SOH).

CHILDREN:

see
p.96 VERNON-5 NEWTON, b. June 14, 1930 (SOH);
    m. Feb. 14, 1954 Joyce Glee Rogers; she was born June 16, 1935 (SOH).

see
p.97 WILLIAM JOE-5 NEWTON, b. Oct. 2, 1932 (SOH);
    m. May 10, 1953 Esther Eileen Day; she was born Dec. 31, 1934 (SOH).

see
p.98 RUTHA LaVERNE-5 NEWTON, b. July 18, 1934 (SOH);
    d. April 23, 1982 (SOH);
    m. March 27, 1953 Robert Clyde Messinger; he was born Feb. 19, 1930;
      he married Melany Hope Mork on April 22, 1984; she was born Nov. 6, 1943
      (SOH).

see
p.99 JAMES LEWIS-5 NEWTON, b. June 22, 1936 (SOH);
    m. June 20, 1959 Carol Iva Campbell; she was born June 18, 1940 (SOH).

see
p.100 LEE ROY-5 NEWTON, b. June 17, 1938 (SOH);
    m. (1st) June 27, 1958 Nellie Joann Spears; she was born June 6, 1940 (SOH).
    m. (2nd) Jan. 2, 1983 Sammy Mae Parker Grimmesey (SOH).

BOBBY D.-5 NEWTON, b. May 21, 1940 (SOH);
    m. Sept. 30, 1961 Hazel Viola Day; she was born Aug. 13, 1944 (SOH).

    CHILDREN: (of Bobby and Hazel)
    BOBBY D.-6 NEWTON, Jr., b. April 5, 1962 (SOH).
    TOBY LYNN-6 NEWTON, b. May 24, 1965 (SOH).
    GREGORY DEAN-6 NEWTON, b. June 30, 1968 (SOH).

JERRY DEAN-5 NEWTON, b. May 27, 1942 (SOH);
    d. Jan. 24, 1943 (SOH).

see
p.101 IRVEN GLYNN-5 NEWTON, b. Feb. 13, 1946 (SOH);
    m. May 21, 1966 Jackie Ruth Bullard; she was born June 27, 1946 (SOH).

LILLIAN LAVONNE-5 NEWTON, b. Feb. 16, 1951(SOH);
    m. Aug. 29, 1970 Terry Lee Jonte'; she was born Aug. 30, 1950 (SOH).

    CHILDREN: (of Lillian and Terry)
    EARL DERICE-6 JONTE', b. Nov. 16, 1971 (SOH).
    WINDY LEE-6 JONTE', b. July 5, 1978 (SOH).
    KLEET KELLY-6 JONTE', b. Aug. 30, 1980 (SOH).

All information concerning this family marked with (SOH) has come from: Reba "Sissy"
Ovalene Harris (Mrs. Gene Harris) of Route 2, Box 2073 Selah, Washington 98942.

page 47

see page 19

MINNIE-4 SUMMERS (Minnie-4, Lou Etta-3, Celia Ann-2, Jesse Abner-1)
b. Oct. 5, 1914 (twin) at Scotland, Arkansas (SOH);
m. Nov. 7, 1937 Edward "Ed" Singleton at Russellville, Arkansas; he was born Nov. 11, 1917 at Bandera, Texas, occupation in US Army, the son of B.F. Singleton and Eva Lee Clark (SOH). "Lived in Lawton, Oklahoma in 1986" (SOH).

CHILDREN: (of Minnie and Ed)
ETTA LEE-5 SINGLETON, b. Feb.1, 1939 at Bandera, Texas (SOH);
m. Feb. 17, 1956 Jo Gary Brooks at Lawton, Oklahoma (SOH).

> **CHILDREN:** (of Etta Lee and Jo Gary Brooks)
> GARY ALAN-6 BROOKS, b. July 25, 1957 at Fort Sill, Oklahoma (SOH);
> m. May 10, 1983 Pamela Sue Parker at Lawton, Oklahoma (SOH).

>> **CHILDREN:** (of Gary and Pamela)
>> MEGHAN LEE-7 BROOKS, b. Nov. 26, 1983 at Lawton, OK (SOH).

> STEVEN JAY-6 BROOKS, b. June 20, 1959 at Walnut Ridge, Arkansas (SOH);
> m. July 28, 1979 Tracy Kaspereit at Lawton, Oklahoma (SOH).

>> **CHILDREN:** (of Steven and Tracy)
>> SHON JOSEPH-7 BROOKS, b. Sept. 8, 1982 at Lawton, OK (SOH).
>> AMY MARIE-7 BROOKS, b. May 11, 1985 at Lawton, OK (SOH).

EMMA JEANNE-5 SINGLETON, b. Jan. 1, 1946 at Morrilton, Arkansas (SOH);
m. Feb. 22, 1969 Samuel Dearment at Lawton, Oklahoma (SOH).

> **CHILDREN:** (of Emma Jean and Samuel)
> STACEY LYNN-6 DEARMENT, b. Feb. 3, 1971 (SOH).
> BRADLEY ALAN-6 DEARMENT, b. July 17, 1976 at Fort Collins, CO (SOH).

All information concerning this family marked with (SOH) has come from: Reba "Sissy" Ovalene Harris (Mrs. Gene Harris) of Route 2, Box 2073 Selah, Washington 98942.

****

see page 23

page 48

MARY ELIZABETH-4 SWAIN, (Mary Elizabeth-4, Charles Dudley-3, William-2, Jessie-1)
   b. March 1, 1902 (NS);
   m. Nov. 29, 1920 Bill Wyrick (NS).

CHILDREN: (of Mary and Bill)
BILL-5 WYRICK, Jr., b. Aug. 29, 1922 (NS);
   m. Treasa Kranc (NS).

   CHILDREN: (of Bill and Treasa)
   JOHN MARVIN-6 WYRICK, b. Sept. 28, 1947 (NS);
     m. Davon Harris (NS).

     CHILDREN: (of John and Davon)
     JERRIED WAYNE-7 WYRICK, b. _____ (NS).
     ANDREW WILLIAMS-7 WYRICK, b. _____ (NS).

   PHILLIP CHARLES-6 WYRICK, b. 1950 (NS).
     m. Brenda Mahan (NS).

     CHILDREN: (of Phillip & Brenda)
     TREASA OLIVA-7 WYRICK, b. _____ (NS).
     NATALIE LOUISE-7 WYRICK, b. _____ (NS).

   GEORGE THOMAS-6 WYRICK, b. Aug. 1959 (NS),
     m. Lana Spellman (NS).

     CHILDREN: (of George & Lana)
     LEAH-7 WYRICK, b. _____ (NS).

****

see page 25

OTIS-4 HORN (Otis-4, Ruthie-3, William-2, Jesse-1)
   b. Aug. 17, 1910 (NS);
   m. Aug. 3, 1935 Bernice Cravens who was born Oct. 9, 1918 (NS).

CHILDREN: (of Otis & Bernice)
CAROLL DEAN-5 HORN, b. June 6, 1936 (NS);
   m. Jan. 4, 1958 Berdie Hendrix (NS).

   CHILDREN: (of Caroll & Berdie)
   DEBORAH LYNN-6 HORN, b. Dec. 19, 1958 (NS);
      m. Feb. 14, 1980 Martin Magana who was born May 17, 1961 (NS).

      CHILDREN: (of Deborah & Martin)
      RYAN MARTIN-7 MAGANA, b. Feb. 17, 1982 (NS).

   BEVERLY DAWN-6 HORN, b. July 12, 1960 (NS);
      m. July 31, 1981 Randal Weatherson (NS).

      CHILDREN: (of Beverly & Randal)
      MICHAEL BRENT-7 WEATHERSON, b. Nov. 8, 1982 (NS).

JOHN WESLEY-5 HORN, B. MARCH 28, 1938 (NS);
   m. June 20, 1959 Dorothy Souza who was born Sept. 29, 1936 (NS).

   CHILDREN: (of John & Dorothy)
   CHERYL ANN-6 HORN, b. June 13, 1961 (NS).
   BRYON OTIS-6 HORN, b. Dec. 25, 1963 (NS).

EUGENE-5 HORN, b. Dec. 5, 1939 (NS);
   m. Sept. 16, 1957 Margaret Idleman who was born May 20, 1938 (NS).

   CHILDREN: (of Eugene & Margaret)
   BARBARA-6 HORN, b. May 3, 1958 (NS);
      m. Oct. 13, 1979 Larry Stewart who was born Oct. 21, 1953 (NS).
   KENNETH EUGENE-6 HORN, b. May 25, 1963 (NS).

****

see page 25

ORIE ELIZABETH-4 HORN (Orie-4, Ruthie-3, William-2, Jessie-1)
b. Dec. 31, 1911 (NS);
m. Arch Varnill (NS).

CHILDREN: (of Orie & Arch)
<u>GLADYS LINDA-5 VARNILL</u>, b. July 21, 1937 (NS);
m. Jan. 22, 1957 Sam Newman (NS).

   CHILDREN: (of Gladys & Sam)
   CALVIN LEE-6 NEWMAN, b. July 8, 1957 (NS);
      m. Sept. 1976 Diane Lazaque (NS).

      CHILDREN: (of Calvin & Diane)
      HEATHER-7 NEWMAN, b. Sept. 2, 1977 (NS).
      NICHOLE-7 NEWMAN, b. Feb. 21, 1980 (NS).
      TIFFANY-7 NEWMAN, b. June 23, 1959 (NS).

   SANDRA KAY-6 NEWMAN, b. Aug. 22, 1959 (NS).

<u>JIMMY HAROLD-5 VARNILL</u>, b. Sept. 22, 1943 (NS);
   d. Jan. 21, 1983 (NS);
   m. Oct. 14, 1963 Ruby Rogers (NS).

   CHILDREN: (of Jimmy & Ruby)
   JIMMY HAROLD-6 VARNILL, Jr., b. Nov. 7, 1964 (NS).
   ARCHIE TERRY-6 VARNILL, b. Feb. 25, 1966 (NS).
   EARL WARREN-6 VARNILL, b. April 6, 1968 (NS).
   IRA WELSEY-6 VARNILL, b. March 7, 1970 (NS).
   CHRISTINE ELIZABETH-6 VARNILL, b. Aug. 6, 1972 (NS).

<u>BENNY CARROL-5 VARNILL</u>, b. March 11, 1946 (NS);
   m. March 6, 1964 Mary Rogers (NS).

   CHILDREN: (of Benny & Mary)
   SHERRY LYNN-6 VARNILL, b. Aug. 13, 1964 (NS).
   BENNY CARROL-6 VARNILL, JR., b. March 8, 1966 (NS).
   DONNA MARIE-6 VARNILL, b. Oct. 4, 1968 (NS).
   TERRESA ANN-6 VARNILL, b. July 11, 1970 (NS).
   STEVEN RAY-6 VARNILL, b. Sept. 2, 1972 (NS).

page 51

see page 25

GERTRUDE-4 HORN (Gertrude-4, Ruthie-3, William-2, Jessie-1)
   b. Dec. 9, 1913 (NS);
   m. March 4, 1933 Tom Sparkman who was born Jan. 3, 1908 (NS).

   CHILDREN: (of Gertrude & Tom)
   DON THOMAS-5 SPARKMAN, b. Feb. 23, 1934 (NS);
        m._____ (NS).

        CHILDREN: (of Don & _____)
        YOLANDE-6 SPARKMAN, b. Feb. 2, 1959 (NS).
          m. _____ Bradley (NS).
        PERRY LEON-6 SPARKMAN, b. May 6, 1960 (NS).

   DOY COLEMAN-5 SPARKMAN, b. June 15, 1936 (NS);
        m. _____ (NS).

        CHILDREN: (of Doy & _____)
        SHEILA DENISE-6 SPARKMAN, b. March 2, 1961 (NS).
          m. _____ Parker (NS).

             CHILDREN: (of Sheila & _____)
             CHENOA JESSICA-7 PARKER, b. Feb. 25, 1978 (NS).
             MARY KATHERINE-7 PARKER, b. April 4, 1981 (NS).

        SABRA DANHAE-6 SPARKMAN, b. Sept. 27, 1964 (NS).
          m. _____ Ford (NS).

   IMMA DELL-5 SPARKMAN, b. Oct. 24, 1939 (NS);
        m. _____ May (NS).

        CHILDREN: (of Imma & _____)
        BRIAN THOMAS-6 MAY, b. June 12, 1959 (NS).
        TRESSIA MYRA-6 MAY, b. April 14, 1961 (NS);
          m. _____ Grant (NS).

   DOLORES IDA RUTH-5 SPARKMAN, b. Jan. 9, 1948 (NS);
        m. _____ Macuse (NS).

        CHILDREN: (of Dolores & ____)
        MARINA EVONNE OLIVAS-6 MACUSE, b. (NS).

   DEBRA ONITA-5 SPARKMAN, b. April 29, 1954 (NS);
        m. _____ Matthews (NS).

        CHILDREN: (of Debra & _____)
        MISTY ANN DAWN LANDEROS-6 MATTHEWS, b. Nov. 3, 1974 (NS).
        JEREMY THOMAS-6 MATTHEWS, b. March 13, 1979 (NS).

****

page 52

see page 27

PAULINE-4 SWAIM (Pauline-4, William Jess-3, William-2, Jessie-1)
b. April 6, 1922 (NS);
m. Oct. 30, 1945 Norman Greenfield, he was born Sept. 16, 1923 (NS).

CHILDREN: (of Pauline and Norman)
CHARLES LaWAYNE-5 GREENFIELD, b. Oct. 4, 1948 (NS);
m. Dec. 30, 1966 Joy Elaine Montgomery (NS).

    CHILDREN: (of Charles and Joy)
    KELLY ANN-6 GREENFIELD, b. Aug. 12, 1968 (NS).
    JERRY LaWAYNE-6 GREENFIELD, b. Aug. 21, 1969 (NS).
    JACKIE FLOYD-6 GREENFIELD, b. Nov. 14, 1972 (NS).

GARY LEE-5 GREENFIELD, b. Feb. 13, 1951 (NS);
m. (1st) May 22, 1972 Karla Durham (NS).
m. (2nd) Oct. 30, 1977 Janet Burrows (NS).

    CHILDREN: (of Gary and Karla)
    MICHAEL LEE-6 GREENFIELD, b. Feb. 15, 1973 (NS).

    CHILDREN: (of Gary and Janet)
    JIRE-6 GREENFIELD, b. June 22, 1979 (NS).
    JOY-6 GREENFIELD, b. March 17, 1981 (NS).
    GARY LEE-6 GREENFIELD, JR., b. Dec. 18, 1982 (NS).

LINDA JOYCE-5 GREENFIELD, b. Dec. 19, 1952 (NS);
m. Dec. 19, 1970 Randall Wayne Cherry (NS).

    CHILDREN: (of Linda and Randall)
    TRACY DON-6 CHERRY, b. Sept. 9, 1972 (NS).

JIMMY LYNN-5 GREENFIELD, b. Oct. 1, 1955 (NS);
m. Dec. 20, 1975 Mary Margaret Weldon (NS).

    CHILDREN: (of Jimmy and Mary)
    JEREMY-6 GREENFIELD, b. Jan. 21, 1977 (NS).
    JESSIE-6 GREENFIELD, b. May 30, 1980 (NS).

TOMMY DON-5 GREENFIELD, b.Feb. 17, 1956 (NS);
m. Dec. 18, 1976 Vickey Stapleton (NS).

    CHILDREN: (of Tommy and Vickey)
    QUINCY JON-6 GREENFIELD, b. May 3, 1979 (NS).

DEBARAH KAYE-5 GREENFIELD, b. Sept. 17, 1959 (NS);
m. April 8, 1978 Rickey Dale Palmutree (NS).

    CHILDREN: (of Debarah and Rickey)
    NATHAN DALE-6 PALMUTREE, b. Jan. 29, 1979 (NS).

****

see page 27

IRENE-4 SWAIM (Irene-4, William-3, William-2, Jessie-1)
  b. Sept. 25, 1923 (NS);
  m. Nov. 25, 1942 Glen Chambers (NS).

  CHILDREN: (of Irene and Glen)
  PHYLLIS-5 CHAMBERS, b. June 12, 1944 (NS);
    m. Harper Fredrick (NS).

    CHILDREN: (of Phyllis and Harper)
    MELODY IRENE-6 FREDRICK, b._____ (NS).

  ROBERT-5 CHAMBERS, b. April 6, 1946 (NS);
    m. Connie Reed (NS).

    CHILDREN: (of Robert and Connie)
    KIMBERLY ANN-6 CHAMBERS, b._____ (NS).

  RONALD-5 CHAMBERS, b. June 5, 1948 (NS);
    m. (1st) Sharon Coffman (NS).
    m. (2nd) Sharon Schlinker (NS);
    m. (3rd) Roberta _____ (NS).

    CHILDREN: (of Ronald and Sharon C)
    SONGA KAYE-6 CHAMBERS, (NS).
    ALLEN DEWAYNE-6 CHAMBERS, (NS).

    CHILDREN: (of Ronald and Sharon S.)
    KEVIN RAY-6 CHAMBERS, (NS).

    CHILDREN: (of Ronald and Roberta)
    BRIDGET-6 CHAMBERS, (NS).

  LARRY-5 CHAMBERS, b. June 5, 1950 (NS).
    m. (1st) Dorothy Harper (NS).
    m. (2nd)Betty Carpenter (NS).

    CHILDREN: (of Larry and Dorothy)
    LARRY-6 CHAMBERS, Jr. (NS).

  STEVEN-5 CHAMBERS, b. June 1952 (NS);
    m. (1st) Alice Scantling (NS);
    m. (2nd) Roberta Dragoo (NS);
    m. (3rd) Debra Cole (NS).

    CHILDREN: (of Steven and Alice)
    CHAD ALLEN-6 CHAMBERS, (NS).

    CHILDREN: (of Steven and Roberta)
    KARLA JEAN-6 CHAMBERS, (NS).

    CHILDREN: (of Steven and Debra)
    JOHNATHAN GLEN-6 CHAMBERS, (NS).

  SHARON-5 CHAMBERS, b. Nov. 6, 1955 (NS);
    m. Clifford Lambert (NS).

this family continued on next page...

CHILDREN: (of Sharon and Clifford)
CHEYANNE ERIN-6 LAMBERT, (NS).

KEITH-5 CHAMBERS, b. Feb. 12, 1956 (NS);
m. Brenda Rice (NS).

CHILDREN: (of Keith and Brenda)
ALISHA DAWN-6 CHAMBERS, (NS).
JASON KEITH-6 CHAMBERS, (NS).

JOHN-5 CHAMBERS, b. Nov. 12, 1958 (NS);
m. Darlene Wilson (NS).

CHILDREN: (of John and Darlene)
ROBERT HEATH-6 CHAMBERS, (NS).

****

see page 27

WILLIAM JOHN "Billy"-4 SWAIM (William-4, William Jess-3, William-2, Jessie-1)
    b.Aug. 1, 1925 (NS);
    m. Sept. 1943 Audrey Hill, she was born Nov. 11, 1923 (NS).

    CHILDREN: (of Billy and Audrey)
    ANGELA-5 SWAIM, b. Aug. 1, 1925 (NS);
        m. Melvin Walker (NS).

        CHILDREN: (of Angela and Melvin)
        WADE-6 WALKER (NS).

    BILLY RAY-5 SWAIM, b. Jan. 22, 1952 (NS);
        m. June Terry (NS).

        CHILDREN: (of Billy and June)
        CODA-6 SWAIM, (NS).

    LYNN-5 SWAIM, b. Sept. 21, 1954 (NS);
        m. Roberta Szarmack (NS).

        CHILDREN: (of Lynn and Roberta)
        BOBBIE-6 SWAIM, (NS).

****

page 56

see page 27

OZELL-4 SWAIM (Ozell-4, William Jess-3, William-2, Jessie-1)
b. Jan. 23, 1933 (NS);
m. Nov. 18, 1948 Joe Apple (NS).

CHILDREN: (of Ozell and Joe)
JOHNNY DEWAYNE-5 APPLE, b. July 1950 (NS);
m. Dec. 7, 1968 Ruth Calhoun (NS).

CHILDREN: (of Johnny and Ruth)
SHERRI-6 APPLE, b. _____ (NS).
SHEILA-6 APPLE, b. _____ (NS).

MICHAEL-5 APPLE, b. Jan. 24, 1954 (NS);
m. (1st) March 17, 1973 Delores Roper (NS);
m. (2nd) Kathy Bowder (NS).

CHILDREN: (of Michael and Delores)
JENNIFER-6 APPLE, b. _____ (NS).
KERRY-6 APPLE, b. _____ (NS).

CHILDREN: (of Michael and Kathy)
JORDON-6 APPLE, b. _____ (NS).

MARCIA DARLENE-5 APPLE, b. March 13, 1956 (NS);
m. Nov. 11, 1944 Dan Terry (NS).

CHILDREN: (of Marcia and Dan)
CASE-6 TERRY, b. _____(NS).

RENEE-5 APPLE, b. May 24, 1957 (NS);
m. April 1, 1977 Richard Morris (NS).

CHILDREN: (of Renee and Richard)
AMANDA-6 MORRIS, b. _____ (NS).

LONNIE JOE-5 APPLE, b. June 5, 1958 (NS).
m. Sept. 15, 1980 Anita Talley (NS).

CHILDREN: (Of Lonnie and Anita)
JESSE JOE-6 APPLE, b. _____ (NS).

****

see page 28

VIRGIL-4 SWAIN (Virgil-4,Joseph Oscar-3,John Abner-2, Jesse Abner-1)
    b. Oct. 22, 1906 (from headstone at cemetary);
    d. June 3, 1972 buried at Pleasant Grove Cemetery near Scotland, AR (JD);
    m.(1st) Lela Guinn (STS); she is buried in Michigan (JD).
    m.(2nd)Mable Lefler (STS).

    CHILDREN: (of Virgil and Lela)
see <u>BILLIE JOE-5 SWAIN</u>, b. Dec. 19, 1933 (JD); resides in Wascom, Texas (JD);
102   d. Dec. 17, 1985, buried in Texas (JD)
       m. (1st)_____Beavers (JD); now divorced (JD);
       m. (2nd) Joyce _____ (JD).

    PAULINE-5 SWAIN, b. _____ (STS)

Left to right:
Virgil, Pauline, Mable
taken about 1961

Left to right:
Virgil, Billy Joe, Lela

see page 28

FAYE-4 SWAIN (Faye-4, Joseph Oscar-3, John Abner-2, Jesse Abner-1)
    b. Sept. 4, 1910 (JD); resides at Scotland, AR (JD);
    m. Ellis Ward (STS); he was born Aug. 5, 1910 and died Sept. 3, 1968 ; he is buried at St.
      Mary's Cemetery at Mt. Vernon, Arkansas (JD).

CHILDREN:
see <u>JIMMY-5 WARD</u>, b. Oct. 16, 1935 (JD); resides in Deering, MO 1985 (JD);
page   m. Betsy Lindsey (JD).
103
see <u>BONNIE-5 WARD</u>, b. Feb. 7, 1937 (JD); resides in Conway, Arkansas (JD);
page   m. E.J. Stracner (JD). spelled "Stracner" not "Strocener" (JD).
104
see <u>GLORIA JEAN-5 WARD</u>, b. Sept. 30, 1946 (JD); reside at Scotland, AR (JD);
page   m. Bobby Love (JD).
105

    "Just south of Scotland and East of U.S. Highway 95 and located among many beautiful shade trees is one of the best cared for rural cemeteries, perhaps, in Arkansas. From its meticulous and well-groomed appearance, one would guess that a couple of men would be involved on a full-time basis in keeping up its good appearance. Happen up around 7:30 a.m. many mornings however, and one would learn differently. Another driver would appear with the trunk of the car opened and with the handles of a wheel-barrow or lawnmower protruding.

    The driver and only care-taker would be none other than Faye Ward of Scotland who has cared for the cemetery a number of years because she says there just is no one elso who will undertake the by no means small task. While this, no doubt, is true, folks more near to the situation state that the long and ardous work Faye spends there is out of the great love she possesses for those kin and neighbors who have gone on to their final resting place.

    Faye's love and concern for those of her community does not end here. Someone dropping by her well-kept home and large lawn might well find her in one of four gardens she tends and where she might be picking a mess of peas for a neighbor whom Faye explains, 'Didn't make any in her garden this year.'

    She has also served as Treasurer of the Pleasant Grove Cemetery for the past 19 years, keeping records on all income and expenses incurred annually, and for a number of years with Faye stating emphatically, 'This is going to be my last year.'

    In her younger years, Faye attended what was then Arkansas State Teacher's College in Conway and taught school for 8 years. She also operated a grocery store at Bragg City, MO and Cleveland, AR for 23 years.

    Faye is a long-time member of the Eastern Star." (VAS)

**Faye Ward
made in 1959**

From left to right:
Faye in her earlier years with her brother, **Dale**,
her mother **Mrs. Gertie Swain**,
and brother **Virgil**.

Faye at the center with grandaughters **Kim** and **Amy** in the front,
their mother **Gloria** at the back, extreme left,
grandaughters **Kathy** and **Sonja** at left and right of their mother, **Bonnie**.

****

see page 28

RAY THOMAS-4 SWAIN (Ray Thomas-4, Joseph Oscar-3, John Abner-2, Jesse Abner-1)
b. Sept. 26, 1915 (from headstone at cemetery)
d. July 31, 1954 buried at Pleasant Grove Cemetery near Scotland, Arkansas (JD);
m. Dorothy Dunsworth (STS). She was born Oct. 26, 1916 at Scotland, AR and now resides
at Oppelo, Arkansas next to her son, Ronnie.

CHILDREN: (of Ray and Dorothy)
PATSY-5 SWAIN, b. 1934 (JD); resides at Glenwood, Arkansas (JD);
m. Pete James (JD).

Ray Thomas Swain

CHILDREN: (of Patsy and Pete)
MICHAEL-6 JAMES, b._____(JD).
PETE-6 JAMES, b._____(JD).
PERRY-6 JAMES, b._____(JD).
DEBBIE-6 JAMES, b._____ (JD).
DONNA-6 JAMES, b._____(JD).

CAROLYN SUE-5 SWAIN, b._____(JD); resides in Danville, Arkansas (JD);
m. Jerome Williams (JD).

CHILDREN: (of Carolyn and _____Williams)
KELVIN-6 WILLIAMS, b._____(JD); resides in Ohio (JD).
KAREN-6 WILLIAMS, b._____(JD).
KIMBERLY-6 WILLIAMS, b._____(JD); m. Gary Brookshear (VAS); they have a
daughter born in 1986 named KAYLA-7 BROOKSHEAR (VAS).

see
page
106 JERRY RAY-5 SWAIN, b. MAY 12, 1939 (VAS); lives at 801 W. Childress, Morrilton, AR.
m. Dec. 27, 1957 Louise Petty, by Rev. C.M. Lewallen
(from Conway County Book 194)

see
page
118 RONNIE JOE-5 SWAIN, b._____(STS); lives at Oppelo, AR.
m. Joan Vinson (JD).

see
page
119 DON HENRY-5 SWAIN, b. Nov. 10, 1948 (SSD Conway Co., Book 5, pg. 454);
m. Jan. 31, 1970 Brenda Marie McArthur of Perry County, Arkansas by Lawrence Maus
(from Conway Co., Book 43). They reside in Oppelo, AR 1985 (JD).

SHARON KAY-5 SWAIN, b._____(STS);
m. Kenny Vinson (JD).
"Sharon, the 6th and last child of Ray and Dorothy Swain is married to Kenny Vinson,
brother of Joann (Mrs. Ronnie Swain) and the couple lives in Ocean Springs, Mississippi.
They have two children, Tammie and Shane." (VAS)

CHILDREN: (of Sharon and Kenny)
TAMIE-6 VINSON, b._____(JD).
SHANE-6 VINSON, b._____(JD).

Donnie, Jerry & Ronnie Swain

Dorothy Swain

****

see page 28

DALE-4 SWAIN (Dale-4, Joseph Oscar-3, John Abner-2, Jesse Abner-1)
    b. July 25, 1925 (JD); middle name is "Draper" (NS); resides in Morrilton, AR (JD);
    m. Mildred Stracner (STS) on Feb. 13, 1943 by Andrew E. Newcomer, Jr.
        (from Conway Co., Book 33, page 596).

"Dale D. Swain was reared in the Gravel Hill Community near Scotland, Arkansas and he graduated from high school in the latter community in 1943. Shortly thereafter he went to work for Community Ice Co. in Morrilton, Arkansas where he was employed for a year as Chief Engineer in charge of ice manufacturing and equipment maintenance.
    From 1944 until 1950 he worked in the same city for Kordsmier Furniture Co. as a salesman and from 1950 until 1952 with Mitchell & Co. in a similar capacity.
    Capitalizing on his sales experience Dale began a sales career in the insurance industry that was to span an overall period of 20 years.
    From 1952 through 1960, he sold life insurance to army personel at military bases located in Oklahoma, and from 1960 through 1965, he changed to the selling of automobile insurance to military personnel covering a territory of six southern states.
    In 1960, Dale and his wife, Mildred, who had also traveled and assisted him extensively in out-of-state sales trips over the years, opened Swain Furniture and Appliance Co. on East Broadway in Morrilton, where they were quite successful in featuring and selling a high-quality line of merchandise.
    While in the furniture business Dale attended Reich School of Auctioneering in Mason City, Iowa and graduated as a licensed and certified auctioneer. Later at home in Arkansas, he conducted a goodly number of auction sales.
    He was approved by the State of Kentucky as a Kentucky Colonel and this honor was bestowed upon him in 1968.
    In 1969, ill health was responsible for the sale of the thriving furniture business and Dale returned to his former career of automobile insurance sales to military personnel. In 1974 he was again forced to retire due to disability.
    Dale and Mildred have been members of the Downtown Church of Christ in Morrilton for the past 40 years, and are members of the AARP" (VAS).

      CHILDREN: (of Dale and Mildred)
see <u>ALMA SUE-5 SWAIN</u>,
page   b.Feb. 29, 1944 resides in Midwest City, Oklahoma (JD);
107   m. Gary Stroud, of Scotland, Arkansas (JD).

DALE

MILDRED

****

see page 31

GLADYS HETTY-4 SWAIN (Gladys Hetty-4, Jesse Abner-3, John Abner-2, Jesse Abner-1)
    b. Dec. 15, 1907 at Cleveland, Arkansas (GR);
    m. August, 1922 Floice Orville Rhoades; he was born Jan. 14, 1905 (GR).

CHILDREN: (of Gladys and Floice)
NOVEL EARNEST-5 RHOADES, b. Oct. 7, 1924 (GR);
    d. Nov. 24, 1943, killed at sea, member of U.S. Navy on U.S.S. Liscome Bay (GR).

NORVIN DALE-5 RHOADES, b. Dec. 28, 1926 at Scotland, Arkansas (GR);
    m. Nov. 18, 1948 Kathryn Berven (GR).
        "Norvin was reared in the Gravel Hill community near Scotland where he graduated
from high school in 1947. While in his high school years, he was an outstanding basketball
player, and in his senior year he was named both to the All-District and All-State teams as
forward.
        Following graduation he lived in the state of California for a number of years and did
ranch-type work. Returning to the Gravel Hill community in the 70's, he owned and
operated a grocery store. Norvin in retired but is an acitve member of the Scotland
Volunteer Fire Dept., now serving as Chairman of the Dept., and as Chief of
Communications.
        He is a veteran of WW II." (VAS)

CURTIS ALVIN-5 RHOADES, b. Dec. 26, 1928 at Scotland, Arkansas (GR);
    d. Jan. 10, 1929 at Scotland (GR).

J.W.-5 RHOADES, b. Jan. 29, 1930 at Scotland, Arkansas (GR);
    d. April 18, 1946 at Scotland (GR).

JEANETTA-5 RHOADES, b. Nov. 24, 1933 at Scotland, Arkansas (GR);
    m. Dec. 11, 1952 Clarence L. Gonzales.

    CHILDREN: (of Jeanette and Clarence)
    TERRI LEE-6 GONZALES, b. Nov. 20, 1953 at Limestone, Maine (GR).
    BOBBY DALE-6 GONZALES, b. July 10, 1960 at Altus, Oklahoma (GR).

"Gladys grew up in the Gravel Hill Community near Scotland, Arkansas and attended the
public schools there. As a young girl she was especially interested in gospel music and attended
singing schools at every opportunity. Her love of music has continued to this date, and for a long
time she has sung in church choirs and gave special songs at worship and funerals.
        Pictured on the next page with her husband, Floice, now deceased, the couple had five
children. The eldest, Novel, lost his life during WW II as a member of the U.S. Navy when the
U.S.S. Liscome Bay, an aircraft carrier, was making its maiden voyage in the Pacific and was
bombed by the Japanese.
        On May 21, 1986, a Blue Star Memorial, erected to the memory of Van Buren County
servicemen who lost their lives during WW II, was dedicated at its new location on U.S. Highway
65 near Clinton, Arkansas. Gladys received special recongition as being the only Blue Star mother
yet residing in the Van Buren County area by U.S. Senator Dale Bumpers who spoke at the
dedication. She was called upon to place a wreath at the site of the memorial.
        Today Gladys enjoys relatively good health and gives of her time unselfishly to her family, to
the local church, and to the Ladies Auxilary of the Scotland Volunteer Dept. particularily in fund
raising events." (VAS)

Floice & Gladys Rhoades

see page 31

page 64

THOMAS EDISON-4 SWAIN (Thomas Elmore-4, Jesse Abner-3, John Abner-2, Jesse Abner-1)
b. July 8, 1921 at Cleveland, Arkansas (GR);
m. Jan. 16, 1951 Alma J. Hardin of Durant, Oklahoma (GR).

CHILDREN: (of Thomas and Alma)
SHIRLEY-5 SWAIN, b. Oct. 12, 1951 at Dennison, Texas (GR).

"Thomas 'Tommy' Swain was reared in the Gravel Hill community near Scotland, Arkansas where he graduated from high school.
At the onset of WW II Tommy volunteered for service in the U.S. Army. In his earlier army years he received training and was classified a Cook. Tommy rose to the rank of Staff Sargeant with most of his military career being spent as a Mess Sargeant in charge of food procurement, menu planning and preparations, and with kitchen personnel working under his supervision.
Retiring in 1964, Tommy returned to the Gravel Hill community where he yet resides with his sister, Gladys, and where he spends much of his time raising beef cattle.
He continues to give of his time and energies freely to neighbors who seek out his help irrespective of the kind of need, and he serves as Ass't Chief and Finance Commissioner in the Scotland Volunteer Fire Dept.
Tommy is an active member of the Scotland Masonic Lodge, and like his father has held varied stations in this benevolent organization." (VAS)

Tommy Swain with his dog, Tip

see page 32

HERVEY-4 SWAIN (Hervey-4, Thomas Elmore-3, John Abner-2, Jesse Abner-1)
  b. Feb. 22, 1904 at Cleveland, Arkansas (HV);
  m. July 3, 1928 Marguerite Haguewood (HV); they live at 1756 Flower St., Escondido,
    California 92027 in 1986 (VAS).

CHILDREN: (of Hervey and Marguerite)
<u>JEAN LEE-5 SWAIN</u>, b. Nov. 1, 1932 (HV);
  m. September, 1968 ? Warren Samuel (HV).

  CHILDREN: (of Jean and Warren)
  EVAN-6 SAMUEL, b. Jan. 25, 1972 (HV).

<u>LINDA SUE-5 SWAIN</u>, b. Aug. 19, 1940 (HV);
  m. (1st) J. Acock (HV);
  m. (2nd) James Lynch (HV).

  CHILDREN: (of J. and Linda Sue)
  TRACY LEE-6 ACOCK, b. May 5, 1962 (HV);
    m. Guy Van Roekel (VAS).
  JENNIFER ANN-6 ACOCK, b. Nov. 15, 1967 (HV).

HERBERT E. SWAIN
RETIRED

'The military career and assignment to various Army bases of his father led to Harvey Swain's attendance in different schools and to his graduation from high school where his father was then stationed at Del Rio, Texas.
  As a teen-ager Hervey worked summer months at military bases for the U.S. Government and upon entering full-time employment, he spent 35 years - 19 for the Army, 10 years with the U.S. Navy Dept. at Long Beach Navel Shipyard, and 6 years in Guam, repairing damages to the nearby base incurred there during World War II - before retiring at age 55 years.
  After 6 months in retirement which Hervey found to be somewhat boring, he joined Douglas Aircraft at Long Beach, California as an Automatic Fueling Facilities Inspector of DC-8 jets emerging from the assembly line. Nine years were to follow in this endeavor, years Hervey describes as the most exciting ones of his life. Acquaintances developing out of a close work relationship were crew chiefs and test pilots led to numerous invitations to accompany them on test flights which were as he describes 'to say the least, hair raising experiences but loving every moment of each flight.' Longer working hours than desired prompted a second retirement at age 65.
  Now at the age of 82 years Hervey and his wife, the former Marguerite Haguewood of Ft. Leavenworth, Kansas and whom Hervey describes as 'his bride of 58 years and his severist critic' live in pleasant year-round weather conditions and in a comfrotable home at 1756 Flower St., Escondido, California 92027.
  As this book goes to press, despite some health problems not at all uncommon to those of his years, Hervey and Marguerite are seriously considering a trip back to Arkansas, Missouri and Kansas for the purpose of renewing acquaintances with friends and visiting with relatives.
  They have 2 daughters, Jean Lee and Linda Sue."
(VAS)

Hervey & Marguerite & Lynda Swain

****

see page 32

HAZEL ALFA-4 SWAIN (Hazel-4,Thomas Elmore-3, John Abner, Jesse Abner-1)
   b. Sept. 30, 1908 at Leavenworth, Kansas (HV);
      lives at Lee's Summit, MO.
   m. Dec. 25, 1931 Richard A.Veatch at Leavenworth, Kansas (HV).

"Hazel Swain Veatch was born in Leavenworth, Kansas. With her father being in the Army, she attended several schools in Del Rio, Texas, San Antonio, Texas, Ft. Sill, Oklahoma and Leavenworth, Kansas, where she went to Leavenworth High School, and also graduated from there and was a sponsor for Co. B. in R.O.T.C. She also attended another year there taking a business course. She worked in the Q.M. office at Fort Leavenworth, also in the Post Exchange, and at the C.M.T.C. Camp there. She was married to Richard Veatch in the Post Chapel in 1931. Hobbies - Bridge and fishing." (HV)

"Richard Veatch was born in Waldron, Mo. and lived in Weston, Mo. while a small boy and then in Leavenworth, Kansas. He was a very outgoing person, President of his High School Class for 3 years, won letters in football, basketball and track. He also attended Kansas University at Lawrence, Kansas, and was a member of Delta Tau Delta Fraternity.

He was married to Hazel Swain in the Post Chapel at Fort Leavenworth, Kansas in 1931. He traveled for many years for Liggett & Myers Tobacco Company, and he and his wife lived in Topeka, Kansas, St. Louis, Mo., Tulsa, Oklahoma, Cincinnati, Ohio and Prairie Village, Kansas. While in Cincinnati, he and his wife belonged to the University Club there, and he also was an Honorary Kentucky Colonel. He and his wife were Charter members of the Sertoma Club in Prairie Village. His hobbies are golf and fishing." (HV)

CHILDREN:
BETTY LOU-5 VEATCH, b. March 25, 1933 at Topeka, Kansas (HV).
   m. Dec. 6, 1957 Elmer Lee Anderson, Jr.; he was born March 5, 1930 in Springfield, Mo.

" Betty Lou Veatch Anderson was born in Topeka, Kansas. As her father traveled for a large company, she moved a great deal as a child, first entering school in Tulsa, Oklahoma, later moving to Kansas City, Missouri where she graduated from J.C. Nichols Grade School and Southwest High School in 1951. In the fall of 1951 she came to Springfield, Mo. to attend Drury College. After attending college for two years she left school to work. She was a legal secretary for many years, and later worked for Continental Insurance Co. for some 17 years, choosing to retire in 1980.

Elmer Lee Anderson Jr. was born March 5, 1930 in Springfield, Mo. to Elmer Lee Anderson and Ethel Simmons Anderson. He has one brother, James Simmons Anderson born in January of 1933. His father was a 1918 graduate of Missouri University School of Engineering. He served in World War I, and participated in the original geodectic survey of the State of Montana and then started a lifelong career with The St. Louis San Francisco Railway Co. (now Burlington Northern) retiring at age 70 in 1957. Shortly there after he was appointed to the City Council of Springfield, subsequently running for office and served on the council for 11 years, 9 years of which he served as Mayor of Springfield, Mo. Ethel Simmons Anderson was born and raised near Buffalo Mo. and in her youth was a "Harvey Girl" working in the Fred Harvey Restaurant here in Springfield before marrying his father. Elmer Lee Anderson passed away December 23, 1977 and Ethel Simmons Anderson died December 19, 1984.

Elmer attended school in Springfield graduating from Greenwood High School and later graduating from Southwest Missouri State University in 1958 with military service in the Air Force during Korea and honorably discharged in Nov. 1954. After graduation Elmer worked for a short time as a commercial photographer, and then went to work for Mellers Photo Labs, Inc. and is presently serving in the capacity of Exec. V.P. with the firm."
(from Betty Lou Veatch Anderson, Feb. 13, 1986 in letter to Robert O. Crossman)

****

page 67

left to right
Hazel (Swain) Veatch
Hervey Swain
and their mother,
Elisa (Meeler) Swain

Richard Veatch

left to right
Elvia Swain
Betty Lou Veatch (age 7, with her grandparents)
Thomas E. Swain
taken in 1940 at the National Cemetary in Baton Rouge, Louisian

Betty & Elmer Anderson
May, 1963

Hazel Swain Veatch, Elizabeth Swain,
and Richard Veatch

page 68

see page 33 & 34

EUEL N.-4 DUNSWORTH (Euel N.-4, Minnie-3, John Abner-2, Jesse Abner-1)
  b. Nov. 16, 1909 (JD);
  d. Jan. 1981 buried at Pleasant Grove Cemetery at Scotland, Arkansas (JD);
  m. Wade Hiland, and resides in Cleveland, Ohio 1985 (JD).

CHILDREN: (of Euel and Wade)
MARY JANE-5 DUNSWORTH, b. Oct. 20, 1938 (JD);
     resides in St. Petersburg, Florida 1985 (JD);
  m. Jimmy Loftis, now divorced (JD).

   CHILDREN: (of Mary Jane and Jimmy)
     JIMMY-6 LOFTIS, b. twin, resides in St. Petersburg, Florida 1985 (JD).
     GEORGE-6 LOFTIS, b. twin, resides in St. Petersburg, Florida 1985 (JD).

JEAN-5 DUNSWORTH, b. Dec. 1940 (JD); resides in Middlefall, Ohio (JD);
  m. Bob Shumate (JD).

****

see page 33 & 34

BRANNON-4 DUNSWORTH (Brannon-4, Minnie-3, John Abner-2, Jesse Abner-1)
  b. June 7, 1912 (JD); resides in Scotland, AR (JD);
  m. Winnie Underwood (STS).

CHILDREN: (of Brannon and Winnie)
BENNIE LOU-5 DUNSWORTH, b.Oct. 28, 1934 (JD); resides in Morenci, Arizona (JD);
  m. Alvin Hamilton (JD).
    Bennie is a music teacher on an Indian Reservation.

  CHILDREN: (of Bennie Lou and Alvin)
  ALVIN-6 HAMILTON, Jr., b._____ (JD). Alvin is an electrical engineer.
  JAMES-6 HAMILTON, b._____(JD).

"Brannon grew up in Scotland, Arkansas where he married Winnie Underwood of the same community.
    The couple moved to Arizona during the depression era and where they lived for 30 years. Brannon worked in a copper mine before a crippling injury to a hand and arm forced him to seek other type of employment. For a period of 10 years he worked at general maintanance in the school system where they resided and worked at a service station for 16 years.
    Their daughter, Bennie Lou is a music teacher at Morenci, Arizona, and their grandson, Alvin Jr. is a graduate electrical engineer.
    Brannon and Winnie, now back in their native community of Scotland, have celebrated a 50th wedding anniversary, and being the happy couple they are, our guess is they would opt for another half century of togetherness.
    They spend much of their time caring for Brannon's 97 year old mother, Minnie, who lives next door." (VAS)

Pictured from left to right: [taken July 2, 1977]
Brannon, Alvin Jr., Winnie, James, Bennie Lou, Alvin Sr.

see page 33 & 34

JERRELL-4 DUNSWORTH (Jerrell-4, Minnie-3, John Abner-2, Jesse Abner-1)
b. Oct. 13, 1914 (JD); resides at N. Hollywood, California, 1985 (JD);
m. Geneva Hall (STS) (JD).

CHILDREN: (of Jerrell and Geneva)
LINDA-5 DUNSWORTH, b. March 2, 1938 (JD);
m. Gary Edwards (JD).

TOMMY-5 DUNSWORTH, b. Dec. 27, 1942 (JD);
m. Jeanne _____ (JD).

CHILDREN: (of Tommy and Jeanne)
GREGORY-6 DUNSWORTH, b._____ (JD).

JERRY-5 DUNSWORTH, b. Aug. 5, 1944 (JD);
m. Charmaine _____ (JD).

CHILDREN: (of Jerry and Charmaine)
BRANDON-6 DUNSWORTH, b. Nov. 16, 1985 (JD).

DANNY-5 DUNSWORTH, b. Oct. 20, 1946 (JD);
m. Mary _____ (JD).

KAREN-5 DUNSWORTH, b. June 20, 1950 (JD);
m. Dave Tunic (JD).

CHILDREN: (of Karen and Dave)
DON-6 TUNIC, b._____(JD).
CHRISTI-6 TUNIC, b._____(JD).
ROBERT-6 TUNIC, b._____ (JD).

**Jerrell, Geneva, Danny &
Carolyn Dunsworth**

see page 33 & 34

JOHN THOMAS-4 DUNSWORTH (John T.-4, Minnie-3, John Abner-2, Jesse Abner-1)
b. June 19, 1921 (JD); resides at Scotland, Arkansas (JD).
m. Norma Dale McCoslin (STS) she died Sept. 15, 1961, buried at Pleasant Grove Cemetery in Cleveland, Arkansas (JD)
John Dunsworth provided all of the information with the initials (JD).

CHILDREN: (of John and Norma Dale)
JACQUELYN DALE-5 DUNSWORTH, b. Nov. 8, 1950 (JD); resides in St. Louis, Mo. 1985 (JD).
m. Mike Murrie (JD).

CHILDREN: (of Jacquelyn and Mike)
DANNY-6 MURRIE, b._____(JD).
BENJAMIN-6 MURRIE, b._____ (JD).
SUSAN-6 MURRIE, b._____ (JD).

KATHRYN GALE-5 DUNSWORTH, b. Feb. 5, 1952 (JD); resides in Little Rock, AR 1985 (JD).
m. Robert Hunt (JD).

CHILDREN: (of Kathryn and Robert)
ROBERT-6 HUNT, Jr., b._____ (JD).

JOHN THOMAS-5 DUNSWORTH, Jr., b. June 27, 1954 (JD); resides in Perryville, AR 1985 (JD);
m.Debbie Gray (JD).

CHILDREN: (of John and Debbie)
ERIN-6 DUNSWORTH, b._____ (JD).
KATIE-6 DUNSWORTH, b._____ (JD).

Jack Dunworth
Made Sept. 4, 1985 at Faye Ward's home
in Scotland, Arkansas on Faye's birthday.

"John Thomas-4 Dunsworth Sr. grew up in the community of Scotland, Arkansas and graduated from high school in 1938.

Amid the depession years he entered the Civilian Conservation Corps and was assigned to Co. 745, Lost Corner, Arkansas where he spent 2 years and where he operated the Post Exchange.

World War II began and John spent 3 years in the U.S. Army serving his country.

With the war having ended, he returned home and entered what is now the University of Central Arkansas where he obtained both his B.A. and a Master's Degree in Education, and where he prepared himself for the teaching profession which was to last 34 years.

In his early years, John taught and coached at Scotland and Plumerville, Arkansas high schools, and for a period of time taught at an elementary school in Arizona.

He served as Superintendent of Schools at Big Flat, Arkansas; Cherry Valley, Arkansas; and, was working in a similar capacity when he retired in May, 1983 at Wonder View High School at Hattieville, Arkansas.

Although he appears young enough to take on another 10 or 15 years, he mentions that governmental red tape demands so much of a school administrator's time and energies that it has become extremely difficult to do that which a superintendent is hired to do, running and operating a school.

John now lives across U.S. Highway 95 from his 97 year old mother near Scotland and devotes his time primarily to her care." (VAS)

****

see page 35

GRADY LAYDUS-4 SWAIN (Grady Laydus-4, John Wesley-3, John Abner-2, Jesse Abner-1)
- b. Dec. 4, 1915 (ROC) at Cleveland, AR (STS);
- d. Dec. 17, 1975 (ROC);
- m. Dec. 24, 1939 Mary Ruth Wright, by Geo. M. Powell (STS),
  Mary was born April 13, 1920 (ROC).

Grady retired from Shell Oil after 36 years of service and Mary retired from teaching school. (ROC).

CHILDREN: (of Grady and Mary)
JOHN EVERETTE-5 SWAIN, b. Sept. 18, 1940. He is a lawyer at Houston, TX (ROC);
    m. June 6, 1964 Ledra Kay Epperson; she was born Oct. 13, 1941 (ROC).

    CHILDREN: (of John and Ledra)
    JOHN DAVID-6 SWAIN, b. Nov. 11, 1967, "adopted" (ROC).
    STEVEN TYLER-6 SWAIN, b. Jan. 24, 1970 (ROC).

RAY ALAN-5 SWAIN, b. Feb. 16, 1946, twin (ROC); "Houston Policeman" (ROC);
    m. Aug. 19, 1972, Susan Elizabeth Brownlee; she was born May 26, 1949 (ROC).

    CHILDREN: (of Ray and Susan)
    ANDREA LEA-6 SWAIN, b. Aug. 22, 1976 (ROC).
    MICHAEL ALAN-6 SWAIN, b. March 7, 1978 (ROC).

RALPH LYNN-5 SWAIN, b. Feb. 16, 1946, twin (ROC); "Private Security Officer";
    m. Dec. 1, 1972, Marsha Kaye Alexander; she was born April 15, 1953 (ROC).

    CHILDREN: (of Ralph and Marsha)
    KAYCIE LYNN-6 SWAIN, b. Dec. 2, 1976 (ROC).

MARY GRACE-5 SWAIN, b. Oct. 26, 1955 (ROC);
    m. May 1, 1982 Glenn Davis Hatcher; he was born Sept. 10, 1948 (ROC);
    "Geologist - Texas Gas Exploration" (ROC).

    CHILDREN: (of Mary & Glenn)
    JUSTIN ELI-6 HATCHER, b. Aug. 18, 1984 (ROC).

Pictured from left to right:
Ray, Mary Grace, Ralph

Information on this page concerning the family of Grady Laydus Swain was provided in January of 1986 by Mary Ruth Swain in a letter to Robert Owen Crossman (ROC).
****

see page 37

EUNICE ALLINE-4 SWAIN (Eunice Alline-4, Sherman-3, John-2, Jesse Abner-1)
>b. April 22, 1918 at Cleveland, Arkansas (STS);
>>"Alline & Oliver live in Blackwell, Arkansas in 1986" (ROC);
>m. July 27, 1938 Oliver Daniel Smirl (STS) by Geo. M. Rowell, see Conway County
>>Arkansas Book 35, page 630 (ROC); Oliver was born Jan. 18, 1914 at Blackwell,
>>Arkansas, the son of Lyndon Biggs Smirl and Hettie Roberta Oliver (STS).

CHILDREN:

see JOE LYNN-5 SMIRL, b. Nov. 30, 1940 at Morrilton, Arkansas (STS);
page
109 m. Sept. 14, 1963 Patricia Marie Ruffiner; she was born on September 11, 1938 at
Morrilton; she is the daughter of Eugene Ruffiner and Mary Margaret Bour (ROC).
Joe and Pat live at 300 Oaklawn Dr., Morrilton, Arkansas 72110 (ROC).

see OLIVIA ANN-5 SMIRL, b. March 19, 1947 at Morrilton, AR (STS);
page
110 m. Nov. 2, 1971 Paul Bernard Allen (STS).

"Eunice Allene Swain Smirl attended the public schools of Cleveland, Arkansas where she
grew up, and later attended Wonder View High School near Hattieville, Arkansas.

During her early working career she taught three terms of school at Cleveland and between
school terms attended State Teacher's College, now known as University of Central Arkansas,
located at Conway, Arkansas.

Allene, as she is better known, graduated from a school of cosmotology in Little Rock,
Arkansas although she has since never worked at this type occupation..

Following her marriage, she and her husband purchased and operated a grocery store in
Morrilton, Arkansas during the years 1947-49. Soon afterward they moved to Houston, Texas
where she was employed with Kress Variety.

Returning to Arkansas in 1952, she became associated with her father in the grocery business
at Blackwell and was appointed Assistant Postmaster. In 1957 she took over ownership of the
business and was named to the position of Postmaster and continued in this dual capacity until her
retirement in 1978.

Oliver, her husband, retired from Crompton Company, Morrilton, Arkansas in 1974 after
working 8 years in the Weaving Department. He previously had served 12 years as an auditor with
the State of Arkansas, Department of Finance and Administration. He spent 19 months in the U.S.
Army during WWII and 2 years with Brown-Root Co., in Houston Texas working in the repair of
U.S. Army tanks. During his earlier working career in addition to operating the grocery store in
Morrilton, Arkansas he farmed for some years in the Blackwell Community." (VAS)

Photo of **Alline & Oliver:**

****

see page 37

VERILL ANSEL-4 SWAIN (Verill Ansel-4, Sherman Norton-3, John Abner-2, Jesse Abner-1)

b. April 13, 1921 at Cleveland, Arkansas (STS);

m. September 3, 1950 Elizabeth Ruth (Hamlet) Kimberlin (STS), at Atkins, Arkansas by Rev. H.C. Minnis; Elizabeth was born Jan. 14, 1921 at Atkins, Arkansas, widow of Donald Kimberlin; she is the daughter of John Turner Hamlet and Velma Katie Johnson (ROC). "Ansel & Elizabeth live in Morrilton, Arkansas in 1987" (ROC)

CHILDREN: (of Ansel and Elizabeth)

see page 111 MARCIA GAIL-5 SWAIN, b. April 26, 1953 at Morrilton, Arkansas in St Anthony's Hospital
m. Feb. 9, 1973 Robert Owen Crossman at Morrilton, Arkansas by Rev. Clyde Parsons at First United Methodist Church; Bob was born Feb. 24, 1953 at Houston, Texas, the son of Paul Judson Crossman and Roberta Frances Mittag. Marcia and Bob Crossman are the compilers of this Swain Family Genealogy. Bob and Marcia live in Prairie Grove, Arkansas in 1987.

see page 114 SHERRY ELIZABETH-5 SWAIN, b. May 6, 1955 at Morrilton, Arkansas (ROC);
m. Dec. 29, 1977 William Michael Lisle of Gentry at Morrilton, Arkansas by Rev. Bob Crossman at First United Methodist Church (ROC); they have no children, and are no longer married (1985). (ROC)

"Amid the latter depression years of the 1930's Verill Ansel Swain left Morrilton High School after his 11th year to financially assist his family and entered the Civilian Conservation Corps at Jacksonville, Arkansas. He graduated from high school while attending night classes at the high school in that city.

After 6 months as a laborer, he was promoted to hospital attendant, which led 15 months later to a civilian job as a clerk with the Medical Department, Base Headquaters, CCC, Little Rock, Arkansas.

Two years were to follow, the second one spent as Chief Clerk of the Department before the outbreak of WWII and the closing of all CCC operations throughout the United States.

He spent three and one half years during WWII as a member of the U.S. Navy Seabees and where he rose to the rank of Storekeeper First Class (Disbursing).

With the return to civilian life in 1946, Ansel, as he is better known in local circles, attended for a period of time both Arkansas Tech University and the University of Central Arkansas.

Between the years 1947 and 1957 he operated a roller rink at Blackwell. Also during 1948-1950 he was the Conway County Draft Board Clerk. In 1950 he was elected to the office of Conway County and Probate Clerk and served almost two years before accepting the position of Personnel Manager with Crompton Company, a manufacturer of unfinished corduroy, in Morrilton and continued in this capacity until 1976 when he was named to a newly created position of Manager of Employee Relations, a job which he held until retirement in 1983.

Ansel is active in community, civic and church affairs and has served as member and President of the Morrilton School Board of Education, member and President of Morrilton Golf and Country Club, member of the Conway County Library Board, member of the Conway County Industrial Development Comm., and at one time or another served in most lay positions including Chairman of the Administrative Board of Morrilton United Methodist Church.

His wife, Elizabeth, retired in 1982 from the U.S. Soil Conservation Service, Watershed Division, Morrilton, Arkansas where she worked 21 years as a Clerk-typist. She previously worked 5 years for the Veterans Administration in Russellville and Little Rock, Arkansas and during WWII she worked almost two years with the Office of Price Administration. Elizabeth was a member of the Conway County Community Service Board for 21 years, and in her retirement continues as a 25 year member and past president of the Morrilton Adelaide Club. Elizabeth has served as President of the Town & Country Garden Club; served as a member of the Church Choir; and, Unit and Circle Chairperson of United Methodist Women for 2 years. Elizabeth attended Arkansas Tech in Russellville following her graduation from Atkins High School in 1939.

The Swains enjoy playing golf and camping, spending most winters in their R.V. at Harlingen, Texas near the Mexican border." (VAS)

page 75

V. Ansel Swain

Elizabeth Ruth Hamlet Swain

Ansel and Elizabeth Swain
at their home in
Morrilton, Arkansas

page 76

Ansel Swain Family

—Horace Crofoot Photography

MRS. SWAIN

Ansel, Marcia
and Elizabeth
at Marcia's
Ordination as
Elder in 1986
in the
North Arkansas
Conference
of the
United Methodist
Church

Mrs. Swain Announces Retirement

Mrs. Elizabeth R. Swain, clerk-typist, Watershed Office, Soil Conservation Service, has retired effective October 29. Mrs. Swain was employed on December 13, 1961, soon after the Watershed Office was opened in Morrilton, and has held this position for the past 21 years.

Previously she spent five years in a similar capacity while working in the Contact Office of the Veterans Administration in

Russellville and Little Rock. During World War II, she was employed in Federal Service at Russellville, in the Office of Price Administration, and in California with the War Department.

Mrs. Swain is a member and past president of the Morrilton Adelaide Club, and she has served since 1962 as a Board member of Conway County Community Service. She is a member of the Morrilton Hospital Auxiliary and is a member of the First United Methodist Church in Morrilton.

On Thursday evening, October 28, a number of Watershed employes, retirees and their spouses joined together at a local restaurant in celebration of her retirement.

Ansel, Elizabeth,
Sherry, and
David Crossman
at Sherry's
home in
Manhattan, KS

page 77

Ansel & Elizabeth Swain
1983

page 78

see page 37

DOYLE THERON-4 SWAIN (Doyle Theron-4, Sherman Norton-3, John Abner-2, Jesse Abner-1)
- b. March 24, 1924 at Cleveland, Arkansas (STS);
- d. June 14, 1980; buried at Fort Smith, Arkansas at the National Cemetery (ROC);
- m. Aug.19, 1947 Mary Alice Cranford (STS), by Clarence Dawson, see Conway County Arkansas Book 36 page 57 (ROC), Mary was born Aug. 10, 1925/6 at Perryville, Arkansas, daughter of 'Gil' Cranford and Lillie May Beard (STS).

CHILDREN: (of Doyle and Mary)
JOHN ANTHONY-5 SWAIN, b. Nov. 7, 1952 at Searcy, Arkansas (ROC).
TIMOTHY "Tim" ALAN-5 SWAIN, b. May 12, 1955 at Searcy, Arkansas (ROC).

In response to a request from Ansel Swain, Mary Alice Cranford Swain Vampola wrote the following biographical information and provided the photographs on December 19, 1985. (ROC)

"Doyle Theron Swain was born at Cleveland, Arkansas on March 24, 1925. He graduated from Morrilton High School, attended Arkansas Tech, the University of Oklahoma, and received a Bachelor of Arts Degree from Harding College in 1949, with a major in Business Administration and a minor in Social Science. He successfully completed all graduate class requirements for a Master of Arts Degree in Social Sciences at Pepperdine University in Los Angeles, California.

Doyle entered the United States Navy in 1943, served in active combat in the South Pacific, and was discharged from the service in 1946.

He was married to Mary Alice Cranford of Perryville, Arkansas, at Perryville on August 19, 1947. To this union John Anthony was born on November 7, 1952, and Timothy Alan was born on May 12, 1955.

Doyle was a member of the Church of Christ. While living in Searcy, Arkansas Doyle and Mary were instrumental in establishing the Westside Church of Christ where Doyle served as a Deacon and teacher and Mary served as a teacher until leaving the area.

Immediately upon his graduation from Harding College, he was employed as Assistant to Director of the Harding College National Education Program. In 1955, he was promoted to Vice President in Charge of Operations in which capacity he served until the end of 1960.

On January 1, 1961, Doyle began work at Pepperdine University in Los Angeles, California, as Director of Civic Services and Research and remained in that position until 1970, when he became Assistant to Executive Director, Center for International Business, an affiliate of Pepperdine University. In 1972 he was promoted to Director of Special Projects, Center for International Business, where he remained until 1973.

In 1973 he was employed by Los Angeles County Mental Health Services in Los Angeles, where he remained until he became ill.

His professional or civic affiliations and memberships include: International Association of Business Communicators, American College Public Relations Society, Los Angeles Area Chamber of Commerce, American Political Science Association, Academy of Political Science, The American Academy of Political and Social Science, Philadelphia Society, Society for International Development, Lion's International, and Toastmaster's Club.

Honors, Distinctions and Directorships include: Distinguished Service Award, Pepperdine University, 1972; Award of Distinction, Harding College, 1961; Board of Directors, Quapau Area Council, Boy Scouts of America; First Vice President and Board of Directors, Southside Chamber of Commerce of Los Angeles; Certificate of Honor and George Washington Medal of Honor, Freedom's Foundation of Valley Forge.

Doyle died on June 14, 1980, and was buried in National Cemetery at Fort Smith, Arkansas."

continued on the next page........

continued from the previous page.....

Mary Alice (Cranford) Swain was born August 10, 1926 at Perryville, Arkansas, to Gil Thompson and Lillie May (Beard) Cranford.

"She graduated salutatorian of her class from Perryville High School in 1944 and attended Harding College, Searcy, Arkansas.

Mary's employment includes: Deputy County, Probate and Circuit Clerk, Perry County; Secretary, County Agricultural Extension Services, Perry County; Secretary, Arkansas State Legislature (1944-45); Secretary to Statistician, Arkansas State Health Department; Secretary, Arkansas Merit System; Secretary, Director of National Education Program, Harding College; Secretary, Business Manager, Harding College; Acquisitions Librarian, Pepperdine College, Los Angeles, California; Junior Manager, Consumer Relations, Continental Airlines, Los Angeles. She took early retirement from Continental Airlines in 1982.

Professional or civic memberships include: Harding Faculty Wives, PTA, Pepperdine Faculty Wives, Associated Women for Pepperdine, Continental Airlines Management Club.

After Doyle's death, Mary was married to Edward Frank Vampola of Manhattan Beach, California, on August 22, 1981. They lived in Redondo Beach, California until August, 1983, when Edward took early retirement and they moved to Ft. Smith, Arkansas.

Mary and Edward are members of the Westark Church of Christ in Fort Smith."

"**John Anthony Swain** was born at Searcy, Arkansas, on November 7, 1952, to Doyle Theron and Mary Alice (Cranford) Swain.

He gradauted from Morningside High School, Inglewood, California, in 1970, where he was an honor student, played clarinet in the High School Band, was President of the Latin Club, and received the Bank of America Award for Outstanding Achievement in the Field of Social Sciences.

John Attended the University of California at Los Angeles, and Pepperdine University at Malibu, California. He graduated Cum Laude from Pepperdine University with a major in Journalism and a minor in History, then studied an additional year at Pepperdine to obtain his California teaching credential.

In 1981, he studied at Cemanahuac School of Languages in Cuernavaca, Morelos, Mexico; and in 1984 he studied at Language Communication Institute in Rosarito Beach, Mexico; and with additional classes at El Camino College, Harbor College, California State University, Long Beach; and California State University, Domimguez Hill, all in the Los Angeles, California area, he obtained his California bilingual teaching certificate. He speaks Spanish fluently.

John has taught in the Los Angeles Public School System since 1979."

"**Timothy Alan Swain** was born at Searcy, Arkansas, on May 12, 1955 to Doyle Theron and Mary Alice (Cranford) Swain.

He graduated from the Lutheran High School of Los Angeles in 1973, where he had won two Varsity Letters with the football team, was track team Co-captian, and was Treasurer of the Letterman's Club. Other activities included Vice-President of the Fellowship of Christian Athletes, Vice-President of the Key (Kiwanis Junior) Club, and Student Council Representative.

Tim attended Harding University at Searcy, Arkansas. He graduated in May of 1978 with a Bachelor of Arts degree in Social Science. He returned to Harding for one year to pursue graduate studies in Secondary Education. His activities at Harding included membership in the Young Americans for Freedom, the Young Republicans, and the Frater Sodalis social club. Tim was the founder of the Harding Rugby Football Club (now defunct) and played for the team from April 1975 until May 1976.

Tim worked for over a year with the Harding University Maintenance Department before joining the United States Army in February 1981. He graduated from the U.S. School of Infrantry in May of 1981, and from the Army Basic Airborne Course in June 1981. His initial assignment was with the 1-504 Airborne Infantry of the 82nd Airborne Division. His duties included Rifleman and Machinegunner. He was eventually moved to the Division Headquarters where he rose to Assistant Operations Sergeant of the entire Division. He was honorably discharged in February, 1985. His awards and decorations included the Parashutist Wings, Jungle Expert Badge, the Army Parachutist Service Ribbon, the Distinguished Paratrooper Award, the Good Conduct Medal, the Army Achievement Medal, and two Army Commendation Medals.

page 80

continued from the previous page.....

Tim began work as a Patrolman with the Fort Smith Police Department in June, 1985, and received his official Police Commission in October, 1985. In November he was selected as a new members of the Department's Special Weapons and Tactics Team (SWAT).

Tim's professional affiliations include the Fort Smith Municipal Police Association, the Arkansas Municipal Police Association, the Fraternal Order of Police, the Police Marksman Association, the National Rifle Association, and the 82nd Airborne Association."

"**Edward Frank Vampola** was born in Omaha, Nebraska, on May 2, 1928, to James, Jr. and Sophie Louise (Bosak) Vampola.

He graduated from South High School in Omaha, Nebraska in 1946 and graduated Cum Laude from Cal State University in Long Beach, California receiving a Bachelor of Science degree with a major in Electronics.

He was married to Donna Jean Abele of Omaha, Nebraska at Omaha, in December, 1948. To this union David James was born on May 17, 1952, Christine Ann was born on November 17, 1957, and Steven Scott was born January 5, 1962. Donna Jean was born September 14, 1931, and died November 18, 1979.

Between 1946 and 1956, Ed was employed by Ballantyne Company in Omaha as a Draftsman/Machinist; Paxton Mitchell Company, Omaha, as a Tool Designer; North American Aviation in Los Angeles as a Draftsman; ITT Gillfillan, Los Angeles, as a Product Engineer.

Ed began his employment with TRW Systems Group in Redondo Beach, California in February, 1956, where he remained until he took early retirement in August, 1983. During his twenty-seven years employment at TRW, he served in various engineering and management capacities, including Engineer, Engineering Section Head, and Department Manager. He was employed in design and engineering in the mechanical and electronics fields. He was awarded several certificates for developing new technology used in equipment for the NASA space programs, specifically the design of transponder equipment used in the shuttle spacecraft. He participated in the design of: Pioneer I - First Commercial Satellite in space; Pioneer 10 - first manmade Satellite to leave the Solar System; Lunar Excursion Module - First manned landing craft on the moon; Design of a spaceborne atomic clock.

Ed was married to Mary (Cranford) Swain of Redondo Beach, California in Redondo Beach, on August 22, 1981. He and Mary moved to Fort Smith, Arkansas, in August, 1983. Since moving to Fort Smith, Ed has started a part-time engineering consulting business.

Ed and Mary are members of the Westark Church of Christ in Fort Smith."

In response to a request from Ansel Swain, Mary Alice Cranford Swain Vampola provided photographs and wrote the biographical information above on December 19, 1985. (ROC)

****

Doyle Theron Swain
1925-1980

Doyle Theron Swain, age 45
&
Mary Cranford Swain, age 43

Wedding Photo
Edward F. Vampola, age 53
Mary Cranford Vampola, age 55

John Anthony Swain
age 24

Timothy Alan Swain, age 19
at Harding College

Timothy Alan Swain, age 25
U.S. Army School of Infantry

see page 37

DALLAS LYNN-4 SWAIN, (Dallas Lynn-4, Sherman N.-3, John Abner-2, Jesse Abner-1)
   b. Oct. 15, 1930 at Cleveland, Arkansas (STS);
   m. April 8, 1951 Nealia Jane Fry in Atkins, Arkansas. Nealia Jane was born Feb. 11, 1931
      in Atkins, the daughter of William Clinton Fry Jr. and Ocie Smith (WSS).
   "Dallas & Nealia Jane live at 505 N. Church St., Atkins, AR 72823 in 1985" (ROC).

CHILDREN:
see
page
115 WILLIAM SHERMAN-5 SWAIN, b. April 4, 1952 in Morrilton, Arkansas (STS).
   m. Nov. 20, 1970 Patricia Ann Farish in Atkins. She was born March 20, 1953.
      They live at Atkins, Arkansas. She is the daughter of Raymond Farish, Jr. and Mary
      Sue Wright (WSS).
      William is an attorney in Russellville, Arkansas and has provided all the material
      throughout this genealogy with the footnote 'WSS'.

   JANICE LYNN-5 SWAIN, b. May 10, 1955 in Morrilton, AR. (WSS);
      d. in infancy (WSS).

   BARRY LYNN-5 SWAIN, b. July 25, 1956 at Morrilton, Arkansas (WSS);
      m. January 5, 1980 Linda Fell in Little Rock, Arkansas. She was born May 28, 1956, the
         daughter of George and Edna Fell. Barry and Linda live in Sheridan, Arkansas (WSS).
         Barry is a Captain in the U.S. Army (WSS).

   BRIAN TODD-5 SWAIN, b. Aug. 21, 1966 in Russellville, Arkansas (WSS); he is a student
      at Arkansas Tech University in Russellville, Arkansas (WSS).

   BRIGITTE LYNETTE-5 SWAIN, b. Aug. 8, 1968 in Russellville, Arkansas (WSS); she is a
      student at Arkansas Tech University in Russellville, Arkansas (WSS).

"**Dallas Lynn Swain**, born Oct. 15, 1930 in Cleveland, Conway County, Arkansas, the
fourth child of Sherman Norton Swain and Stella Trimble Swain attended school in Cleveland,
Blackwell, Morrilton and Atkins graduating in May 1948 from Atkins High School. Dallas entered
the U.S. Navy in January of 1949. He served aboard the U.S.S. Chevalier in the Korean War,
participating in the first evacuation of war in August, 1950 and the Inchon invasion in October,
1950. Dallas was discharged honorably November, 1955.
   He graduated from the Draughon School of Business in September, 1957. Dallas and Nealia
Jane resided in Sheridan, Arkansas for six years before moving to Atkins in November of 1963.
   Dallas is the owner of a Public Accounting firm and partner in an insurance agency.
He was elected Mayor of Atkins, with his term beginning on January 1, 1983 and expiring
December 31, 1986 (WSS).

"**Barry Lynn Swain**, second son of Dallas and Nealia Swain, was born July 25, 1956 at St.
Anthony's Hospital in Morrilton, Arkansas.
   He attended elementary school at Sheridan in 1962-1963 and moved to Atkins, Arkansas in
November of 1963. He attended Atkins Public Schools until graduation in May, 1974. He entered
Arkansas Tech University in September, 1974, majoring in History and Political Science. During
the time Barry was at Arkansas Tech he was a member of the R.O.T.C. in his Sophomore, Junior
and Senior years receiving the Distinguished Military Award and a commission in the regular
Army. During his Senior year, Barry served as President of the Student Government Association.
Barry was a charter member of Sigma Phi Epsilon fraternity at A.T.U. He graduated from A.T.U.
in May, 1978 and entered the University of Arkansas in September, 1978, majoring in Public
Administration on a two year military delay. Barry graduated from the U of A in May of 1980.
   Barry was married to the former Linda Fell at the Pulaski Heights United Methodist Church in
Little Rock, Arkansas on January 5, 1980. Barry reported for army duty at Fort Benjamin
Harrison in August of 1980 as a Second Lieutenant and was later transferred to Fort Hood, Texas

page 84

serving with the First Calvalry Division until July, 1984 attaining the rank of Captain. Upon completion of duties at Fort Hood, Barry was assigned as Opperations Officer at the Military Entrance Processing Station in Little Rock, Arkansas for a three year tour of duty.

Barry and his life, Linda, presently reside at Sheridan, Arkansas.

"**Brian Todd Swain**, son of Dallas and Nealia Swain, was born August 21, 1966 at St. Mary's Hospital, Russellville, Arkansas.

He entered elementary school at Atkins, Arkansas in September 1972 and graduated from Atkins High School in May of 1984. Brian was a member of the Atkins High School Choir for five years. He also served as President of the Senior Class and Letterman's Club, as well as Parlamentarian for the Student Council. Brian was also a member of the Atkins High School Tennis Team for 4 years. Among the honors Brian received in High School are: AHS Honor Graduate; 1983 Boys State Delegate; 1984 American Government Award; 1984 Presidential Academic Fitness Award; 1984 District Singles Champion (Tennis); 1984 Business Award; and 1982-1984 Society of Distinguished American High School Students.

Brian is presently attending Arlkansas Tech University, Russellville, Arkansas majoring in Journalism with a Public Relations emphasis. Brian's involvement in college life includes: 1984-1985 Student Government Association Freshman Senator; 1985-1986 S.G.A. Executive Committee Administrative Assistant; 1985-1987 Sigma Phi Epsilon Fraternity; 1984-1985 Studer Activities Board; 1986-1987 Chairman Fine Arts Committee; 1985-1986 Bacchus member; and, 1986-1987 Treasurer; 1984-1985 Outstanding Freshman Journalism Major; 1984-1985 Charter Member President's Leadership Program; 1985 Delegate to NACA National Student Government Workshop; 1985-1986 ATU Performance Scholarship Recipient; 1985-1986 Delegate to NACA National Convention; and, 1987 Who's Who Among Students in American Universities and Colleges.

Brian is an avid tennis fan, and he plays and teaches tennis. He is a member of the Atkins United Methodist Church, has served as President of United Methodist Youth Fellowship and Secretary of Atkins United Methodist Men's Club.

Brian plans to pursue post-graduate work leading to a master's degree in Public Administration or a master's degree in City and Regional Planning leading to a position in Municipal Management." (DLS)

"**Brigitte Lynette Swain**, daughter of Dallas and Nealia Swain, was born August 8, 1968 at St. Mary's Hospital, Russellville, Arkansas.

She entered elementary school at Atkins, Arkansas in September 1974 and graduated from Atkins High School in May of 1986. Brigitte was a member of the High School Band for 7 years, serving as Band Captian her senior year. She was also a member of the High School Choir for 6 years, serving as Soprano Section Leader her senior year. Brigitte was a member of the Betta Club (Honor Society), F.L.B.A. & F.H.A.

Brigitte is a member of the Atkins United Methodist Church and was president of the Youth Fellowship.

Brigitte is now attending Arkansas Tech University, Russellville, Arkansas on an A.C.T. Scholarship. She is majoring in Business Administration with Management and Marketing option. She plans on pursuing a career in Hospital Administration after post-graduate work. She is employed part-time as a Wal-Mart Associate." (DLS)

**Pictures of the Dallas Lynn Swain and family
may be found on page 115-116.**

****

see page 37

SHIRLEY ANN-4 SWAIN, (Shirley Ann-4, Sherman Norton-3, John-2, Jesse Abner-1)
    b. May 10, 1934 at Cleveland, Arkansas (STS);
    d. "lives at 1253 W. 20th Street, Merced, California 95340 in 1979" (ROC);
    m. Donald G. Tedder on April 10, 1954; Donald was born Aug. 28, 1933, son of John
       Tedder (STS).

CHILDREN:
ALLEN-5 TEDDER, b. May 31, 1951 ROC);
    d. Oct. __, 1976 (ROC).

"**Shirley Ann**, the fifth and last child of Sherman and Stella Swain, was born at Cleveland, Arkansas on May 10, 1934. The family moved to Blackwell, Arkansas in 1937 and Shirley attended elementary school there. She transferred to Atkins School in the 6th grade and graduated from high school in 1952. In her junior year in high school, she was one of two girls selected for Girl's State in Little Rock, Arkansas. In her senior year she reigned as Annual Homecoming Football Queen.

Following graduation she worked for more than two years as a clerk and bookkeeper for Cheek's Wholesale Grocery in Atkins.

On April 10, 1954, Shirley married her former high school classmate and sweetheart, Donald Gene Tedder, then a member of the U. S. Navy and stationed at Memphis, Tennessee. Donald was later transferred to Pensacola, Florida. Before the birth of their only child, Shirley was employed as a clerk for an office equipment company. Their son, Alan Gene, was born at Pensacola Naval Hospital on May 31, 1955.

With Don's discharge from the U. S. Navy in 1957, the young family moved to Atkins, Arkansas for two years where Donald owned and operated a radio and television repair shop. They moved to Little Rock in 1959 and Donald completed a course in electronics at Business College. He accepted employment with Boeing Aerospace Division in Seattle, Washington in 1960 where he worked as an electronic technician at the Missile Production Center until 1963. Since then, Shirley and Don have lived in Merced, California where Don has worked, mostly in the capacity as Service Director for Bruce's Television and Repair.

For a period of years, Donald played a guitar with a string band in Merced and still enjoys joining friends for an evening of music making.

Shirley enjoys attending garage sales and derives a lot of pleasure in discovering a 'treasure in the rough' and then restoring the item as much as possible to its original state" (VAS).

"**Alan Gene Tedder** was born May 31, 1955 at Pensacola Naval Hospital, Pensacola, Florida. He started school (Kindergarten) in Seattle, Washington. During his 3rd grade, his school continued at Mercid, California, where he graduated from Yosemite High School in 1973. He was on the wrestling team in Junior High sports. His favorite hobbies were collecting old Laurel & Hardy movies, a stamp collection, music and guitar. Some favorite trips he enjoyed taking with his parents were to Yellowstone National Park and Vancouver British Columbia. One of his pastimes was restoring a '63 MG auto that he owned. A special pet was a black dachsund named "Suzi" that remained with the family for 15 years. At age 21, Alan was in his second year at Merced College with plans to major in Psychology when he met untimely death in a car accident Oct. 16, 1976. His place of burial is Merced District Cemetary." (SAS)

Shirley, Don, & Allen
in their front yard

Allen Tedder
in his backyard

Shirley & Don

Shirley & Don

Shirley
about 1952
High School Homecoming Queen

see page 40

WILLIAM O'NEAL-4 SWAIN (William O'Neal-4, William-3, John Abner-2, Jesse-1)
b. May 22, 1928 (STS);
m. Dixie Yadon, Seminole, Oklahoma (VAS).

CHILDREN: (of William and Dixie)
TERRI-5 SWAIN, b. March 21, 1955 (VAS);
m. Steven C. Miller (VAS).

CHILDREN: (of Terri and Steven)
JUSTIN O'NEAL-6 MILLER, b. Jan. 2, 1982 (VAS).
STEPHANIE NACOLE-6 MILLER, b. Oct. 27, 1984 (VAS).
ALANA SHEA-6 MILLER, b. April 29, 1986 (VAS).

GINGER LEE-5 SWAIN, b. Feb. 15, 1957 (VAS);
m. Bradley Allen Roberts (VAS).

WILLIAM RALPH-5 SWAIN, b. Sept. 17, 1960 (VAS).

"Following graduation from high school in Bowlegs, Oklahoma, William O'Neal "Bill" Swain served a two-year term with the United States Marine Corps and held the distinction of graduating at the top of a class fo 120 recruits.

In 1954 he began a career that was to span a period of 30 years in U.S. Civil Service at Tinker Air Base near Oklahoma City, Oklahoma. After 15 years as a sheet metal mechanic he was promoted and worked a similar period as an Aircraft Aerospace Inspector before retiring on Oct. 31, 1984.

In 1977 Bill decided to enter into a monumental undertaking, that of a complete scroll of the Bible in his own handwriting. In 1980 after many cast-away fountain pens and after filling pounds of paper the task as picture below was completed. For the successful completion of his herculean task, Bill was featured in the local Midwest City, Oklahoma Newspaper.

From that newspaper article, we learn of what an interesting person Bill is. 'Bill Swain wanted to see just how difficult it was for scribes to copy the scriptures by hand, without making an error in a single 'jot or tittle.' Swain, member of Meadowwood Church in Midwest City, has written the entire Bible in long hand. It occupies a continuous unspliced scroll 3,485 feet long and it took him nearly three years to complete. 'I found out it's rather difficult,' he said about copying accurately. Copying error free was important to Bill Swain who worked several hours each night after his work as a sheet metal inspector at Tinker Field, all day most Saturdays and long hours on Sunday. Living with the scripture as he did for so many months, Swain learned a lot and accumulated a lot of questions. He said he found 32 'errors' in the King James Version edition he copied from. A reason for his starting the project was his special interest in numerics, a practice that assigns number value to each letter, space or punctuation in the Bible to discern patterns.' The article ended by complimenting Bill on his serious regard for scripture.

Dixie, his wife, has been employed the past 8 school terms in the cafeteria of Midwest City Public Schools.

In his leisure hours and as he says when motivated to do so, Bill writes poetry and does woodcarving. A quality most likely inherited form his grandfather O'Neal is that he is a 'pretty fair carpenter' and on one occasion built a house in which his mother and grandmother would reside.

A sad commentary, indeed, is the fact that this (ghost) writer and a first cousin after too many years has just come to know William 'Bill' Swain.. Two recent visits, both altogether too brief it seemed, led to the conclusion that he is a person of exceptionally fine character, one who loves and cares for his family, and a devoted son to this mother, and as citizen a credit to his community.

This too brief acquaintance is most assuredly treasured and we trust that the future will bring about a much closer and more enriching relationship."(VAS).

page 88

The William 'Bill' O'Neal Swain family of 2237 S. Webster Drive, Midwest City, OK 73130.
Pictured are:
[front row, left to right]
**Terri Lynn Miller, Alana Shea Miller, Dixie Lee Swain, Justin O'Neal Miller,
and Ginger Lee Swain.**
[back row]
William Ralph Miller & William O'Neal Swain.

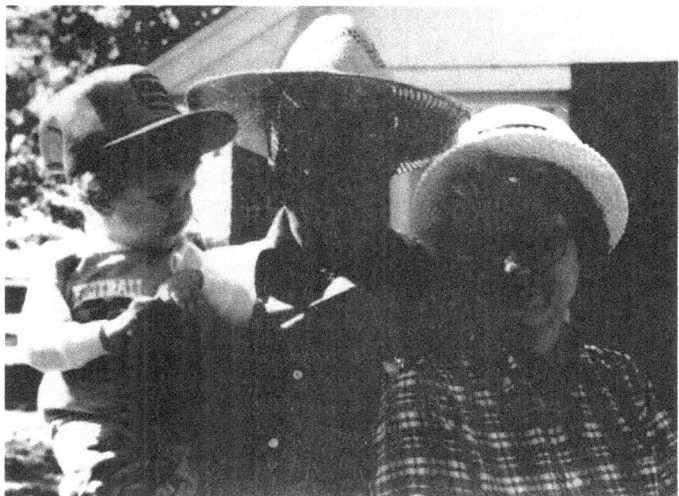

This scroll of the Holy Bible
was handscribed by
William O'Neal Swain.

Justin O'Neal Miller,

Willaim O'Neal Swain & Dixie Lee Swain

Our

Fifth

Generation

page 89

see page 26

JAMES WILLIAM-5 SWAIN, (James William-5, James Albert-4, James-3, William-2, Jessie-1)
b. Aug. 31, 1937 (NS);
m. Jan. 5, 1957 Georgia Raye Ragsdale; she was born Oct. 9, 1939 (NS).

>**CHILDREN:** (of James William and Georgia Raye)
>JAMES ROBERT-6 SWAIN, b. July 17, 1960 (NS);
>>m. March 8, 1980 Lena Ann Cropper (NS).

>>**CHILDREN:** (of James and Lena)
>>TANISAH MARLENE-7 SWAIN, b. April 15, 1981 (NS).
>>AMBER SUSETTE-7 SWAIN, b. April 15, 1981 (NS).

>SUSAN NORENE-6 SWAIN, b. Oct. 3, 1961 (NS);
>>m. Oct. 6, 1979 Richard Dwight Neal (NS).

>>**CHILDREN:** (of Susan and Richard)
>>JAMES DWIGHT-7 NEAL, b. Dec. 23, 1982 (NS).
>>BARBARA SUZANNE-7 NEAL, b. Nov. 15, 1983 (NS).
>>JARRED CRAG-7 NEAL, b. Oct. 2, 1984, twin (NS).
>>JUSTIN ROBERT-7 NEAL, b. Oct. 2, 1984, twin (NS).

>GEORGE EDWARD-6 SWAIN, b. Sept. 25, 1964 (NS);
>>m. Feb. 27, 1982 Vickie Allen (NS).

>>**CHILDREN:** (of George and Vickie)
>>KARI DAWN-7 SWAIN, b. Oct. 8, 1982 (NS).

>JERRY MILTON-6 SWAIN, b. Oct. 12, 1970 (NS).

****

see page 41

page 90

IRENE-5 KINCANNON, (Irene-5, Pearl Ann-4, Lou Etta-3, Celia Ann-2, Jesse Abner-1)
b. Feb. 11, 1923 at Scotland, Arkansas (SOH) at Cleveland, Arkansas (SOH);
m. Sept. 4, 1943 William Campbell at Little Rock, Arkansas; he was born Oct. 8, 1923 at
Montcoal, West Virginia (SOH). "lives in Port Orange, Florida, 1985" (SOH)

CHILDREN: (of Irene and William)
CARROLL EUGENE-6 CAMPBELL, b. July 25, 1944 at Clinton, Arkansas (SOH);
m. in 1964, Linda Cook, at Washington D.C. (SOH). "live in Virginia, 1985" (SOH).

CHILDREN: (of Carroll and Linda)
JEFFERY-7 CAMPBELL, b. Aug. 20, 1967 at New Haven, CT (SOH)
DAVID-7 CAMPBELL, b. June 9, 1969 at New Haven, CT (SOH)

NORMA DEAN-6 CAMPBELL, b. Sept. 1, 1945 at Clinton, Arkansas (SOH);
m. in 1965, Richard Terrace, at East Haven, CT (SOH).

CHILDREN: (of Norma and Richard)
MARK RICHARD-7 TERRACE, b. Nov. 21, 1966 at New Haven, CT (SOH)
KATHY LYNN-7 TERRACE, b. April 21, 1969 at New Haven, CT (SOH)

JOE ANN-6 CAMPBELL, b. Dec. 11, 1949 at Naoma, West Virginia (SOH);
m. June 12, 1984, Fred Massare, at Las Vagas, Nevada (SOH);
"lived in New Haven, CT in 1985"; "no children" (SOH).

JOHN MARK-6 CAMPBELL, b. June 29, 1952 at Charleston, West Virginia (SOH);
m. June 7, 1975 Joyce Christianna at Norwalk, CT. (SOH).

CHILDREN: (of John and Joyce)
JOHN MARK-7 CAMPBELL, JR., b. April 9, 1981 at New Haven, CT (SOH).

All information concerning this family marked with (SOH) has come from: Reba "Sissy"
Ovalene Harris (Mrs. Gene Harris) of Route 2, Box 2073 Selah, Washington 98942.

****

see page 41   page 91

ARNOLD-5 KINCANNON, (Arnold-5, Pearl Ann-4, Lou Etta-3, Celia-2, Jessie-1)
  b. March 19, 1924 at Scotland, Arkansas Van Buren County (SOH);
  m.(1st) April 1942 Moatte Dodd at Harrison, Arkansas the daughter of Delas Dodd and
    Winnie Chewing, Moatte was born Feb. 20, 1925 at Everton, Arkansas and she died June
    24, 1981 at Mt. Home, Arkansas with burial at Bruno Cemetery at Bruno, Arkansas. She
    was a member of the Church of Christ (SOH). Her other husbands were (2nd) _____,
    (3rd) Glenn Green, and (4th) C.R. Gilbert (SOH).
  m.(2nd) Sept. 1957 Pauline Oberlander (SOH);
  m.(3rd) June 12, 1976 Joyce Barker Weston (SOH).

CHILDREN: (of Arnold and Moatte)
MARY ANN-6 KINCANNON, b. March 15, 1943 at Little Rock, Arkansas (SOH);
  m. May 19, 1961 Joe Dillard; he was born Feb. 11, 1943 (SOH).

  CHILDREN: (of Mary and Joe)
  JOE BRANDT-7 DILLARD, b. July 21, 1967 at Mt. Home, Arkansas (SOH).
  CANDICE PAIGE-7 DILLARD, b. March 21, 1973 (SOH).

ALICE MARIE-6 KINCANNON, b. Nov. 24, 1944 at Scotland, Arkansas (SOH);
  m. Dwayne Clark (SOH). "divorced" (SOH).

  CHILDREN: (of Alice and Dwayne)
  KATHY-7 CLARK, b. June 15, 1964 at Yakima, Washington (SOH);
    m. May 22, 1982 Tony Erickson at Mt. Home, Arkansas (SOH).

    CHILDREN: (of Kathy and Tony)
    ALICIA KAY-8 ERICKSON, b. Nov. 20, 1983 at Mt. Home, AR (SOH).

  RONNIE CLARK-7 ERICKSON, b. Sept. 17, 1966 at Yakima, Washington (SOH).

****

page 92

see page 41

REBA "SISSY" "Judy" OVALENE-5 KINCANNON (Reba-5, Pearl Ann-4, Lou
Etta-3, Celia-2, Jesse Abner-1)
b. March 26, 1925 at Scotland, Arkansas (SOH);
m. March 26, 1946 Eugene Delbert Harris at Piggott, Arkansas; he was born Jan. 24, 1922 at
Truman, Arkansas; he served in U.S. Army from Oct. 1942 to Dec. 1945 (SOH).
"left Libourn, MO Dec. 1947 for Yakima, Washington" (SOH).
"live at: Rt. 2 Box 2073, Selah, Washington 98942 in 1986" (ROC).

CHILDREN: (of Reba and Eugene)
RODGER DAVID "DAVE"-6 HARRIS, b. Jan. 20, 1947 at Lilbourn, MO (SOH).
   m.(1st) Carol Ready on Jan. 22, 1966 at Yakima, Washington (SOH);
   m.(2nd) Kathryn Lamb on September 7, 1977 at Coeur D'alene, ID (SOH);
      "live at Selah, Washington in 1985" "divorced 1980" "no children" (SOH).

LINDA DARNELLE-6 HARRIS, b. Feb. 18, 1948 at Yakima, Washington (SOH);
   m.(1st) David Snider, Jan. 21, 1967 at Yakima, Washington(SOH);
   m.(2nd) Gerald Edwards, May 9, 1975 at Yakima, Washington (SOH).

   CHILDREN: (of Linda and David)
   CINDY SNIDER-7 EDWARDS, b. July 19, 1972 (SOH);
      "lived at Yakima, WA, 1985" (SOH).

PHYLLIS JEANNE-6 HARRIS, b. Aug. 10, 1949 at Yakima, Washington (SOH);
   m.(1st) Charles Schlect, Sept. 7, 1968 at Yakima, Washington (SOH); "lived at
      Yakima, WA, 1985" "divorced Oct. 5, 1973" (SOH).
   m.(2nd)LaVern Fredrick Barnes, Jr. on Jan. 24, 1986 (SOH).

   CHILDREN: (of Phyllis and Charles)
   JANELLE-7 SCHLECT, b. May 1, 1971 (SOH).

All information concerning this family marked with (SOH) has come from: Reba "Sissy" Ovalene
Harris (Mrs. Gene Harris) of Route 2, Box 2073 Selah, Washington 98942.

The Harris Family:
[left to right]
Phyllis, Linda, Ovalene, Gene, David [taken 1963]

see page 41

CARLELL "Carl"-5 KINCANNON, (Carlell-5, Pearl Ann-4, Lou Etta-3, Celia-2, Jessie-1)
b. Nov. 8, 1928 at Scotland, Arkansas (SOH);
m. May 5, 1947 Mary Wales at Scotland, Arkansas; she was born May 3, 1928 at Scotland,
Arkansas, daughter of Hugh Wales and Gladys Lindsey. Mary was also married to
Leonard Fisher (SOH).

CHILDREN: (of Carlell and Mary)
CAROLYN-6 KINCANNON, b. Feb. 5, 1949 at Yakima, Washington (SOH);
m. June 10, 1972 Michael Wies at Yakima, Washington (SOH).

CHILDREN: (of Carolyn and Michael)
MICHAEL-7 WIES, b. Sept. 8, 1976 (SOH).
CARRY-7 WIES, b. Aug. 12, 1981 at Yakima (SOH).

DEBORAH-6 KINCANNON, b. Jan. 29, 1952 at Yakima (SOH);
m.(1st) Roy Andras (SOH);
m.(2nd)Adair Shear (SOH);
m.(3rd) Bill Pate (SOH).

CHILDREN: (of Deborah and Roy)
ROBERT-7 ANDRAS, b. Feb. 1, 1970 at Yakima (SOH).
ERICK-7 ANDRAS, b. Oct. 14, 1973 at Yakima (SOH).

CHILDREN: (of Deborah and Adair)
DAWN-7 SHEAR, b. June 7, 1975 (SOH).

CHILDREN: (of Deborah and Bill)
SARAH JANE-7 PATE, b. Feb. 12, 1982 (SOH).

CARLA-6 KINCANNON, b. June 30, 1953 at Yakima (SOH);
m. March 10, 1973 Mark Izzett at Yakima (SOH).

CHILDREN: (of Carla and Mark)
MILLISA-7 IZZETT, b. Jan. 5, 1977 at Portland, Oregon (SOH).
SAM-7 IZZETT, b. Oct. 28, 1979 at Portland, Oregon (SOH).

RICHARD LYNN-6 KINCANNON, b. Dec. 30, 1954 at Yakima, Washington (SOH);
m. April 26, 1975 Linda E. Dunn at Yakima (SOH); "no children" (SOH).

****

page 94

see page 41

CARMEL E.-5 KINCANNON, (Carmel-5, Pearl Ann-4, Lou Etta-3, Celia-2, Jessie-1)
  b. April 30, 1932 at Scotland, Arkansas (SOH); "Baptist" (SOH);
  m.(1st) Oct. 8, 1947 Gerald Whorton at Yakima, Washington the son of Calvin Whorton and
      Wilma Franklin (SOH);
  m.(2nd) Jan. 14, 1971 James Trimm (SOH).

  CHILDREN: (of Carmel and Gerald)
  DWAYNE-6 WHORTON, b. July 10, 1948 at Ventura, California (SOH);
    d. Nov. 28, 1963, died in Service, Vietnam War (SOH); "no children" (SOH).

  REX-6 WHORTON, b. Dec. 10, 1952 at Yakima (SOH);
    m. Karie Oiler on Nov. 5, 1977 (SOH).

    CHILDREN: (of Rex and Karie)
    TYLER JEFFERSON-7 WHORTON, b. March 15, 1984 at Nashville, Tennessee (SOH).

  DANNY-6 WHORTON, b. Aug. 20, 1954 at Arcata, California (SOH);
    m. Bonnie Johnson on April 20, 1974 (SOH); "now divorced" (SOH);

    CHILDREN: (of Danny and Bonnie)
    CHRISTIE-7 WHORTON, b. Nov. 30, 1975 at Arcata, California (SOH).
    MISTY-7 WHORTON, b. June 7, 1977 at Arcata, California (SOH).

****

see page 45

TILLMAN-5 OSBORNE (Tillman-5, Dessa Mae-4, Lou Etta-3, Celia-2, Jesse-1)
b. Aug. 30, 1930 (SOH);
m. June 13, 1953 Ellen Louise Dujardin.

CHILDREN: (of Tillman and Ellen)
VALETA-6 OSBORNE, b. Jan. 18, 1955 at Everett, Washington (SOH);
m. Sept. 22, 1973 Willard Ralph King (SOH).

    CHILDREN: (of Valeta and William)
    RUSSELL LEE-7 KING, b. June 28, 1978 (SOH).
    AMANDA LOUISE-7 KING, b. July 28, 1980 (SOH).

KEVIN LOYLE-6 OSBORNE, b. July 23, 1957 at Everett, Washington (SOH);
m. Oct. 23, 1976 Suzanne Hanson Marsal (SOH).

    CHILDREN: (of Kevin and Suzanne)
    HEATHER MICHELLE-7 OSBORNE, b. Jan. 28, 1978 (SOH);
      d. at birth (SOH).
    NICHLOS LARKIN-7 OSBORNE, b. May 4, 1979 (SOH).
    PAUL CHRISTOPHER-7 OSBORNE, b. Sept. 13, 1982 (SOH).
    ELIZABETH MARIE-7 OSBORNE, b. Dec. 4, 1984 (SOH).

DOYLE MARLON-6 OSBORNE, b. Sept. 10, 1958 at Mt. Vernon, Washington (SOH);
m. Feb. 4, 1978 Velda Mae Broxson (SOH).

****

see page 46

VERNON-5 NEWTON, (Vernon-5, Dovie-4, Lou Etta-3, Celia-2, Jessie-1)
   b. June 14, 1930 (SOH);
   m. Feb. 14, 1954 Joyce Glee Rogers; she was born June 16, 1935 (SOH).

   CHILDREN: (of Vernon and Joyce)
   ROSELEE JOYCE-6 NEWTON, b. Oct. 6, 1955 (SOH).

   CELESTIAL DOVIE-6 NEWTON, b. March14, 1958 (SOH);
      m. June 19, 1976 KERRY LEE HODGES who was born July 20, 1956 (SOH).

      CHILDREN: (of Celestial and Kerry)
      MATTHEW LEE-7 HODGES, b. Oct. 18, 1977 (SOH).
      JASON DEREK-7 HODGES, b. June 20, 1981 (SOH).

   TAMMY RAE-6 NEWTON, b. May 30, 1960 (SOH);
      m. Dec. 6, 1978 Charles Henry Pelroy who was born July 28, 1959 (SOH).

      CHILDREN: (of Tammy and Charles) "divorced now" (SOH).
      CHRISTOPHER LEE-7 PELROY, b. Dec. 18, 1978 (SOH).
      CHARTAM MARIE-7 PELROY, b. July 4, 1980 (SOH).

   VENETTA MAE-6 NEWTON, b. Nov. 10, 1962 (SOH);
      m. Jan. 16, 1982 Aaron David Anderson, he was born March 18, 1959 (SOH).

      CHILDREN: (of Venetta and Aaron)
      AMANDA JO-7 ANDERSON, b. Feb. 10, 1983 (SOH).
      ALISHA RAYNEEE-7 ANDERSON, b. April 10, 1985 (SOH).

   VERNON MARK-6 NEWTON, b. Dec. 20, 1964 (SOH).

   DANIEL ROGER-6 NEWTON, b. June 11, 1966 (SOH).

****

page 97

see page 46

WILLIAM JOE-5 NEWTON, (William-5, Dovie-4, Lou Etta-3, Celia-2, Jessie-1)
   b. Oct. 2, 1932 (SOH);
   m. May 10, 1953 Esther Eileen Day; she was born Dec. 31, 1934 (SOH).

CHILDREN: (of William and Esther)
DOROTHY NADINE-6 NEWTON, b. March 5, 1954 (SOH);
   m. June 30, 1973 David Luther Ipock (SOH).

   CHILDREN: (of Dorothy and David)
   JASON LUTHER-7 IPOCK, b. March 21, 1975 (SOH).
   TAWNYA DE ANN-7 IPOCK, b. April 2, 1978 (SOH).

WILLIAM JOE-6 NEWTON, Jr., b. July 9, 1956 (SOH);
   m. Feb. 24, 1979 Mary Helen Leamy who was born Sept. 8, 1957 (SOH).

   CHILDREN: (of William and Mary)
   WILLIAM JOE-7 NEWTON, III, b. Sept. 16, 1979 (SOH).
   CRYSTAL DAWN-7 NEWTON, b. July 20, 1982 (SOH).

KATHLEEN FAYE-6 NEWTON, b. June 3, 1958 (SOH);
   m. Nov. 25, 1978 Brian Keith Badley who was born Feb. 19, 1957 (SOH).

   CHILDREN: (of Kathleen and Brian)
   AMBER KAYE-7 BADLEY, b. April 17, 1980 (SOH).
   RYAN DANIEL-7 BADLEY, b. April 24, 1984 (SOH).

MARGARET EILEEN-6 NEWTON, b. Jan. 3, 1960 (SOH);
   m. March 11, 1978 Grant Arther Guenthner who was born May 14, 1960 (SOH).

   CHILDREN: (of Margaret and Grant)
   ALISA EILEEN-7 GUENTHNER, b. Dec. 4, 1979 (SOH).
   BRENT ARTHUR-7 GUENTHNER, b. Nov. 5, 1981 (SOH).

PATRICIA LOUISE-6 NEWTON, b. April 27, 1962 (SOH);
   m. Aug. 8, 1981 Darryl Paul Koerschgen who was born Feb. 20, 1950 (SOH).

   CHILDREN: (of Patricia and Darryl)
   DARRYL PAUL-7 KOERSCHGEN, II, b. Aug. 10, 1982 (SOH).
   DANIELLE PATRICIA-7 KOERSCHGEN, b. May 25, 1984 (SOH).

****

see page 46

page 98

RUTHA LaVERNE-5 NEWTON, (Rutha-5, Dovie-4, Lou Etta-3, Celia-2, Jessie-1)
    b. July 18, 1934 (SOH);
    d. April 23, 1982 (SOH);
    m. March 27, 1953 Robert Clyde Messinger; he was born Feb. 19, 1930 and married (2nd)
       Melany Hope Mork on April 22, 1984; she was born Nov. 6, 1943 (SOH).

CHILDREN: (of Rutha and Robert)
TERRY La VERNE-6 MESSINGER, b. May 15, 1954 (SOH);
    m.(1)John Grumbo (SOH). "divorced now " (SOH).
    m.(2)July 17, 1978 Jack O. Smith who was born Aug. 13, 1939 (SOH).

    CHILDREN: (of Terry and John)
    JOHN LEON-7 GRUMBO, b. Sept. 8, 1972 (SOH).
    JEANETTE La VERNE-7 GRUMBO, b. April 4, 1974 (SOH).

MARY ELAINE-6 MESSINGER, b. Feb. 3, 1956 (SOH);
    m. Jan. 2, 1973 Mark Allen Pruett (SOH).

    CHILDREN: (of Mary and Mark)
    JEANNIE MARIE-7 PRUETT, b. Oct. 8, 1973 (SOH).
    JANIE ELAINE-7 PRUETT, b. Aug. 9, 1974 (SOH).
    JAMIE ANN-7 PRUETT, b. Dec. 17, 1976 (SOH).

DEBORA RUTH-6 MESSINGER, b. March 4, 1958 (SOH);
    m. Oct. 3, 1977 Theodore William Harkleroad, III, who was born Aug. 9, 1947 (SOH).

    CHILDREN: (of Debora and Theodore)
    JEREMY LYNN-7 HARKLEROAD, b. Feb. 18, 1976 (SOH).
    TED WILLIAM-7 HARKLEROAD, b. Nov. 18, 1978 (SOH).

ROBERT JAMES-6 MESSINGER, b. Oct. 14, 1959 (SOH);
    m. June 15, 1979 Lorenda Lee Ford who was born Feb. 1, 1961 (SOH).

DIANNA BELL-6 MESSINGER, b. Sept. 21, 1960 (SOH);
    d. Oct. 30, 1962 (SOH).

DONALD CLYDE-6 MESSINGER, b. Sept. 17, 1963 (SOH);
    m. June 18, 1983 Rosemarie Lois Turner who was born Dec. 11, 1961 (SOH).

****

page 99

see page 46

JAMES LEWIS-5 NEWTON, (James-5, Dovie-4, Lou Etta-3, Celia-2, Jessie-1)
b. June 22, 1936 (SOH);
m. June 20, 1959 Carol Iva Campbell; she was born June 18, 1940 (SOH).

CHILDREN: (of James and Carol)
ANDREW JAMES-6 NEWTON, b. March 10, 1961 (SOH);
    m. July 12, 1980 Thesa Louise Ferrell who was born June 22, 1963 (SOH). divorced June
    13, 1983 (SOH).

   CHILDREN: (of Andrew and Thesa)
   KENNETH ANDREW-7 NEWTON, b. April 15, 1981 (SOH).

JOSEPH LEWIS-6 NEWTON, b. Jan. 1, 1971 (SOH).

IVARENE BELLE-6 NEWTON, b. Sept. 30, 1972 (SOH).

****

page 100

see page 46

LEE ROY-5 NEWTON (Lee Roy-5, Dovie-4, Lou Etta-3, Celia-2, Jessie-1)
    b. June 17, 1938 (SOH);
    m.(1st) June 27, 1958 Nellie Joann Spears, she was born June 6, 1940;
        "divorced July 30, 1980" (SOH).
    m.(2nd) Jan. 2, 1983 Sammy Mae Parker Grimmesey who was born Aug. 25, 1931 (SOH).

CHILDREN: (of Lee Roy and Nellie)
CURTIS LEE-6 NEWTON, b. Oct. 1, 1959 (SOH);
    m. July 24, 1982 Kathi Ann Gatlin who was born March 29, 1962 (SOH).
BARNEY SANFORD-6 NEWTON, b. May 9, 1962 (SOH).

****

page 101

see page 46

IRVEN GLYNN-5 NEWTON, (Irven-5, Dovie-4, Lou Etta-3, Celia-2, Jessie-1)
b. Feb. 13, 1946 (SOH);
m. May 21, 1966 Jackie Ruth Bullard; she was born June 27, 1946 (SOH).

CHILDREN: (of Irven and Jackie)
SHERI LANETTE-6 NEWTON, b. June 9, 1967 (SOH).
RONDA JA ANN-6 NEWTON, b. Oct. 17, 1971 (SOH).
IRVEN GLYNN-6 NEWTON, Jr., b. Feb. 16, 1973 (SOH).
BRADLEY JAY-6 NEWTON, b. Jan. 9, 1975 (SOH).
ROXANN RANAE-6 NEWTON, b. Oct. 19, 1976 (SOH).
KEVIN JAMES-6 NEWTON, b. March 17, 1978 (SOH).
JEFFERY SCOTT-6 NEWTON, b. Dec. 16, 1979 (SOH).
COREY WADE-6 NEWTON, b. Aug. 9, 1982 (SOH).
JASON WAYNE-6 NEWTON, b. March 4, 1985 (SOH).

see page 57

BILLIE JOE-5 SWAIN (Billie Joe-5, Virgil-4, Joseph Oscar-3, John Abner-2, Jesse Abner-1)
  b. Dec. 19, 1933 at Cleveland, Arkansas (JD); resided in Wascom, Texas (JD);
  d. Dec. 17, 1985, buried in Texas (JD);
  m. (1st)_____Beavers (JD); now divorced (JD);
  m. (2nd) Joyce _____ (JD).

CHILDREN: (of Billie Joe)
  ART L.-6 SWAIN, b. _____; "resides in Wascom, Texas (JD).
  PHILLIP J.-6 SWAIN, b. _____; "resides in Wascom, Texas (JD);
    m. Joyce _____ (JD).

"Billie Joe Swain died at his home in Wascom, Texas on Dec. 19, 1985 because of a heart ailment at the age of 51 years. He was the only child of Virgil and Lela Swain and was born at Cleveland, Arkansas.

At an early age Billie Joe moved to Detroit, Michigan where he became employed at General Motors Corporation and where he retired as a supervisor.

At the memorial services held in his memory at Wascom, Texas on December 19, 1985 the eulogy read in part:

> Billie was a people person ... he loved to be with his family and friends. His home was their home, and the door never locked, nor did anyone ever need to knock before entering. He loved children and worked continously with the Grotto in Youngstown (Ohio) helping the retarded. While in Shreveport (Louisiana) he worked with the Shriners in raising money to build a new hospital.

He was a member of Masonic Lodge No. 5 of Rochester, Michigan, the Scottish Rite of Youngstown, Ohio, and the El Karubah Shrine Temple of Shreveport, Louisiana." (VAS)

JOYCE & BILLIE JOE SWAIN

****

see page 58

JIMMY-5 WARD (Jimmy-5, Faye-4, Joseph Oscar-3, John Abner-2, Jesse Abner-1)
   b. Oct. 16, 1935 (JD); resides in Deering, MO 1985 (JD);
   m. Betsy Lindsey (JD).

   CHILDREN: (of Jimmy and Betsy)
   MARK-6 WARD, b. _____ (VAS).
   KEITH-6 WARD, b. _____ (VAS).

   "Jimmy is the oldest of three children born to Ellis and Faye Ward.
   In High School he excelled in basketball and attended Arkansas State University as Jonesboro, Arkansas on a basketball scholarship, graduating with a degree in physical education. Following graduation, he coached high school basketball for several years in eastern Arkansas.
   Some years ago he and his family moved to Deering, Missouri where he farms with his younger son, Keith. Mark works in hospital maintenance at Haith, Missouri." (VAS)

**JIMMY AND BETTY WARD
WITH THEIR TWO SONS** (FROM LEFT TO RIGHT) **KEITH AND MARK.**
Pictured in December, 1963

Keith, Wynette, Karessa, & Nathan

****

see page 58

page 104

BONNIE-5 WARD (Bonnie-5, Faye-4, Joseph Oscar-3, John Abner-2, Jesse Abner-1)
b. Feb. 7, 1937 (JD); resides in Conway, Arkansas (JD);
m. E.J. Stracner (JD). spelled "Stracner" not "Strocener" (JD)

CHILDREN: (of Bonnie and E.J.)
SONJA-6 STRACNER, b. _____ (JD).
KATHY-6 STRACNER, b. _____ (JD).

"Following high school, Bonnie attended Harding College in Searcy, Arkansas for two years and later graduated from the University of Central Arkansas in Conway, Arkansas.
For 12 years she taught business courses in high schools, and for a period of time she worked at the Arkansas Children's Colony in Conway. Bonnie now works for the Arkansas Department of Education in Little Rock.
Sonya, the older daughter, graduated from Southern Technical College in Little Rock and Kathy has attended the University of Central Arkansas.
Since high school days, Sonya has sung country and western music and both daughters now reside in Nashville, Tennessee where Sonya works for a recording studio and where she has ambitions of becoming a recording artist." (VAS)

BONNIE AND HER TWO DAUGHTERS,
(left to right)
SONJA & KATHY

****

see page 58

GLORIA JEAN-5 WARD (Gloria-5, Faye-4, Joseph Oscar-3, John Abner-2, Jesse Abner-1)
b. Sept. 30, 1946 (JD); reside at Scotland, AR (JD);
m. Bobby Love (JD).

CHILDREN: (of Gloria Jean and Bobby)
KIMBERLY-6 LOVE, b. Oct. 12, 1968 (VAS).
AMY-6 LOVE, b. May 3, 1977 (VAS).

"Gloria Ward Love graduated from Wonderview High School, Hattieville, Arkansas in May of 1948 and later attended Petit Jean Vocational Technical School in Morrilton while taking a business course.

With her two daughters reaching sufficient age, Gloria worked in a secretarial position with the Arkansas Department of Social Services at Clinton, Arkansas for 8 years. During the past 5 years she has worked as a Teacher's Aide at the high school in Scotland, Arkansas.

Her husband, Bobby, raised in the Scotland area and also a graduate of Scotland High School, is a carpenter and home builder. Bobby formerly taught carpentry at Petit Jean Vocational Technical School and worked at this trade in Little Rock for a period of time.

The family resides in a spacious and comfortable home surrounded by some beautiful acreage at Scotland and which was built entirely by Bobby." (VAS)

****

page 106

see page 60

JERRY RAY-5 SWAIN, (Jerry-5, Ray-4, Joseph-3, John-2, Jessie-1)
    b. May 12, 1939 (VAS); lives at 801 Childress in Morrilton, Arkansas;
    m. Dec. 27, 1958 Louise Petty, by Rev. C.M. Lewallen (from Conway County Book 39,
        page 194)

    CHILDREN: (of Jerry and Louise)
    TIM-6 SWAIN, b.   (JD).
    SCOTT-6 SWAIN, b.   (JD).
    RENEE-6 SWAIN, b.   (JD).

"As a youth **Jerry Ray-5 Swain** attended the Morrilton Public Schools, and in December of 1956 he enlisted in the U.S. Air Force. During his military career of 20 years his achievements included receipt of a high school diploma in 1958, two tours of overseas duty in Vietnam, training for and lengthy service as a Flight Engineer and with promotions leading to the rank of Technical Sergeant.

In December 1958, Jerry was married to a former high school classmate and sweetheart, Louise Petty, of Morrilton and the couple have three children: Tim, now 28 years of age, a resident of Morrilton and one of the better bowlers of the area; Renee, age 27, now Mrs. Dennis McCoy; and Scott, age 15 years, and a 9th grade student.

Since retiring from the Air Force, Jerry worked 6 years for a Morrilton lumber firm and is currently performing general maintenance for the Morrilton Housing Authority.

Jerry's favorite pastime includes hunting and fishing, and he has a workshop behind the neat brick and frame house where the family resides at 801 W. Childress Street in Morrilton and where he builds such items as gun cases and suctom made kitchen cabinets.

Louise is employed as Pace Setter Inn in Morrilton and is in charge of Maid Service." (VAS)

****

page 107

see page 61

ALMA SUE-5 SWAIN, (Alma-5, Dale-4, Joseph Oscar-3, John Abner-2, Jesse Abner-1)
   b.Feb. 29, 1944 resides in Midwest City, Oklahoma (JD);
   m. Gary Stroud, of Scotland, Arkansas (JD).

CHILDREN: (of Alma and Gary)
PAUL KELLY-5 STROUD, b. July 15, 1968 (VAS).
GREGORY TODD-5 STROUD, b. June 26, 1970 (VAS).
DANIEL SCOTT-5 STROUD, b. March 24, 1973 (VAS).

"Quite early in life, Alma Sue Swain brought distinction and honor to herself, to her family and to the Swain family name as an expert horsewoman. From early childhood, Sue, as she is better known, demonstrated a great love for horses and soon began to excel in the art of horseback riding. During her early high school and college years she and her favorite horse, Gypsy, began to perform at rodeos throughout the state where she won numerous events in pole-bending, barrel pick-ups, and barrel racing. In 1965, at Conway, Arkansas, she won the Arkansas Rodeo Championship in pole bending, and placed 5th in the Arkansas and Oklahoma Rodeo Sweetheart Contest.
   In the same year, 1965, Sue graduated from Plumerville High School where she starred as a forward on the Senior Girl's high school team. She was elected FFA Sweetheart and was also Miss Plumerville High School.
   Sue enrolled at the University of Central Arkansas in Conway in September of 1965 and attended for three years while majoring in physical education.
   Beginning in September 1968 and continuing for the next three terms she taught school and coached girl's basketball at Scotland High School.
   It was during this time that she came to know and later married Gary Stroud of the Scotland Community and also a UCA student who obtained a B. S. Degree in Electrical Engineering and later earned a Master's Degree in Business Education.
   With Gary's education completed the young couple moved to Mobile, Alabama where he accepted a position as an electrical engineer with the U. S. Air Force Civil Service. A later assignment of a similar nature followed at Biloxi, Mississippi and the family including three young sons now live at Oklahoma City where Gary continues his U. S. Civil Service career.
   In 1983, Sue returned to college where she obtained a B. S. Degree in Elementary Education and she is currently in her second year teaching at the elementary level in Oklahoma City." (VAS).

Alma Sue Swain Stroud

****

see page 73
page 108

JOE LYNN-5 SMIRL (Eunice Alline-4,Sherman Norton-3, John Abner-2, Jesse Abner-1)
b. Nov. 30, 1940 at Morrilton, Arkansas (STS);
m. Sept. 14, 1963 Patricia Marie Ruffiner, she was born on September 11, 1938 at
Morrilton, she is the daughter of Eugene Ruffiner and Mary Margaret Bour (ROC).
Joe and Pat live at 300 Oaklawn Dr., Morrilton, Arkansas 72110 (ROC).

"Joe Lynn Smirl graduated from Atkins High School in May, 1958 where he played tackle and
lettered in football 2 years in Junior High and 2 years in Senior High. He was also President of the
Student Council in his senior year. He later attended Arkansas Tech University in Russellville for
2 years.

During his high school and college years Joe worked part-time at the Blackwell Roller Rink
and at the Atkins Pickle Plant.

Full-time jobs following his college years have included one and one half years with Interstate
Manufacturing Company in Romeo, Michigan; two years as a parts clerk with Maus Implement
Company in Morrilton; nine and one half years as Purchasing Agent and Parts Department
Manager with Crompton Company in Morrilton; and, in 1977 Joe returned to the parts department
at Maus Implement Company where he has only recently been elevated to Parts Department
Manager.

On September 14, 1963 Joe and Patricia Ruffiner of Morrilton were united in marriage.

Pat graduated from Sacred Heart High School in Morrilton in 1956 where she lettered in volley
ball during her last four years. She was Class Secretary while in her junior year and served on the
Yearbook Staff and was a member of the Dramatics Team during her senior years.

Following high school Pat spent 10 years as a Bookkeeper with Morrilton Packing Company
and she has been employed in the office of Dr. Norman Gray in Morrilton as a Veterinary
Technician since December, 1966.

Pat and Joe are members of Sacred Heart Church and Pat's church activities include past
membership in Catholic Youth Organization (CYO), Student Mission Crusade during high school
years and she is now an active member of the Altar Society.

Joe is a member of the Knights of Columbus and in 1977-78 was honored as Knight of the
Year.

Joe is an avid fisherman and does some bird and squirrel hunting.

The Smirls own their home at 600 Oaklawn Drive in Morrilton. Both have developed wide
acquaintances in the surrounding areas and being the especially well-liked persons that they both
are, they enjoy many many friends. "(VAS)

Joe with a prize catch

Joe & Pat Smirl

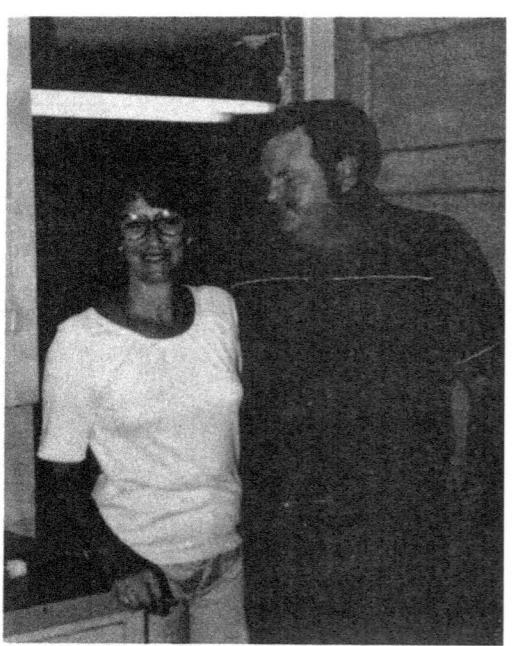

page 110

see page 29

OLIVIA ANN-5 SMIRL, (Olivia-5, Eunice Alline-4, Sherman Norton-3, John-2, Jesse-1)
    b. March 19, 1947 at Morrilton, AR (STS);
    m. Nov. 2, 1971 Paul Bernard Allen (STS).

CHILDREN:
DANIEL CRAIG-6 ALLEN, b. Austin, Texas (STS).
CHRISTI DAWN-6 ALLEN, b. Austin, Texas (STS).

"Born and reared at Blackwell, Conway County, Arkansas, Olivia Ann Smirl Allen graduated from nearby Atkins High School in 1965 and attended Petit Jean Vocational Technical School training in office practices and the operation of business machines.

With the completion of this course in 1966, she became employed wit G. E. Credit Corporation in Little Rock, and later accepted employment in a similar capacity with Ford Motor Credit Corporation, also in Little Rock. It was there that she came to know and later married her husband, Paul B. Allen.

At Carthage, Mississippi, where the family resides, Olivia is busily engaged in rearing her two children, Craig and Christie, and in managing the family household. Additionally, she finds the time to teach the Young Ladies' Class each Sunday morning at First Baptist Church at Carthage where the family are members. Olivia works part-time as a bookkeeper in her husband's business, and she also is employed part-time as an Interviewer with the Mississippi State Welfare Department.

Her husband, Paul, was born January 28, 1940 at Noxapater, Winston County, Mississippi and graduated from high school in that city in 1958. In the following fall he enrolled at Mississippi State University where he graduated in 1962 with a B. S. Degree in Business Administration.

From 1962-1971, Paul was employed with Ford Motor Credit Corporation in Little Rock and later worked in a similar position in Austin, Texas until 1978.

Since 1978 to the present time, Paul has been President and General Manager of Frontier Ford, Inc., a new and used car sales agency located in Carthage.

He is a Deacon at First Baptist Church in Carthage, and Paul is a member of the Gideon's International. Paul is also an active fisherman and plans much of his vacation time in and around the crappie-biting season in Arkansas.

Daniel Craig Allen is 13 years of age and in the 8th grade at Leake Acadamey in Madden, Mississipi. He is an active member of Carthage First Baptist Church. Craig is on the B Football Team. His favorite sports are fishing, camping, tennis, basketball, and swimming.

Christie Allen is 11 years of age and a 6th grade student at Leake Academy, Maddea, Mississippi. She is an active member of Farthage First Baptist Church. Her favorite sport is swimming.

Paul & Olivia
Christi & Craig

****

see page 30

MARCIA GAIL-5 SWAIN (Marcia Gail-5, Verril Ansel-4, Sherman-3, John-2, Jesse-1)
   b. April 26, 1953 at Morrilton, Arkansas in St Anthony's Hospital
   m. Feb. 9, 1973 to Robert Owen Crossman at Morrilton, Arkansas by Rev. Clyde Parsons
   at First United Methodist Church. Bob was born Feb. 24, 1953 at Houston, Texas
   son of Paul Judson Crossman and Roberta Frances Mittag. Bob Crossman is the
   compiler of this Swain Family Genealogy. Bob and Marcia live in Prairie Grove,
   Arkansas in 1985. Bob is an eleventh generation descendant of John Crossman of
   Taunton (Robert-11, Paul Judson-10, Nelson Kennedy-9, Samuel Peleg-8, Samuel-7,
   Samuel-6, Stephen-5, Nathaniel-4, Robert-3, Robert-2, John-1 Crossman). A
   complete genealogy of the Crossman family is available in "A Genealogy of The
   Crossman Family, Descendants of John & Robert Crossman of Taunton,
   Massachusetts", pp. 1-212, (1977), and Supplement #1 pp. 213-470, (1982) both
   compiled by Bob Crossman. (ROC)

CHILDREN:
CHARLES ROBERT-6 CROSSMAN, b. Aug. 3, 1978 at Dallas, Texas in Presbyterian
   Hospital (ROC).
DAVID NATHAN-6 CROSSMAN, b. Nov. 2, 1981 at Fayetteville, Arkansas in
   Washington Regional Hospital (ROC).

Marcia Swain Crossman

David & Charlie Crossman

page 112

Marcia Gail Swain Crossman attended public school in Morrilton, Arkansas and graduated from Morrilton High School in May of 1971.

In her high school days, Marcia worked part time at the local movie theatre selling tickets at the box office and at a drive-in restaurant. Marcia loved mini-skirts, knee boots, records, dating and twirling a baton for the high school band. Marcia, along with her sister, Sherry, and Patricia Farish Swain (also in this genealogy) were in a majorette line together. It was said by many that the girls all made, "quite an impressive team." Marcia was active in the Methodist Church and enjoyed participating in the Youth Fellowship.

In the summer 1972, after attending the University of Arkansas for a year and while working at Morrilton First United Methodist Church as secretary for a second summer, Marcia met Robert Owen Crossman who was working at the same church as Director of Youth Ministries. In February of 1973 Marcia and Bob were married. Marcia and Bob moved to Mayflower where Bob became pastor of four small United Methodist Churches in the area while the two of them finished undergraduate school in Conway. Marcia graduated in 1975 from the University of Central Arkansas with a B.S.E. in Home Economics. Bob graduated in the same year with a B.A. in Religion from Hendrix College.

Marcia and Bob moved to Dallas, Texas in 1975 living in Moore Hall while Bob attended classes and Marcia worked at Highland Park United Methodist Day Care Center. Marcia enrolled in the Masters of Divinity Degree program at Perkins School of Theology, Southern Methodist University in January of 1976 and completed her degree in May of 1983. During the eight years Marcia was in seminary, she also served for a summer as Co-Pastor of the Brightwater/ Avoca/ Tucks Chapel United Methodist Churches; Intern Minister of First United Methodist Church of North Little Rock nine months; pastor of the Belleville UMC for two years; and pastor of the Weddington/ Cincinitti/ Rheas Mill United Methodist Churches for two years. Marcia also worked with the Southern Methodist University Housing Office as Director of Perkins and Smith Graduate Dormitories.

On August 1 of 1978, Charles Robert was born at Presbyterian Hospital in Dallas, Texas. Marcia traveled to Israel and Egypt in the winter of 1981 with Educational Opportunities, a non-profit organization. Her second child, David Nathan, was born on November 2, 1981 at Washington Regional Hospital at Fayetteville, Arkansas.

After graduating with a Masters of Divinity in 1983, Marcia was appointed as Director of Cooperative Parish Ministries for the Benton County United Methodist Churches (18 in all) in Northwest Arkansas. The following year her responsibilities were enlarged to include Washington County. In 1985 Marcia was appointed as Associate Minister of the largest United Methodist Congregation in the North Arkansas Annual Conference, Central UMC in Fayetteville.

Marcia was ordained a Deacon in the United Methodist Church in 1977 at the regular session of the North Arkansas Annual Conference held at First United Methodist in Jonesboro, Arkansas. She was ordained an Elder and elected a full member of the North Arkansas Annual Conference in May of 1986 at First United Methodist Church in Conway, Arkansas.

In her leisure hours, Marcia enjoys aerobic exercise and sculpting and painting Christmas ornaments made of salt and flour dough. Marcia also enjoys designing computer art work and word processing. In 1986 she began a successful business in graphic design called The Communication Shoppe.

Robert Owen Crossman, son of Paul Judson and Roberta Frances Mittag Crossman, was born February 24, 1953 in Houston, Harris County, Texas.

Bob attended Lula M. Stevens Elementary School in Houston, Texas through the fifth grade; Lee Elementary School and Lakeside Elementary School, both of Robbinsdale, Minnesota through the sixth grade; Robbinsdale Junior and Senior Highs through the ninth grade; University of Minnesota summer entomology courses in 1967 and 1968; and, graduated from Russellville Senior High in May of 1971. Bob attended Arkansas Tech University in Russellville, Arkansas; University of Central Arkansas in Conway, Arkansas; and received a Bachelor of Arts degree in Religion from Hendrix College of Conway in May, 1975. Bob attended Southern Methodist Universities' Perkins Graduate School of Theology from 1975 until 1980, and received a Master of Theology degree. Bob returned to SMU and completed a Doctor of Ministry in 1984.

As a child, Bob helped his parents occasionally when they owned and operated Crossman Bakery and Catering Service in Houston, Texas. As a teenager, Bob owned Crossman Honey

page 113

Company from 1965 until 1968; he worked as a sales clerk with Pet World Stores, Inc. of Robbinsdale, 1965-68; with The Little Pet Shop of Russellville, 1968 until 1970; with Minute Man Resturant in Russellville from 1970 until 1971; with Morton Frozen Foods in the summer of 1971; with First United Methodist & First Presbyterian of Morrilton as Summer Youth Worker in the summer of 1972. It was during that summer that Bob and Marcia met.

Bob was pastor of four United Methodist Churches in the Faulkner County Parish from 1973 until 1975; he worked as Director of SMU's Mary Hay Hall, 1975-6; in the Perkins Library at SMU, 1976-78; co-pator of the Brightwater-Tuck's Chapel United Methodist Churches during the summer of 1978; as Intern Minister at Pulaksi Heights U.M.C., 1978-79; and as Director of Martin Hall at S.M.U., 1979-1980.

After completing his Master's Degree, Bob served as pastor of the Pottsville United Methodist Church in Pottsville, Arkansas from April 1980 until June of 1981. Since that time he has served as pastor of the Viney Grove and First United Methodist Churches in Prairie Grove, Arkansas.

Bob's hobbies have included genealogy, stamp collecting, aquariums, coin collecting, and beekeeping. Bob received numerous ribbons for his bees at the Minnesota State Fair and trophies for his aquariums from the Arkansas Aquarium Society. Bob has held membership in the Minnesota Hobby Beekeepers Acssociation; the Arkansas Aquarium Society; University of Arkansas Tech President's Council; President, Arkansas Tech Wesley Foundation; Past Master Counselor and State Chaplain, Order of Demolay; Board of Directors, Arkansas Tech Wesley Foundation; Worship Chairperson, Conway District Council on Ministries; Director, West Washington County Cooperative Parish Ministry; President/Treasurer, Prairie Grove Ministerial Alliance; Prairie Grove Chamber of Commerce; Fayetteville District Council on Ministries; Registrar, North Arkansas Conference Board of Diaconal Ministry; North Arkansas Conference Board of Discipleship; North Arkansas Conference Worship Committee; Board of Directors, U. of A. Wesley Foundation; Room Dad, 2nd Grade; and, Den Leader, Cub Scouts.

In his leisure hours, Bob enjoys wrestling with Charlie and David, helping Charlie's Cub Scout Den, and working with Marcia's computer laser publishing and printing enterprise.

Charles Robert (Charlie) Crossman is a happy healthy third grader (1986). At age eight, Charlie, slender with blond hair and blue eyes, is a very smart little boy who loves the Cub Scouts, 't-ball' and is an "honorary" member of the Prairie Grove United Methodist Youth Fellowship and manager of their choir, "GOING UP". Charlie is very smart in mathematics, spelling and has received many compliments on his ablilty to print well.

David Nathan Crossman is a smiling, healthy, blond haired and blue eyed five year old (1986). David is a happy-go-lucky type of person. He enjoys playing with toy characters and having them to talk to each other. It is interesting to note that David has inherited his grandfather Ansel (-4) Swain's natural curly hair and left handedness.

Charlie, Bob, Marcia (Swain), David
taken October, 1985

Charles Robert Crossman

David Nathan Crossman

page 114

see page 75

SHERRY ELIZABETH-5 SWAIN (Sherry-5, V. Ansel-4, Sherman-3, John-2, Jesse-1)
   b. May 6, 1955 at Morrilton, Arkansas (ROC);
   m. Dec. 29, 1977 William Michael Lisle of Gentry at Morrilton, Arkansas by Rev. Bob
        Crossman at First United Methodist Church (ROC); they have no children, and are no
        longer married (1985). (ROC)

   "**Sherry Elizabeth Swain Lisle** attended public school in Morrilton, Arkansas and
graduated from Morrilton High School in May of 1973.
   In her teen years, Sherry was active in the Methodist Church and enjoyed participating in the
Youth Fellowship. Sherry also enjoyed attending dances, wearing mini-skirts and knee boots
popular in the late '60's, dating, and twirling a baton for the Morrilton High School Band. Sherry
along with her sister, Marcia, and Patricia Farish Swain (also in this genealogy) were in a majorette
line together. It was said by many that the girls all made, 'quite an impressive team.'
   In her high school days, Sherry worked part-time as a waitress at a local restaurant and at the
city's drive-in theatre consession building.
   Sherry, an attractive young woman, 5' 3" tall, blond hair, blue-eyed, and slender was
Morrilton's Junior Miss in 1972 and had the honor of lighting the town's Christmas tree. In 1973,
upon entering college at Arkansas Tech University in Russellville, Sherry was awarded a
scholarship from Crompton- Arkansas Mills of Morrilton. Sherry was in the Arkansas Tech
marching band for a year and was their Feature Twirler. In 1978, Sherry graduated from the
University of Central Arkansas in Conway with a BSE in Speech Pathology. While studying at
UCA, Sherry enjoyed the marching band and was also a member of the twirling team. During
college years, Sherry worked part time for Wal Mart in Morrilton and several summers at the
Morrilton Country Club as lifeguard.
   On December 28, 1977 Sherry and William Michael Lisle were married at First United
Methodist Church of Morrilton by Rev. Robert O. Crossman. As "Sparky" was stationed in
various localities with the U. S. Army, Sherry taught speech therapy and individual children who
had learning disabilities in public schools. Sherry was a teacher in Ft. Leonard Wood, Missouri
(two years), in Enterprise, Alabama (one year), in Junction City, Kansas (two years), and in
Manhattan, Kansas (four years). In 1986, Sherry has almost completed a Master's Degree in
Speech Therapy at Kansas State University in Manhattan and continues to make her home in
Manhattan, KS.
   In her leisure hours, Sherry has enjoyed bicycle riding, aerobic exercise, dancing, arranging
flowers and tending to a special pet dog named 'Gusty'." (MGSC)

Sherry Swain

****

page 115

see page 83

WILLIAM SHERMAN-5 SWAIN (William-5, Dallas-4, Sherman-3, John-2, Jesse Abner-1)
  b. April 4, 1952 in Morrilton, Arkansas (STS).
  m. Nov. 20, 1970 Patricia Ann Farish at the Atkins United Methodist Church by Rev. M.J.
    Pollard. She was born March 20, 1953. They live at Atkins, Arkansas. She is the daughter
    of Raymond Farish, Jr. and Mary Sue Wright. (WSS).

CHILDREN:
  BELINDA KAYE-6 SWAIN, b. March 19, 1971 in Russellville, AR (WSS).
    "Attends Atkins High School, currently a Freshman" (WSS).
  BRITTANY NICOLE-6 SWAIN, b. Sept. 3, 1980 in Russellville, AR (WSS); "attends
    Atkins Elementary School, kindergarten student" (WSS)

William Sherman Swain was born in Morrilton, Arkansas at St. Anthony's Hospital on
April 4, 1952. Bill graduated from Atkins High School as Salutatorian of his class in May of
1970. He attended Arkansas Polytechnic College, now Arkansas Tech University, majoring in
history and political science and minoring in accounting. He was a Dean's List student and a
member of Blue Key National Honor Fraternity, and graduated on May 11, 1974, receiving a
Bachelor of Arts Degree. During his senior year in college, he was a Senior Fellow in the
Department of Social Sciences. Bill graduated from the University of Arkansas at Fayetteville
School of Law in December of 1976 receiving a Juris Doctor Degree. He was admitted to practice
law in the State of Arkansas on March 24, 1977, and has practiced continuously since that time
with the firm of Laws, Swain & Murdoch, P.A., located in Russellville, Arkansas. The firm
recently moved into a new two-story office building at the corner of Second and Arkansas. Since
1979 he has served as city attorney for the cities of Atkins and Pottsville. Bill was President of the
Atkins Jaycees for the year 1985, has served as Chairperson of the Administrative Council of the
Atkins United Methodist Church for the years 1980 through 1985, and has served as Chairman of
the George S. Jones Trust, a trust fund to support girls athletics at Atkins High School, since the
trust was formed in 1978. He has held many other offices in his local church including Chairman
of the Building Design Committee for the Atkins United Methodist Church constructed in the late
1970's. Bill is presently Vice-President of his local church's United Methodist Men's Club and
Vice-President of the Arkansas River Valley Methodist Men. He and his wife, Pat, are members of
the Arkansas Arts Center and the Arkansas River Valley Art Center. While in high school and
college, Bill worked at Crompton Mills in Morrilton, where his uncle, Ansel Swain, was employed
in a supervisory capacity.
  Bill's wife, **Patricia Ann Swain** , was born March 20, 1953, in Morrilton, Arkansas at St.
Anthony's Hospital. She graduated from Morrilton High School in 1971. While attending high
school, she played the flute in the MOrrilton High School Band and was a majorette in the same
line with Marcia Swain and Sherry Swain. Pat previously worked at C & D Drug Store in Atkins
as a clerk and bookkeeper. She ius now a homemaker, and her activities include leading aerobics,
decorating cakes, baking and studying taekwondo karate. Pat is currently a blue belt working her
way up to red and then black. Pat is active in her local United Methodist Church, serving on the
nominating and memorial committees, volunteering as a Bible School teacher, and serving as
co-chairman along with Bill, on the Charcoal Hamburger Cookout Committee, a successful project
held annually for the last seven years to raise money for the building fund. All of the Swains living
in Atkins help with this project.
  Belinda Kaye Swain was born March 19, 1971, in Russellville at St. Mary's Hospital.
She is currently a sophomore at Atkins High School. She is a member of the Atkins High School
Band and plays the same flute that her mother Pat played. Just like her mother, Belinda is a
majorette in the band. Belinda is a Bible School assistant and is a member of the Future
Homemakers of America, the Science Club, and the Beta Club. She has a pet guinea pig named
Peanut Butter. Although all her ancestors on both sides of her family have dark hair, Belinda's hair
is blonde.
  Britanny Nicole Swain was born September 3, 1980, in Russellville at St. Mary's
Hospital. She is a first grade student at the Atkins Elementary School. She enjoys swimming,
gymnastics, and roller skating. Britanny enjoys school and loves her first grade teacher.

page 116
Belinda and Britanny both enjoy playing with the family pets, Cookie, Candy, and Taffy.
Cookie, a dachshound, is the mother of Candy and Taffy, both of which are dachshund-chihuahua
mix. Pat retrieved Cookie over 11 years ago in Fayetteville when Cookie has been dumped by
someone along the side of the highway.

William Sherman-5 Swain
Patricia Ann (Farish) Swain

Belinda Kaye-6 Swain

Brittany Nicole-6 Swain

William Sherman-5 Swain
Patricia Ann (Farish) Swain
Belinda Kaye-6 Swain
Brittany Nicole-6 Swain

****

page 117

standing, left to right
Linda, Barry, Brian, Belinda, Brigitte, Pat, William
[sitting, left to right]
Dallas, Brittany, Nealia

[standing, left to right]
Barry, Brian, Brigitte, William
[sitting, left to right]
Dallas & Nealia

**Brigitte Swain
Graduation Picture
Atkins High School**

page 118

see page 60

RONNIE JOE-5 SWAIN, (Ronnie Joe-5, Ray Thomas-4, Joseph Oscar-3, John Abner-2,
Jesse Abner-1)
b.Jan. 30, 1945 (STS); lives at Oppelo, AR.
m. Joan Vinson (JD).

   CHILDREN: (of Ronnie and Joan)
   RONNY JOE-6 SWAIN, Jr., b.March 13, 1973 (VAS).
   ERICA ASHLEY-6 SWAIN, b.Dec. 7, 1976 (VAS)

"Ronnie Joe-5 Swain, was born at Morrilton and graduated from Morrilton High School in
May, 1963. He later completed a course in Drafting and Surveying at Petit Jean Vo Tech in
Morrilton, Arkansas.
   In his earlier years he spent two years in the U.S. Army where he attended a Telecommunica-
tions School and served as a Mores Code and Radio Teletype Operator.
   For several years Ronnie has been employed by the Woodland Division of Arkansas Kraft
Corporation, first working as a land surveyor, and in more recent years as a Timber Buyer.
   He is married to the former Joann Vinson of Morrilton, and they have two children, Ronnie
Jr., born March 13, 1973 and Erica Ashley, born Dec. 7, 1976.
   Ronnie and his family reside in a recently completed brick home which he and Joann
themselves largely built on two pine studded acres near the community of Oppelo in Conway
County, Arkansas.
   His mother, Dorothy, is also comfortably situated in a trailer, located just next door.
   Ronnie enjoys outdoor life and spend as much time as possible hunting and fishing." (VAS)

Ronnie Joe Swain

Joan & Erica

Ronnie Joe Swain Jr.

Erica Ashley Swain

****

see page 60

DON HENRY-5 SWAIN (Don Henry-5, Ray Thomas-4, Joseph Oscar-3, John Abner-2, Jesse Abner-1)
b. Nov. 10, 1948 (SSD Conway Co., Book 5, pg. 454);
m. Jan. 31, 1970 Brenda Marie McArthur of Perry County, Arkansas by Lawrence Maus (from Conway Co., Book 43). They reside in Oppelo, AR 1985 (JD).

CHILDREN: (of Don and Brenda)
ANGELA LEE-6 SWAIN, b.Dec. 30, 1970 (VAS).
GREGORY DON-6 SWAIN, b.June 11, 1976 (VAS).
ERIN DANIELLE-6 SWAIN, b. MARCH 2, 1978 (VAS).

"Any friend or relative of the **Don Henry Swain's** would tell you invariably that the family is one 'That has it all together'.
Don, the fifth child of Ray and Dorothy Swain is a Supervisor at Arrow Automotive Industries, a manufacturing plant in Morrilton, and he has been employed there 13 years.
Born at Kennett, MO. November 10, 1948, and now in his late thirties, he is a quiet, easy going and perfectly relaxed individual, and seemingly very much at ease with the world.
Don's wife, the former Brenda McArthur, a member of a prominent South Conway County family, is a friendly and personable person who makes any visitor to their home feel readily at ease.
The couple lives at Rt. 1, Perry Arkansas in the Oppelo Comunity in a comfortable rock and frame combination home located on a beautiful 20 acre tract of land formally owned by Brenda's parents.
They have 3 children, Angela, born December 30, 1970, now a 10th grader who demonstrates her mother's same personable charms; Gregory Don, born June 11, 1976, a bright and intellectual 5th grader, and who has put together an impressive genealogy of his maternal ancestors, the McArthurs; and lastly, Erin Danielle, born March 2, 1978, a third grader, and a pretty lass already involved in softball and other sports.
Don and Brenda graduated from Morrilton High School and Don has diplomas in two courses taken as a student at Petit Jean Vo-Tech, one in Data Processing and one in Appliance Repair. He also spent 3 years in the U.S. Army and was a Supply Sergeant.
Brenda has 20 years of employment to her credit in the secretarial field and is currently employed at Winrock International Communications.
Getting to better know this young family as well as any other children of the Ray Swain family would indeed be an enriching experience." (VAS)

**BRENDA
AND
DON SWAIN**

**ERIN,
GREGORY,
& ANGELA**

****

INDEX

page 122

page 124

page 125

page 126

Appendix Two:

"The Life and Times Of

John Turner Hamlet"

Atkins, Arkansas Merchant, Early 1900's

Research & Writing by
Marcia Swain Crossman

Granddaughter of Velma Kate Johnson & John Turner Hamlet

Last updated 2022

This volume is included
for family interested in learning more about
Atkins, AR & the family of Elizabeth Ruth Hamlet Swain.

The Life and Times of

JOHN "TURNER" HAMLET

Atkins, Arkansas Merchant
Early 1900's

Research and Writing by Marcia Swain Crossman • 2022
Granddaughter of John Turner & Velma Johnson Hamlet

THE PARENTS OF JOHN TURNER HAMLET
Written by Marcia Swain Crossman   2022   Granddaughter of John Turner Hamlet

John Ernest Hamlet, father of **John Turner Hamlet**, was born in **Galla Rock, Arkansas** on May 8, 1851 and died in Galla Rock on May 29, 1889, age 38. There is little known of the early years of John E. At age 19, John E. lived in the home of his sister, Margaret Louisa and Amos Johnson. A young brother, Archie Hamlet, age 7 then, also lived in the home of his sister. (EHS)

Elizabeth Frances Turner Hamlet, mother of **John Turner Hamlet**, was born on August 3, 1856 and died on January 21, 1914, age 57 years. She was born in Hanna State, Alabama and was the daughter of William B. Turner and Martha Reed Turner. She had two siblings, **John O. Turner**, who died 1911 and **Mary-anne Turner Stubbs,** who died 1884.

From an obituary of **Martha Reed Turner**, wife of **William B.** and mother of **Elizabeth F.** records the family arriving in Arkansas in 1859. When the Civil War broke out, the father of Elizabeth F. joined the Confederate Army. He took measles, came home and died January of 1862. Elizabeth F. was around six years old. The mother of Elizabeth F., Martha Reed Turner, lived to be 81 years old, a widow over 45 years. Martha died in 1907 and is buried in Carden Bottoms, Arkansas in Yell County. The family was active in the Methodist Episcopal Church, South.

As my sister, **Sherry Swain Borck**, and I grew up, we visited the home of our grandparents, **Turner and Velma Hamlet** of Atkins every Sunday of every week. On their back porch was a trunk

Elizabeth Frances Turner Hamlet

under a table. We were told never to open or touch the trunk. After our grandparents death the trunk was given to me, granddaughter **Marcia Swain Crossman**. It was in here that our grandfather, **John Turner Hamlet** kept an old family Bible. The very large book was tied together to hold the pages in. The tying also kept tiny tin photos from falling out.

The Bible had been given to Elizabeth F. after she was married to John E. In the Bible is the marriage certificate of **Elizabeth Frances and John Ernest** dated July 3, 1872. There are two pages that give dates of the birth and deaths of their children. On one of these pages it states John was 21 years old when he professed religion. This was witnessed and signed by Elizabeth F., September 1, 1872. Perhaps the relationship of the couple depended on this confession.

In the old Bible were found many tiny tin photos of people not labeled in any way that had come loose from insert pockets. Yet it is predictable that several of these photos are specific family members. I will share these photos and comments along the way in this paper. The only tiny tin photo that was labeled was one of **Elizabeth F.** It described her eyes being brown and her complexion was fair. Her hair sample was "enclosed." Some artist had taken this tiny tin photo and made it into a large pastel portrait, *(seen on next page)*, that was also originally stored in the trunk.

Elizabeth F. was only a child herself, at the age of 16, when she married **John E.** Their first child, **Wm. Thomas**, came at her age 18. Other children came at two to three years apart: **Samuel** at age 20; **Mary** at around age 22; **Charley** at age 25; **Albert** at age 28 and **John Turner** at age 30.

In their young adult years, John and Elizabeth F. had two children of three that died. What great sorrow they must have had to lay their two youngest children to rest in the **Galla Rock Cemetery** not too far from the Arkansas River, outside of Atkins. Precious Mary L. died on Aug. 29, 1882, only a baby at the age of 3. Young Samuel J. Hamlet passed away four years later on Nov. 1 in 1886 at the tender age of 9 years. William Tom, in his teen age years must have been a great help to console his parents in their sadness. In 2022 the grave markers of Samuel and Mary still exist at the cemetery. A small rock left by Mary's grave has her initials carved in it, "MLH."

Around the age of 33, Elizabeth F. also laid her husband to rest. John E. died at the early age of 38. He was probably a farmer most of his life. We think John was also buried on the banks of the Arkansas River in the community of Galla Rock between the two children. There is no marker at his grave. There were two stories of what happened to the body of John E. Hamlet. One is that his body was carried across the frozen over Arkansas River by wagon to be buried. This is unlikely as he died in May. The second tells about a flood. His body was washed away and lost into the Arkansas River. Both are unusual. The washed away story is also unlikely to be true. There is a handwritten note that says he is buried "by" his two children. (EHS) We believe we have found his unmarked grave between the children. (MSC '22)

Large Pastel Portrait of Elizabeth F. Hamlet with her Family Bible
photo by
Elizabeth R. Hamlet Swain

There is no record of what illnesses took these three family members. What tragedy to be a young widow with four surviving sons. A reminder, our grandfather, John Turner Hamlet whom this story is about, was the last child to be born. My sister, Sherry, and I found it strange as we visited our grandparents, "Turner," as he was called, never mentioned these three deaths. It is probably because the children were deceased before he was born and he was only two years old when his father passed away.

There are family stories of Elizabeth F. taking care of Methodist circuit riding preachers, making sure they had food before the children did. She gave money "too generously" to the circuit riders as told by Elizabeth Hamlet Swain, granddaughter. Elizabeth F. died in 1914 at the age of 57. Her obituary stated, "she was a patient Christian. Her faith was steadfast, and ready to cross death's river. Heaven was her home." She is buried in the Atkins City Cemetery near three sons, John Turner, Charley and Wm. Thomas.

The fifth born child, Albert Ernest Hamlet is buried with his wife, Mary Emma, in Roselawn Memorial Park in Little Rock. He was the owner of Hamlet Variety Store at Stifft Station in Little Rock, Arkansas. Albert and Mary Emma had two daughters. All were active in Pulaski Heights Methodist Church. We know very little of his life.

(EHS) is Elizabeth Hamlet Swain
Daughter of John Turner Hamlet

(MSC) is Marcia Swain Crossman
Granddaughter of John Turner Hamlet

Marriage Certificate of John Ernest Hamlet and Elizabeth Frances Turner

From the Bible of Elizabeth Frances Turner Hamlet

THE LIFE OF YOUNG JOHN TURNER HAMLET

Written by Marcia Swain Crossman   2022   Granddaughter of John Turner Hamlet

John Turner Hamlet (called Turner) lived his early life at Fowler, Arkansas in Yell County. There is nothing about Fowler in 2022 on the internet. It no longer exists. From maps, it was across the Arkansas River from a larger community called Galla Rock (sometimes spelled incorrectly Galley Rock as locals pronounced it). There was a community building at Fowler used as a school and for other social gatherings. Jim Fowler had come from Gumlog in Pope County (next county over) and built a store in Fowler. There was no mention of a church building. A circuit rider did pass through Fowler and stayed with the Hamlet family. A few families lived in Fowler. It was mostly a trading community off the Arkansas River.

Turner was the last child born into the family of John E. and Elizabeth Frances Hamlet. At the time of Turner's birth, his parents John E. and Elizabeth F. had two children who had died. The reason for their deaths is unknown. They are buried at the Galla Rock Cemetery. They were Mary Louise Hamlet, who died at age two, and Samuel J. Hamlet who died at the of age nine years. I do not remember my grandparents, Velma Johnson or Turner Hamlet, or our mother, Elizabeth Ruth Hamlet Swain, ever speaking of these children, My mother did have knowledge of them in her notes, genealogical charts and book. Her research is where this story comes from.

It was only, at the age of 69, (2022) that I, Marcia Swain Crossman daughter of Elizabeth Hamlet Swain, learned of the deceased siblings from cemetery records on the internet. My husband, Bob, and I visited the Galla Rock Cemetery near Atkins. We drove a few miles south of Atkins and easily found the cemetery. Upon locating the graves, we found two beautiful little headstones that belonged to Mary and Samuel. We cleaned the graves and reset the headstones of the two children. We also found, buried under the ground, a small headstone shaped rock with the initials "MLH" carved into it. This rock had been underground for a long time. We accidentally hit it poking around the headstone. Surprised, we dug it out, cleaned it up and placed it by little Mary's headstone. We also questioned why the graves of the children were so far apart. Elizabeth Swain had documented that John E. was buried in an unmarked grave. At the same time we were leaving our visit with the children, we were very sad to think these children had been buried so far from their mother.

We believe this photo was made at the time of death of Mary L. Hamlet, age three. People in early Arkansas had lifelike pictures of deceased family members as lasting mementos. Notice Mary's head is nodded. Her small hands have been placed together. She is wearing very nice clothing. Her body was propped up on a fancy rug. This is sad, but so obvious. She is not asleep. Samuel, age 5 in the photo, is standing next to his little sister guarding her with a toy gun in his hand.

The cemetery was about five miles of the cemetery in Atkins where their mother had been placed in eternal rest. We left the cemetery sadly thinking about the children being so far from their mother. We were also puzzled about such a large space between them. We had marked off a space between the two children's graves large enough for another grave to be between the children. On the way out of Atkins, we went by Lemley Funeral Home to find out what it would cost us to have the children's graves moved. We strongly felt the children should be in the Atkins City Cemetery next their mother. After all, three of her sons were buried next to her, why not have two more children moved there? We gathered the costs and learned what it takes in Arkansas to legally move a grave. Driving home we toyed with the idea of just picking up the headstones of Samuel and Mary, moving what was left of these next to their mother. We left Atkins with many questions in our minds. We let some time pass to think about the idea of moving the graves. We did not move the graves or headstones.

Turner's father, **John E. Hamlet** died, at the early age of 38, leaving his wife a widow, age about 35, with four children. **Tom** was a 15 year old teenager. The other boys were young. **Turner** was two; **Albert** was four; and **Charley** was seven years old. We do not know what happened to John E. that caused him to die at this early age. We did find burial records in **Elizabeth Ruth Hamlet Swain**'s notes that the children's father, John E. Hamlet was "buried between them in an unmarked grave." Her notes also said, "His body was taken across (from Fowler) the frozen river (the Arkansas) by wagon to Galla Rock and it was washed away by the river." Yet, he died in May. Whose story is this? So we find two very different stories of the burial of John E. Hamlet, the father of John Turner Hamlet. I will leave this to your imagination as to what happened to "father John."

John E. Hamlet

In 1887, **John Turner Hamlet** was the youngest child born to the family of John E. and Elizabeth F. Hamlet. He was born just two years before his father's death. There were four living sons at John E.'s death. In order of birth, were Tom, Charley, Albert and Turner. **Elizabeth F.** had become a young widow strapped with four growing boys. They were a farm family. This must have been a hard life. She had been a life long member of the Methodist Episcopal Church, South. It was said in her obituary she was kind and generous. Her church life and personal attributes must have helped her endure this hard life. She lived with her children and lived to be 58 years old.

At the age of 15, being the eldest son, **William Thomas Hamlet** (we later called him "Uncle Tom") took over the task of being a father to his younger three brothers. Much later after Tom's death his niece **Elizabeth Hamlet Swain** wrote, "His life became devoted to helping others in the family. Of those who knew him best, there was nothing of pretense or affliction in his manner. He had a kind and gentle disposition."

Looking at Elizabeth Frances Hamlet, *(in the photo)* we see that birthing six children, raising the four remaining children and working as mother and father aged her very much. A year before his mother's death, Elizabeth F. lived with Tom until her death at age 58. "Uncle Tom" lived his last years in the home of his brother, Turner. To my knowledge he had never married or had children. We will say more about William Thomas Hamlet later.

Back Left to Right: "Tom" and Elizabeth Frances
Front Left to Right: Charley, Albert and "Turner"
It was obvious there was no wealth in the family.
These photos came from Elizabeth F. Hamlet's
family Bible owned by Marcia Swain Crossman.

THE ADULT YEARS OF JOHN TURNER HAMLET
Written by Marcia Swain Crossman   2022   Granddaughter of John Turner Hamlet

As a young man, before WWI, around 1912, **Turner Hamlet**, worked for Darr & Lemley General Merchandise in Atkins He either rode by horse from Fowler or lived briefly with someone he knew in Atkins. The company sold furniture, coffins, hardware, and farming implements. Friends of the company had been asked for references on Turner. Perhaps he was attempting to get a business loan.

> •**November 13th, 1912**; To Whom It May Concern:
> "The bearer, Turner Hamlet, has been in our employ for the past three months, and during that time we have found him to be worthy of any confidence that may be bestowed upon him. We found him honest and willing to work, and to any one needing a young man of good habits and character, we think that Mr. Hamlet will give satisfaction to the utmost of his ability. Yours truly, J. E. Darr & Lemley."

> •**November 13th, 1912**; To Whom It May Concern, a second letter was written:
> "I have worked daily with Mr. Turner Hamlet while he was in the employ of Darr & Lemley, and I think that he will conscientiously and honestly perform any duties he may agree to perform. I take pleasure in saying that I, at all times, found him to be truthful, honest, and courteous in his business dealings. I never have heard him use profane or vile language, and have not known of his using intoxicating beverages in any form. Very truly, Irl R. Darr, Bookkeeper for Darr & Lemley."

> •**November 13, 1912**; the President of the Bank of Atkins, whose letterhead said "Paid up Capital in Cash $50,999, Surplus & Dividends Profits $5,000.00" wrote:
> "I have known Mr. Turner Hamlet, for a number of years, and know him to be throughly honest. Any courtesies shown him will be appreciated, as well as myself. Yours very truly, President, Bank of Atkins."

> •**March 16, 1914**; A Letter of Recommendation was written by a friend from Elk Drug Store in Atkins:
> "To Whom It May Concern — I take pleasure in offering this letter of recommendation to Mr. J. Turner Hamlet who I have known for about three years and being associated with him to be strictly business, honest, sober, and a conscientious man in every aspect. President J. Hal Bradley, Manager of Elk Drug Store.

Around 1989, **Elizabeth Hamlet Swain** daughter of Turner Hamlet rewrote contents from a book from the Russellville, Arkansas Library, "Lest We Forget, 43 Years Brief History." There is a brief section explaining how the Hamlet brothers got into the mercantile business:

"Early in life, **Charley and Tom** had been stock owners in the **Fowler Mercantile Co**. in Fowler, Arkansas. In the early part of 1913, **Charley Hamlet** *(second oldest son)* sold his stock in Fowler and purchased a one-half interest in the **A. D. Stubbs Mercantile Company** located one mile south of Atkins on Bottoms Road." *(See photo next page.)*

In the fall of 1913, **Tom** sold his farming interest and moved with their mother to Atkins. Elizabeth Hamlet Swain noted that they lived across the road from the store and the house was still standing in 1989. The book continued, "In, 1913, **Tom and Turner** bought the other half of **Stubbs' store**. They came over from Fowler and started work at Stubbs. All three brothers then owned the A. D. Stubbs Store. The book continued, "During the ten years we were in that location it was not an uncommon thing to see 50 to 60 wagons and teams come from out of the bottoms with cotton and goods." Later there began to be more cars. The brothers were in that location for ten years and changed the name to the **W. T. Hamlet and Company** with respect to William Thomas Hamlet, the oldest brother.

Sadly, both **Charley Hamlet** and mother **Elizabeth F. Hamlet** passed away in the early part of 1914. The reasons of their deaths were unknown. Since they then lived in Atkins, both were buried next to each other in the **Atkins City Cemetery.** The remaining two brothers, Tom and Turner, bought Charley's stock interest from his widow, Maggie. Maggie Hamlet later remarried and became an early telephone worker connecting customers. Her sons were Charlie *(currently Charles, Jr.)* and Garret Hamlet.

By 1913, Tom, Charley and Turner became full owners of the A. D. Stubbs Store in Fowler, Arkansas. The name was later changed to the W. T. Hamlet Store. Upon looking closely at the photo, Turner Hamlet is seen to the left of the door with a hat on. Look to the left of the photo and you will see a woman standing on the porch. There is a double glider swing to the left of the house.

Dated May 21, 1917, Russellville, Ark. a postcard arrived from Sheriff Chambers, Sheriff of Pope County and Chairman of the Registration Board of Pope Co. It informed Turner: "The President, by Proclamation, has fixed Tuesday, June 5, 1917, as **Registration Day**. As one of the Registrars appointed by the County Registration Board, you are hereby notified to be in Russellville, Saturday, May 16, 1917, at 9 o'clock A.M. to take the oath of office provided by law, to receive instructions pertaining to your duties, and to set the Registration Blanks for your precinct. Be here Without Fail. No excuses will be accepted. By authority of law, W. J. Chambers"

Another postcard arrived: "Dear Sir: You are hereby notified that you have been selected as one of the **Registrars of your Township** to register all Male Citizens in your township who are subject to Select Draft Bill, on date to be named by the President. You will therefore hold yourself in readiness to come at a moment's call to Russellville to get instructions and take the oath of office. Acknowledge receipt of this communication by signing and returning enclosed card. Yours Truly, W. J. Chambers, Sheriff; W. A. Montgomery, County Health Officer; and D. A. Thomasville."

It was the beginning of World War I. In 1917, Turner was called to help gather a list of men from his area to go. Then he was called to the U.S. Army as an artillery soldier. He was sent to Jackson Barracks, New Orleans, LA. Turner went to the army in 1918 and returned in 1919.

The war started for many young men in Arkansas at Camp Robinson in North Little Rock was then Camp Pike. They left there their hometowns by train and ship to fight the Germans. From **Wikipedia** we learn what it was to be artillery:

"An artillery soldier was in trench warfare. It was an important factor in the war. These soldiers fought at the front of the battle. Artillery would fire explosive shells that caused fire explosions. Because of this, enemies in trenches were no longer always safe, and could constantly be fired upon. In some areas, artillery meant using smaller guns fired onto an area such as a line of trenches, each gun firing several rounds per minute for hour

Artillery was also used directly in battle. The artillery would distract the enemy. They would fire on enemy reinforcements to keep the enemy from reaching front lines."

What was it like to be in the artillery of WWI? From the **Butler Center** in Little Rock, Arkansas researchers of Arkansas history, we gain some insight on what it was like for Arkansas soldiers in WWI:

"You remember how an elevated trains sound when you are standing underneath them and hear an express go by. Multiply the speed considerably and imagine the accompanying whine of a big shell. Then imagine that the roar ceases abruptly near you and explodes with a violence and concussion of tons of dynamite. This repetition would go on for hours. There are the accompanying whine of shell fragments flying by you. You hear the cries of help from comrades who you are unable to help. You feel the horror at seeing a companion fall at your side. There is also deafening noises; the deadly gas; the flash and roar of your own guns. Then there are the prayers of those who are giving their lives for their cause. Your personal equation is forgotten. You are merely a part of a huge machine with one idea: to get the other man before he gets you."

John Turner Hamlet, WWI

By the end of WWI, 2,183 Arkansas boys had died and another 1,751 sustained wounds. **Influenza** and other illnesses flourished during war camps, killing more U.S. troops than battle wounds did. The deadly influenza Pandemic followed the soldiers home after the war, too, killing 7,000 Arkansans — more than three times the number killed in the war itself. On Nov. 11, 1918, more than four years since the world erupted into warfare and just over 18 months since the United States declared war on Germany, it was over.. Finding the way back home often took months with travel on ships, trains, and by foot.

On May 6, 1919, **Turner Hamlet married Velma Kate Johnson**. From an old newspaper clipping, "An interesting wedding took place at 3 o'clock Tuesday afternoon at the home of the bride's parents at Atkins, Arkansas. The house was prettily decorated in flowers and palms. The ceremony was performed in the presence of the immediate family and a few friends. The bride, who was given in marriage by her father, wore a traveling costume of dark blue with gray accessories. Mr. and Mrs. Hamlet left immediately after the service for Little Rock where they were the guests of Mr. and Mr. Albert E. Hamlet *(older brother of the groom)*. They will be at home after June 1, *(1919)* in Atkins." Whether they traveled the 65 mile trip by car or train, we do not know. *The honeymoon must have lasted around three weeks.*

Velma Kate Johnson Hamlet,
wife of John Turner Hamlet, daughter of Flonnie Odella Evans and Horace LaFayette Johnson of Atkins.

On January 14, 1921 baby **Elizabeth Ruth** was born. The family of four, including **"Uncle Tom Hamlet"** was living in a small house near the store.

Three years later, in January of 1924, the **W.T. Hamlet and Company** moved to the downtown of the big city of Atkins, Arkansas. The family also moved to town. The railroad had been built right through the middle of the city. The Hamlet mercantile occupied one of the E.A. Darr Estate buildings on the south side of the railroad track.

By that time **Wm. Thomas, "Uncle Tom" Hamlet** had become a permanent resident in the home of Velma and Turner Hamlet. By all means, the family was not rich. Velma had become cook, maid and laundry keeper for the two older men. I almost want to say she had two husbands. They occupied a five room house with two porches, a chicken house, smoke house, garden, and outhouse.

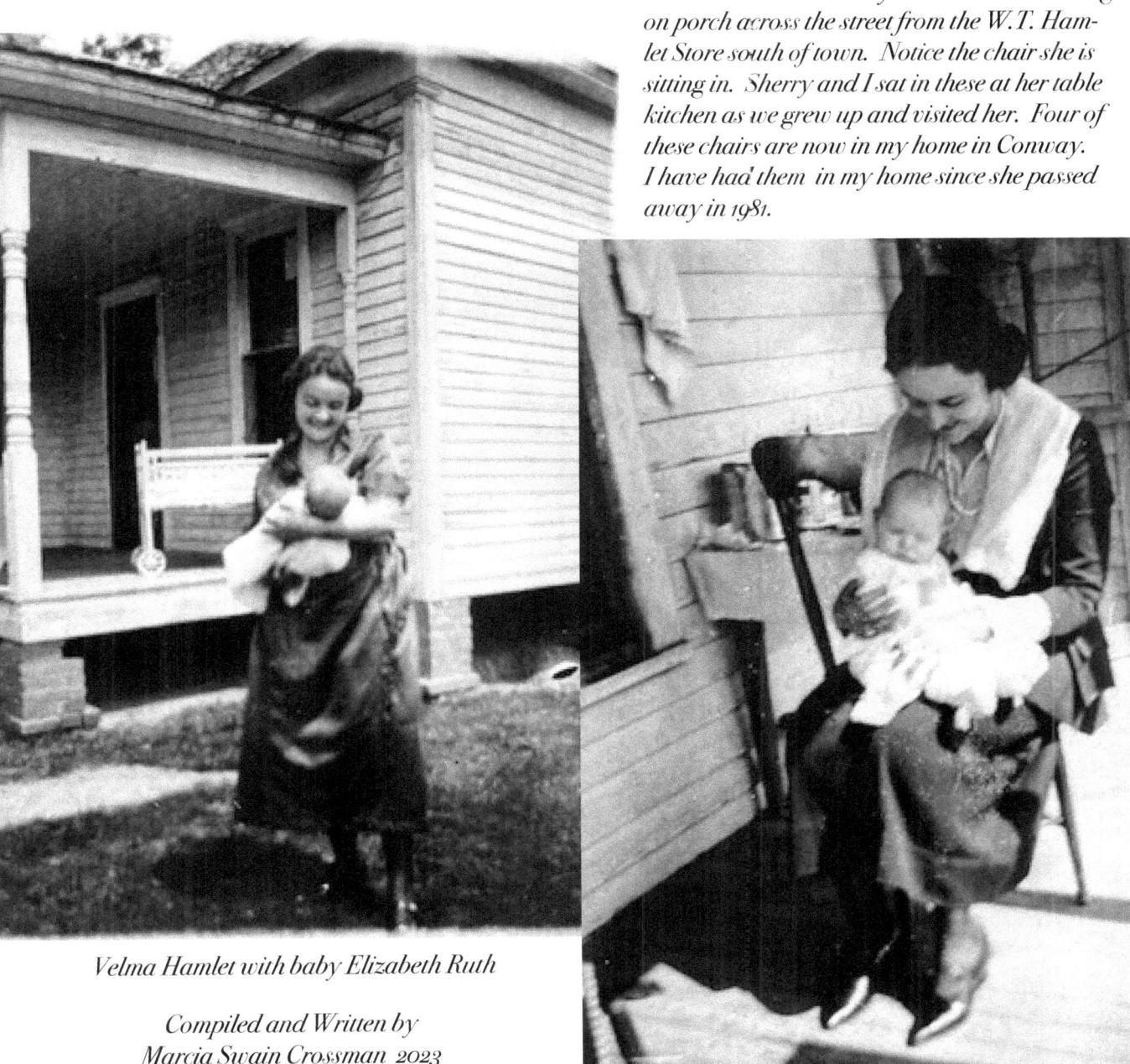

Velma Hamlet with baby Elizabeth Ruth sitting on porch across the street from the W.T. Hamlet Store south of town. Notice the chair she is sitting in. Sherry and I sat in these at her table kitchen as we grew up and visited her. Four of these chairs are now in my home in Conway. I have had them in my home since she passed away in 1981.

Velma Hamlet with baby Elizabeth Ruth

*Compiled and Written by
Marcia Swain Crossman 2023
Granddaughter of John Turner Hamlet*

The remainder of the life of Turner Hamlet comes from obituaries and tributes saved from the Atkins Chronicle, newspaper of the Atkins and surrounding area. Also included are family recollections.

Because of Tom Hamlet's declining health and Turner Hamlet's bad eye sight they decided to close the store. This ended a continuous business of 43 years in Atkins, south of Atkins and the Fowler areas. The two were quite proud of their record of business under the **W.T. Hamlet & Company** name. They thanked their customers and friends for long and faithful business with their firm, closing their doors on August 1, 1956.

In his retirement, Turner had cataract surgery in both eyes at the veteran's hospital in North Little Rock. Each eye surgery required him to lie flat on his back with his head between sandbags for ten days. His favorite past time was playing the game of Dominoes with other men at the "Domino Hut" downtown, Atkins. On April 27, 1971, at the

age of 83 Turner died at the veteran's hospital of lung cancer, probably from smoking Camel Cigarettes since his WWI days. He is buried in the Atkins City Cemetery by Velma, Tom, Charley and his mother, Elizabeth Frances. Velma would survive him for ten years until her death at 83 years.

In his obituaries we find: "**Turner Hamlet** was a Methodist and served as secretary for the Men's Bible Class for a number of years. He was a 50 Year Mason and served as secretary for Atkins Lodge 172 for more than 25 years. As a veteran of WWI, he was a member and active worker in the American Legion serving in the Loyd Stout Post 34 years as adjutant for over 25 years."

From the Arkansas Legionnaire, Newspaper of the American Legion we read, "...He lived in Atkins most of his life, was in business there for 43 years before retirement, an active Methodist and served as secretary for the Men's Bible Class. Turner was a 50 year mason and served as secretary of Atkins Lodge 172 for more than 25 years. As a veteran of World War I, he was a member and active worker in the American Legion. He served as Adjutant for over 25 years. He was a worker who assisted many veterans with papers and claims for service benefits."

From the Atkins' Chronicle: "**Turner Hamlet** is going to be missed here. You don't participate in church and civic affairs like he did without being missed. He was a familiar figure in Atkins every day for many years — while in business and after retirement — with a cheery greeting for young and old. Turner sort of grew up with Atkins. When cotton was king and the river bottoms was full of it, he operated a store at old Stubbs-town, later moving the business on the south side of Atkins and saw it flourish. In Atkins he saw the economy shift. He outlived most of those. With his death went a certain amount of Atkins "*back when.*"

> I enjoyed so very much sharing about my grandparents, John Turner Hamlet and Velma Johnson Hamlet; also about my mother, Elizabeth Ruth Hamlet Swain. I hope by reading this, you gain a greater understanding what life was like in their day.
> By Marcia Swain Crossman

Velma, Elizabeth & Turner Hamlet

PHOTOGRAPH ALBUM OF HAMLET FAMILY

Compiled by Marcia Swain Crossman   2022   Granddaughter of John Turner Hamlet

*Left: Brothers
Tom, Turner and Albert Hamlet*

*Bottom Right:
Velma Kate Johnson Hamlet
wedding photo, Aug 19, 1897
Wife of John Turner Hamlet
Mother of Elizabeth Ruth Hamlet
Daughter of Flonnie Odella Evans
& Horace Lafayette Johnson of
Atkins, Arkansas*

*Bottom Left:
Elizabeth Ruth Hamlet Swain*

Wife of Verill Ansel Swain; Mother of Marcia Swain Crossman, Grandmother of Charles & David Crossman, great grandmother of Grayson, Blake, Marlie, Owen & Cooper Crossman and mother of Sherry Elizabeth Swain Borck, grandmother of Bailey Borck Bachamp, great grandmother of Dylan & Brooks Bachamp and grandmother of Raquel Elizabeth Borck. (the name of 'Elizabeth' was handed down through the generations.)

Left: Elizabeth Ruth and Velma Hamlet, around 1923.
Right: Ernest John and Ruth Johnson Lemley Sister of Velma;
Velma and Turner Hamlet. Photo was in mid 1960's.

President Velma Hamlet   American Legion Auxiliary Department of Arkansas
Velma Hamlet, President, represents Arkansas in New York City parade, around 1930.
She attended three national parades and served in various national leadership capacities.

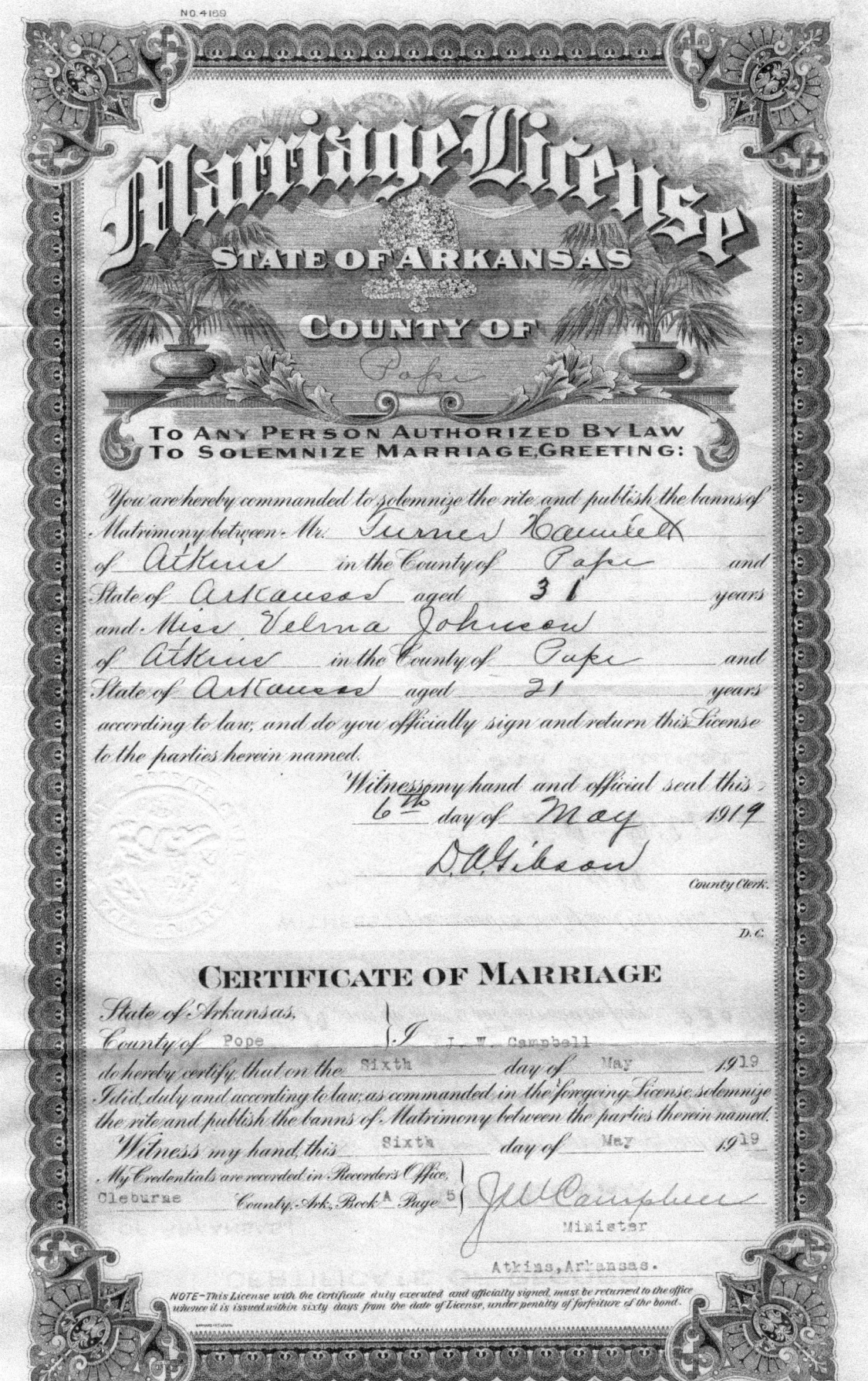

CERTIFICATE OF RECORD.

STATE OF ARKANSAS,

County of _____ } I, *D. A. Gibson*

_____ Clerk of the County Court of said County, certify that the above license

for and Certificate of the Marriage of Mr. *Turner Hamlett* and

Miss *Velma Johnson* was filed in my office on the 7th

day of *May* 1919, and the same is duly recorded on page *530* of Book

L of Marriage Records.

WITNESS my hand and the seal of said Court this 9th

day of *May* 1919

D. A. Gibson

Clerk.

By Iva Etheridge D.C.

MARRIAGE CERTIFICATE.

Mr *Turner Hamlett*
TO
Miss *Velma Johnson*

RECORDED BOOK *L* PAGE *530.*

RETURNED AND FILED THIS *7* DAY OF

May 19*19*

_____ CLERK

BY _____ D.C.

Velma Kate Johnson Hamlet

Velma Johnson Hamlet
Obituary

The funeral for Mrs. Velma Kate Johnson Hamlet, 83 of Atkins, Arkansas was held Wednesday, May 6, 1981 in the Atkins First United Methodist Church. The Rev. Jerry Nichols, the Rev. Alan Hilliard, and the Rev. Robert Crossman officiated. Burial was in the Atkins City Cemetery.

Velma was an active member of First United Methodist Church, Atkins. She was a member of the church choir; taught Sunday School class for years; and served as a president of the United Methodist Women.

Velma was a charter member of the Lloyd-Stout Unit No. 34 of the American Legion Auxiliary and served an active part in the Girls State Program. In 1947, she was elected president of the Arkansas Chapter of the American Legion Auxiliary, and was appointed to the national office as national executive committeewoman in 1948. Velma was past president of the Atkins Order of the Eastern Star and a member of the Atkins Garden Club.

Left:
Velma Hamlet and daughter, Elizabeth Ruth

Right:
Elizabeth Ruth and mother, Velma Hamlet

Elizabeth Ruth Hamlet Swain

BIRTH 14 JAN 1921 • *Atkins, Pope Co., Arkansas, USA*
DEATH 4 JANUARY 1997 • *Conway, Faulkner Co, Arkansas, USA*

When **Elizabeth Ruth Hamlet Kimberlin Swain** was born on January 13, 1921, in Atkins, Arkansas, her father, **John Turner Hamlet**, was 33, and her mother, **Velma Kate Johnson**, was 23. Elizabeth had no siblings. She grew up the daughter of a local merchant, never with too much need during her early years.

Elizabeth was a player on the Atkins High School Basketball. As an only child she was overwhelmed with love and affection by her parents. Her father's brother, **Wm. Thomas Hamlet**, business partner of Turner Hamlet lived in the home with the family until his death, having a special relationship with this niece.

In 1921, when Elizabeth was born, her grandparents **Flonnie Odella Evans Johnson and Horace Lafayette Johnson**, also gave birth. Their son, **Raymond Horace Johnson**, was Elizabeth's uncle, but with both being in the same class at Atkins schools, the two were more like brother/sister. Elizabeth and Raymond both graduated from Atkins High School in 1939.

Elizabeth attended college for a short while at Arkansas Tech in Russellville. She soon married her Atkins High classmate sweetheart, **Donald Eugene Kimberlin**. The young Kimberlin couple soon moved to California to allow Donald to serve in the US Air Force in pilot school. Elizabeth was active in various groups and served in the USO while Donald trained. In a tragic accident, Donald and several young men were killed when their plane went down in the mountains in CA. Elizabeth moved back to Atkins after becoming a widow.

Elizabeth Ruth
Hamlet Swain
Wife of
Verill Ansel Swain

Mother of
Marcia Gail
Swain Crossman
&
Sherry Elizabeth
Swain Borck;

Grandmother of
Charles & David Crossman,
Bailey Borck Bachamp
& Raquel Elizabeth Borck;
Great grandmother of
Blake, Grayson, Marlie, Owen &
Cooper Crossman and
Dylan & Brooks Bachamp
(children of
Bailey Borck & Cole Bachamp)

During the remainder of WWII, Elizabeth worked two years with the Office of Price Administration, and five years with the Veteran's Administration in Russellville and Little Rock, Arkansas.

It was during this time when Elizabeth met **Verill Ansel Swain**, a Navy Seabee who returned to Blackwell after his service in WWII. Between his continued education in college and owning a roller rink in Blackwell the two began courting and talking marriage. They married on Sept. 3, 1950 and spent the rest of their lives in Morrilton, Arkansas.

Elizabeth and Ansel were parents of two daughters, **Marcia Gail Swain Crossman**, born April 26, 1953 and **Sherry Elizabeth Swain Borck**, born May 6, 1955. They were an active family in the Morrilton First United Methodist Church. Elizabeth was a member of the choir for many years. She was also a member and two year president of the Women's Society of Christian Service later named United Methodist Women. The family resided at 101 North West Street. They later built a large new home (*paying cash*) in 1960 at 3 Magnolia Drive.

Elizabeth was also a faithful daughter. She rarely missed spending a Sunday afternoon in Atkins with her family. She made sure her daughters were there, too.

Elizabeth was employed as a clerk/typist for 21 years with the US Soil Conservation Service in Morrilton, retiring in 1982 earning at most $3500 per year. She was also a 21 year volunteer for the Conway County Community Service Board. Elizabeth served as a member and past president of the Morrilton Adelaide Club, a service organization for women. She also served as member and president of the Town & Country Garden Club.

Elizabeth was a wonderful mother and wife. Most of the money she earned in her job with the Soil Conservation Service provided a better life for the family, like the "icing on the cake." The family had nicer furnishings in the home and the family was able to afford clothing and transportation much more easier. She spent a great deal of time sewing for her and the girls. Around 1950, Ansel challenged Elizabeth to win a sewing contest by constructing a beautiful silk 3 piece suit. She won the contest. He purchased her a brand new Singer sewing machine.

Elizabeth saw to it that both girls were given baton twirling lessons, both becoming majorettes for the Morrilton High School Band. The parents never missed a football game. The Swains chaperoned many high school parties and sorority proms for their girls, often signing as responsible in the event of misuse of the country club building (which never happened). They welcomed their daughter's friends into the home. They were good examples to live by, showing much love and friendship to family and friends.

To their credit Ansel and Elizabeth paid for both daughters to receive degrees at the University of Central Arkansas. As more time went along, they had the pleasure of knowing well their grandchildren, **Charles Robert and David Nathan Crossman & Bailey Erin and Raquel Elizabeth Borck**.

After Elizabeth's retirement, she and Ansel took up golfing. They spent winters in So. Texas with friends. In her 70's Elizabeth saw Ansel die with cancer over a four year illness. During the later part of Ansel's illness, Elizabeth also developed ovarian cancer. She died in her daughter, Marcia's, home, on January 4, 1997 amid friends and family just 10 month after Ansel's death.

Elizabeth and Ansel are buried in **Elmwood Cemetery in Morrilton**. They share a memorial headstone with the words, **"No Tears."** Ansel and Elizabeth had many happy years together as a married couple.

FAMILY OF JOHN ERNEST & ELIZABETH FRANCES TURNER HAMLET

Compiled by
Marcia Swain Grossman
August 30, 2022

John Ernest Hamlet
b. May 8, 1851; m. July 3, 1872, age 21
d. May 29, 1889, age 38
buried at Galla Rock Cemetery between Mary and
Samuel. No monument.
m. Elizabeth Frances Turner

Elizabeth Frances Turner
b. Aug. 3, 1856; m. July 3, 1872, age 16; d. Jan. 21, 1914, age 58; Owner of the "Big
Bible;" large watercolor of her; *buried in Atkins City Cemetery next to Thomas, Turner*
and Charley; Age babies born: Tom 18, Samuel 21, Mary 23, Charley 26, Albert 29,
Turner 31; Left a widow age 33 with four children; youngest Turner age 2, oldest Tom

2) Samuel J. Hamlet
b. Jan. 11, 1877
d. Nov. 1, 1886
Samuel was a child who died at
the age of 9 yrs., 9 mos.
Buried at Galla Rock Cemetery

5) Albert Ernest Hamlet
b. Feb. 18, 1885
d. Feb. 23, 1948, age 63
m. Mary Emma
b. Oct. 21, 1893; d. May 10, 1988, age 94
2 children; couple buried in Roselawn
Memorial Park, Little Rock, Ark.

3) Mary Louise Hamlet
b. Oct. 15, 1879
d. Aug. 29, 1882, age 3
Mary was a child who died at
the age of 2 yrs., 10 mos.
She died before Samuel
Buried in Galla Rock Cemetery outside Atkins

4) Charles Henry "Charley" Hamlet
b. Aug. 8, 1882
d. June 23, 1914, age 32; buried Atkins City Cemetery
m. Maggie Ellis, buried at Lewisburg Miss. Bapt. Cem.
children: Garret Henry Hamlet, b. Sept. 30, 1910;
Charles Wilson Hamlet, b. Jan. 12, 1912
Maggie remarried. Her Mother, Emma, lived with her
many years.

1) Wm. Thomas Hamlet
"Uncle Tom"
b. Dec. 29, 1874
15 years old when father died
d. Jan. 17, 1956, age 82,
Buried in Atkins City Cemetery;
Never married

6) John Turner Hamlet
b. Oct. 18, 1887, youngest child
age 2 when father died
(He never knew Mary or Samuel.)
d. Jan. 22, 1971, age 83
m. Velma Kate Johnson
May 6, 1919
b. Aug. 10, 1897
d. April 27, 1981
Couple buried in Atkins
City Cemetery
One child, Elizabeth Ruth
b. Jan. 14, 1921
d. Jan. 4, 1997

Sequence of deaths:
~**Mary**, age 3, 1882
~**Samuel**, age 9, 1886
~**Father John E**., age 38, 1889
~**Charley**, age 32, 1914
~**Mother Elizabeth Frances**, age 57, 1914

Tom "Uncle Tom" goes into mercantile business
to support mother and three brothers. Later Charley, Albert and Turner join him.

~**Albert**, age 63, 1948
~**Tom**, age 82, 1957
Lived his adult life with
Turner and Velma,
~**Turner**, 83, 1971
~**Velma**, 83, 1981

Sources:
History of the Hamlet Family by
Elizabeth Hamlet Swain
and various internet sources.

Hamlet & Johnson Family Tree

Source: Ancestry.com: Marcia Swain Crossman's Family Tree, 2024

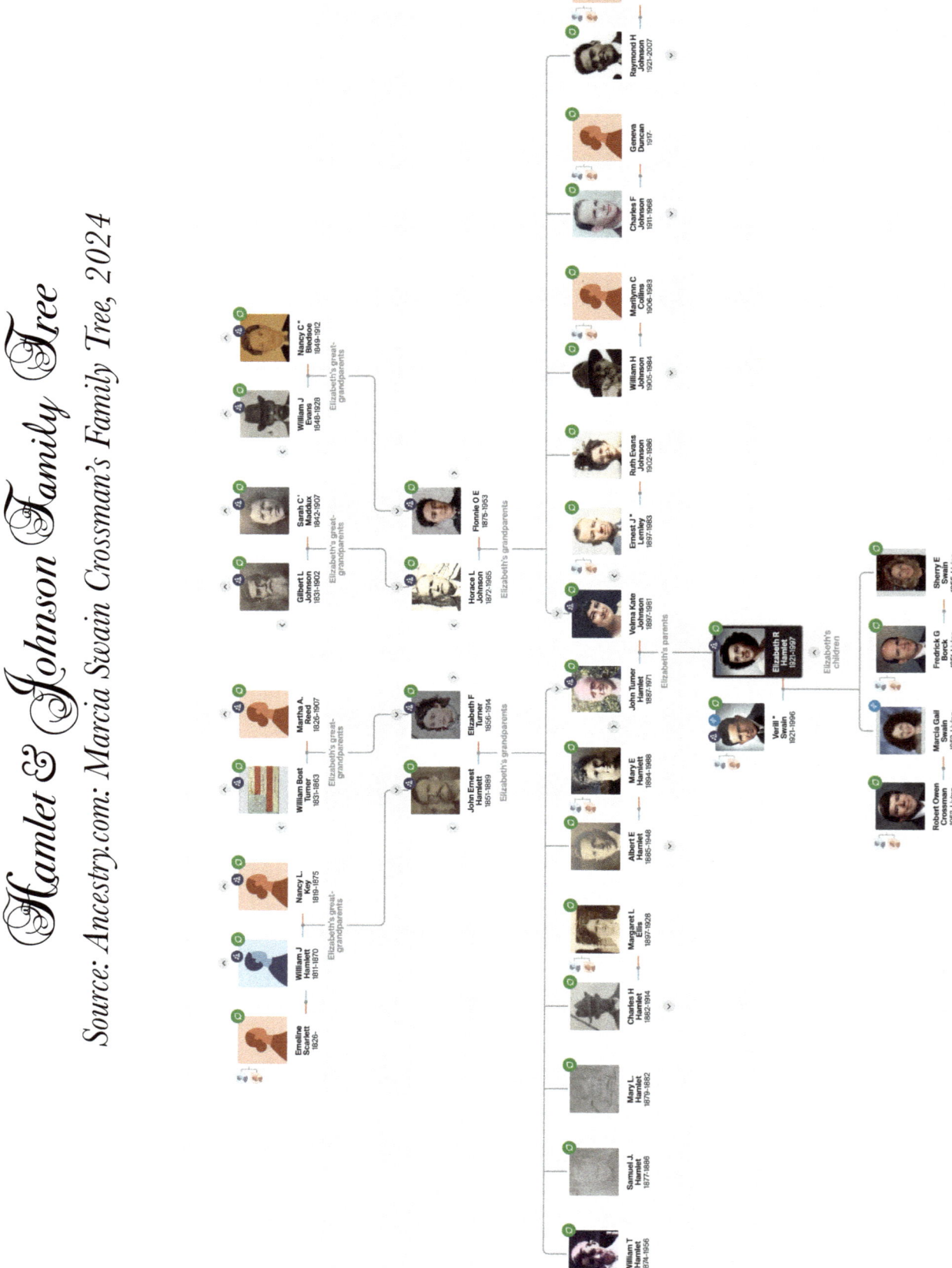

Appendix Three:

"*Lucinda Elizabeth Norman*

and

John Mason Liner"

Great Great Grandparents of
This Generation of Swains

Lucinda & John Liner were the parents of
Great Grand Mother Teresa Mason Liner

Teresa Mason Liner Trimble (later Treadaway) became the
Mother of Grandmother Stella Thomas Trimble

Stella Thomas Trimble Swain became the Mother of
Allene, Ansel, Doyle, Dallas & Shirley Swain

Research & Writing by
Marcia Swain Crossman
Last updated 2022

This volume is included
for family interested in learning about the ancestors
of Stella Thomas Trimble, not included in
the 1987 Swain Genealogy in Appendix One.

Lucinda Elizabeth Norman
&
John Mason Liner

"Our Great Great Grandparents"

By
Marcia Swain Crossman, 2024

Introduction

References to "our" in this story refer to me, my sister, and our first cousins. Our surname is Swain. This story was written for our generation and for future generations. We are the grandchildren of **Stella Thomas Trimble Swain** *and* **Sherman Norton Swain**. *We are so fortunate, in our past,* **V. Ansel Swain** *and* **Robert "Bob" Crossman** *researched the Swain side of our family giving us,* ***"A Genealogy of the Swain Family: Descendants of Jesse Abner Swain"*** *(1987); Jesse Abner Swain was the grandfather of Sherman "Sam" Swain). A great deal of Swain family, living at that time, contributed stories and facts to this effort. It is truly a great history of our family to read. Future generations will learn a great deal about the Swain side of our family through this gift.*

There is little to no information written about the other side of our **Stella Trimble-Sam Swain** *grandparents. My goal was to find out about the* **Trimble** *side of the marriage of Stella and Sam. This piece of the story goes back two generations to the grandparents of Stella Thomas Trimble Swain who are our great great grand parents,* **Lucinda Elizabeth Norman Liner** *and* **John Mason Liner**.

Lucinda and John Liner's daughter, **Teresa Marie Liner**, *married* **Thomas Mason Trimble**. *They bring us forward another generation by being our great grandparents. Teresa and Thomas's daughter,* **Stella Thomas Trimble** *married* **Sherman "Sam" Norton Swain** *becoming our paternal grandparents. Our parents are the children of Sam and Stella.*

We cannot see the faces or places of these ancestors. Our generation doesn't remember stories of these people. The only information we have comes from bits and pieces found in US Census Records and other on line sources where our distantly related cousins have made family trees. Results from this research doesn't make interesting reading. I have attempted to compile these bits and pieces into a story, to be more interesting, rather than a list of names and dates. I hope our family and future generations will enjoy reading a slice of our story. This is the story of Lucinda and John, our great great grandparents.

1

The Story of John & Lucinda

John Mason Liner *(1831-1862)*, our great great grandfather, was the son of **Sarah Martin** *(1807-1882)* and **Christopher Dickson Liner** *(1793-1875)*. John Mason Liner was born in 1831 in Walton Co. Georgia. He was raised in **Tallapoosa, Haralson County, GA**. His Liner family made their home for many years in Tallapoosa. We know John had 15 siblings. Sarah, John's mother, gave birth to 16 children in a 26 year time span. John's parents, Christopher and Sarah, lived to be very elderly for that day and time. They are buried in the Liner Cemetery in Tallapoosa, GA.

Before our great great grandmother **Lucinda Elizabeth Norman** *(1835-1901)* was married to **John Mason Liner**, he was first married to **Lemila Elizabeth "Millie" Chandler** *(1833-1856)*. John Mason Liner and Millie Chandler were married in 1850 in Calhoun, AL. Millie was only 17 years old. John Mason was 19 years old. John and Millie were blessed with two children, **William O. Liner**, born 1853 in GA and **Rhoda Malissa "Mae" Liner** *(later Edwards)*, born 1854, in Heflin, Cleborne Co., AL. With the older child born in Georgia, it seemed the young couple had struck out on their own for a short while. As the second child came, they moved back to Tallapoosa, GA. Millie was a mere 23 when she died in 1856, perhaps from childbirth. John, a widower, was left with two small children.

Our great great grandmother was **Lucinda Elizabeth Norman** *(1835-1901)* second marital partner of **John Mason Liner**. Lucinda was born in Benton, Cleburn Co., AL. Her father, **Charles Norman** *(1798-1874)*, was 36 and her mother, **Jane Elizabeth Reid** *(1805-1895)*, was 30 years old when she was born. Lucinda's mother, Jane, gave birth to 13 children. Before Lucinda's father, Charles, was married to Jane, he had been widowed from another woman, with the last name of Pounds. Several children had been born to Charles in this marriage. Charles and second wife, Jane, had large amounts of land and money. When Charles died, he had left a will with instructions of what was to become of the estate. The estate was not settled until nearly thirty years after his death, several years after Jane had died. There is a nearly 200 page paper on line describing court proceedings regarding the division of the Norman estate. By the time of division Lucinda had become an older woman living in Arkansas married to a second husband. She received $48.31. More about Lucinda's second marriage to come.

Lucinda Norman and **John Mason Liner** were married on May 3, 1859, six years after Millie Liner's death. At their marriage, John was 28 and Lucinda was 25 years old. John's children with Millie Liner, **William** and **Rhoda**, then ages six and five became part of the new **John/Lucinda household**. This new Liner family moved back to John's home area in Tallapoosa, GA. US Census Records report that John and Lucinda Liner were farmers. The value of their real estate

2

at that time was $200. The value of their personal property brought the value of their estate to $460. John Mason and Lucinda Elizabeth were blessed by the birth of their first daughter, **Martha Rose Liner** *(1860-1945)* on October of 1860, born in Tallapoosa, GA.

From history we know **politics** of that day were in heat all over the country. In 1861, **Abraham Lincoln** became the United States' 16th President. Extreme tension brewed between the **northern** and **southern states**. Differing beliefs led the nation's young men to make harsh decisions on living, dying, possession of slaves, and at the ultimate price for many. Confederates soldiers from the South and Union soldiers from the North would go to war fighting to their deaths. The **Civil War** raged across the country. In total, 618,222 young men, 360,222 from the North and 258,000 from the South died. **John Mason Liner** enlisted in the Georgia Voluntary Infantry in the southern Virginia Army.

John and **Lucinda** might still be considered "newlyweds" when John marched off to war. John Mason and Lucinda Elizabeth had been married less than four years. **John Mason Liner** enlisted as s a private in **Company A of the 35th Infantry** *(Confederate)*. His muster *(arrival)* was March 4, 1862. John was killed in the war in Gordonsville, Orange County, Virginia on August 9, 1862. There are no records where John Mason, 31 years old, was buried. It was probably near the battlefield where he died.

At the time, **Lucinda Elizabeth Liner** was left behind with **three young children**. She was step mother to John and Millie Chandler's children. Her own toddler, **Martha Rose**, needed constant care. When John was off fighting in the war, Lucinda was pregnant with her second baby, **Teresa Mason Liner** *(1862-1953)*. Teresa was born April 19, 1862. John Mason never met his second daughter, Teresa. Four months before his death, **Teresa Mason Liner** had been born. John was killed in the Civil War before the time of her birth.

Back home in Tallapoosa, GA, **Lucinda Elizabeth Liner, a widow**, was left with four *(or five)* children, a house, cleaning and tending to what was left of their farm. A US Census Record shows that Lucinda had a third child with John Mason, a daughter, named **Leroi** *(or Leavy)*. Her birth year was 1862, just like her sister Teresa's birth year. Was this a twin who died in infancy? I have found only one on line record of her. We may never know who she was or really if she was.

This was not the end of the story. **Lucinda Liner**, age 36, married a second husband, a widower and farmer, **Joseph W. Williams** *(1824-1872)*, age 47, May 24, 1871. Joseph married Lucinda only four months after the death of his first wife **Narcissa Amelia Davis** *(1825-1871)*. Joseph and Narcissa Davis Williams had six children including Jonah John *(1842-)*, Sarah Frances *(1844-)*, Mary Elizabeth *(1850-)*, Andrew Jackson *(1861-)*, Nancy Jane *(1862-)*, and Catherine Louise *(1864-)*. Lucinda and Joseph had a son of their own, **Jackson** *(1872-)*.

3

Take a closer look at the volume of children throughout Lucinda's life. The children included two step children from John Liner's first wife, Millie; two or three children with Lucinda's first husband, John Liner; six more step children from Joseph William's first wife; then add one last child from Lucinda and Joseph's marriage. There were many children that passed through Lucinda's household during her lifetime. **Lucinda** became a **step mother of eight children** and a **biological mother of possibly four children**. All of these children did not live in Lucinda's household at the same time.

Lucinda and her daughters eventually moved into an area of Arkansas where my generation of **Swains** is most familiar. That is **Liberty** and **Scotland** in Van Buren County, AR. Lucinda and John Liner's daughter, **Martha Rose Liner** married **John Stobaugh** a farmer who lived in Scotland, AR. We can credit **Martha Rose Liner Stobaugh** for bringing part of our family into Arkansas. She lived to be 84 years old. We will learn more, at a later time, when we look into the next generation.

Joseph W. Williams lived to be 73 years old. He died in Georgia, in 1897, leaving Lucinda, once again, a widow. Probably seeking care in her old age is what brought **Lucinda** to Arkansas to live with daughter **Martha Rose Stobaugh**. The 1900 US Census records **Teresa Liner Trimble**, who became our great grandmother, plus several children lived very near to Martha Rose and Lucinda Williams. Teresa's household included our grandmother **Stella Trimble**.

Lucinda died in 1901, living to be 67 years old. Records show **Lucinda** and **Martha Rose** are buried in **Old Liberty Cemetery** in Scotland, AR. **Teresa Mason Liner Trimble Treadaway**, Lucinda's other daughter and our great grandmother, is buried at **Mt. Pleasant Cemetery** near Scotland, AR. These cemeteries are only a few miles from the other. Our grandfather, Sherman Norton Swain is buried at Old Liberty. Grandmother Stella Trimble Swain is buried at Mt. Pleasant, each desiring to be near their families.

Such is the story of our great great grand parents, **Lucinda Norman** and **John Mason Liner**. Included is some information about their descendants. It's our collection that I have found about these ancestors in 2024. Gathering this information was quite a journey. It is my pleasure to share it with our family. Perhaps, some of you or our children will add more information to this history in the future. I plan to continue this history with the story of **Teresa Mason Liner** and **Thomas Milton Trimble**, our great grandparents.

Last Minute Addition to Book
The photos on the following pages were added after I finished my paper on Lucinda Norman and John Mason Liner. I could not print this book without the addition of these new photos, some shared to be by Teri Bethge, a new found second cousin who lives here in Arkansas. Here are some descendants of Lucinda and John ...

4

Teresa Mason Liner & Thomas Milton Trimble
"Our Great Grandparents"
Teresa Liner was a daughter of Lucinda Elizabeth Norman & John Mason Liner.

Teresa Mason Liner married Thomas Milton Trimble. They were parents of
Lucinda "Lula" Trimble Bost, John Milton Trimble, Luther Gordon Trimble,
Ardella "Della" Agnes Trimble Newton, and Stella Thomas Trimble Swain.

We gratefully thank our cousin, TERI BETHGE for so generously sharing the following photos and helping me identify ones I had.

I met Teri through Ancestry and look forward to meeting her in person soon. She is also from Arkansas.

Teri sent me the bottom photo, identified as, "Stella's parents." With the assistance of Photoshop and Artificial Intelligence, "AI" we see the first glimpse of our **great grandparents**.

This is drawing, not a photograph. Notice what the couple are wearing. He has on a shirt with a lace collar tied with a ribbon. She has on a lace bow in her hair and very nice jewelry. Seen on a computer screen, one can see the ruffles built in her dress with a lace collar on top. Surely, this was made near the time of their wedding. I will gladly email anyone a copy of this computer file so its detail can be enjoyed. *Photos continue on next page ...*

5

Mr. Treadway   Grand mother Treadwa[y]

Thanks to cousin **Teri Bethge**, we have another photo of **Teresa Trimble**, our great grandmother, who also married **Samuel Benjamin Treadway**.

Thomas Milton Trimble, first husband, died around the age of 36 near the time their last daughter, Stella, was born. After some time, Teresa remarried and added another child, **Chester**, with **Benjamin Treadway**.

Teresa died on **September 15, 1953**, at the **age of 91**. *She knew the generation of our parents and a few of our cousins born by then.* Her home was in Scotland, Arkansas, where she is buried in the **Pleasant Grove Cemetery**. The name on her monument and in the photo above is **Treadway**, not Treadaway *(with the extra a,)* as part of the family has spelled it.

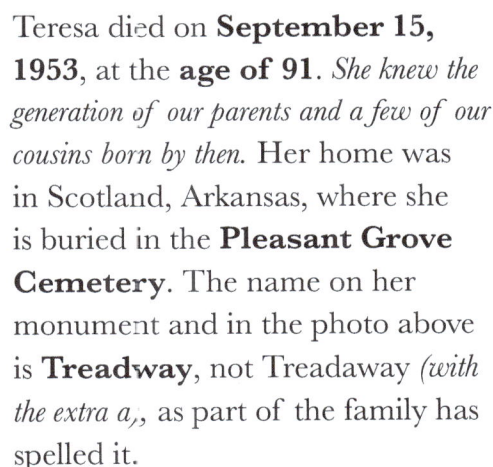

Stella Thomas Trimble
&
Ardella Agnes Trimble

Shown as teens, at left, they were the last two daughters born to Teresa Liner & Thomas Milton Trimble.

This photo was a gift of cousin Teri Bethge.

6

A mystery finally solved!

This is Lucinda Trimble Bost "Aunt Lula"

This 8 x 10" photo has been in my possession and unidentified for many years. The photo was very well cared for. I though she must have been someone very special. She was special. She was the older sister of Stella Trimble Swain, my grandmother!

Thanks to cousin Teri Bethge, we now know who she is.

Lucinda "Lula" Elizabeth Trimble Bost
&
Teresa Trimble Treadway

Lucinda was the first child born to Teresa Mason Liner & Thomas Milton Trimble.

This photo was a gift of cousin, Teri Bethge.

7

Luther Gordon Trimble

*At right: Luther Gordon Trimble was the third child of Teresa Liner and Thomas Milton Trimble. Luther lived to be 81 years old. His son, **Luther Grady Trimble** was a dentist in Little Rock for many years. Luther Grady's daughter, **Glennie Earnestine Trimble Hardy** is the mother of **Teresa "Teri" Hardy Bethge**, a second cousin who assisted with photographs in this appendix.*

John Milton Trimble

At left: There is not much found about John Milton Trimble. John was the second child of Teresa Liner and Thomas Milton Trimble. His death was recorded at his age 34 years in 1935.

An Interesting Trimble Monument

*At the **Pleasant Grove Cemetery** near Scotland, AR, where many Trimbles are buried, is this double monument. On the left is the memorial of John Milton Trimble with the above photo on its front. On the right is the memorial of Thomas Milton Trimble, who was John's father. John died in 1935 and Thomas died in 1896.*

8

One Last Photo

From Left to Right: **Stella Thomas Trimble Swain, Verill Ansel Swain, Teresa Liner Trimble Treadway, Dallas Lynn Swain, Lula Trimble Bost and spouse Charles Bost.** *Lula Bost and Stella Swain were sisters, being born 15 years apart. Stella Swain is the mother of Ansel and Dallas Swain. This photo was probably taken around 1950-1953 when Dallas was home from his Naval Service in Korea. Thanks again to our cousin, Teri, for sharing this photograph.*

9

Milton Keynes UK
Ingram Content Group UK Ltd.
UKHW051358011224
451734UK00005B/87